Macromedia Flash™ MX 2004 For Dummies®

GW00982808

Common Keyboard Shortcuts

File Menu Commands

Command	Windows	Mac	Command	Windows	Mac
New	Ctrl+N	⌘+N	Save	Ctrl+S	⌘+S
Open	Ctrl+O	⌘+O	Publish Settings	Ctrl+Shift+F12	Option+Shift+F12
Import to Stage	Ctrl+R	⌘+R	Publish	Shift+F12	Shift+F12
Import to Library	Ctrl+Shift+O	⌘+Shift+O	Quit	Ctrl+Q	⌘+Q
Close	Ctrl+W	⌘+W			

Edit Menu Commands

Command	Windows	Mac
Undo	Ctrl+Z	⌘+Z
Redo	Ctrl+Y	⌘+Y
Cut	Ctrl+X	⌘+X
Copy	Ctrl+C	⌘+C
Paste in Center	Ctrl+V	⌘+V
Paste in Place	Ctrl+Shift+V	⌘+Shift+V
Clear	Delete/Backspace	Delete/Clear
Duplicate	Ctrl+D	⌘+D
Select All	Ctrl+A	⌘+A
Deselect All	Ctrl+Shift+A	⌘+Shift+A
Copy Frames	Ctrl+Alt+C	⌘+Option+C
Paste Frames	Ctrl+Alt+V	⌘+Option+V

Tools Panel

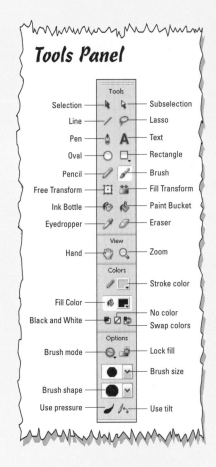

For Dummies: Bestselling Book Series for Beginners

Macromedia Flash™ MX 2004 For Dummies®

Cheat Sheet

View Menu Commands

Command	Windows	Mac	Command	Windows	Mac
Magnification 100%	Ctrl+1	⌘+1	Snap to Objects	Ctrl+Shift+/	⌘+Shift+/
Magnification: Show All	Ctrl+3	⌘+3	Work Area	Ctrl+Shift+W	⌘+Shift+W

Insert Menu Commands

Command	Windows	Mac	Command	Windows	Mac
New Symbol	Ctrl+F8	⌘+F8	Keyframe	F6	F6
Frame	F5	F5	Blank Keyframe	F7	F7

Modify Menu Commands

Command	Windows	Mac	Command	Windows	Mac
Document	Ctrl+J	⌘+J	Distribute to Layers	Ctrl+Shift+D	⌘+Shift+D
Convert to Symbol	F8	F8	Group	Ctrl+G	⌘+G
Break Apart	Ctrl+B	⌘+B	Ungroup	Ctrl+Shift+G	⌘+Shift+G
Add Shape Hint	Ctrl+Alt+H	⌘+Option+H			

Control Menu Commands

Command	Windows	Mac	Command	Windows	Mac
Play	Enter	Return	Test Movie	Ctrl+Enter	⌘+Return
Rewind	Ctrl+Alt+R	⌘+Option+R	Enable Simple Buttons	Ctrl+Alt+B	⌘+Option+B
Step Forward	. (period)	. (period)			
Step Backward	, (comma)	, (comma)			

Window Menu Commands

Command	Windows	Mac	Command	Windows	Mac
Properties	Ctrl+F3	⌘+F3	Info	Ctrl+I	⌘+I
Timeline	Ctrl+Alt+T	⌘+Option+T	Transform	Ctrl+T	⌘+T
Tools	Ctrl+F2	⌘+F2	Actions	F9	F9
Library	Ctrl+L/F11	⌘+L/F11	Behaviors	Shift+F3	Shift+F3
Align	Ctrl+K	⌘+K	History	Alt+F10	Option+F10
Color Mixer	Shift+F9	Shift+F9	Movie Explorer	Alt+F3	Option+F3
Color Swatches	Ctrl+F9	⌘+F9	Hide Panels	F4	F4

Macromedia Flash™ MX 2004 FOR DUMMIES®

by Ellen Finkelstein and Gurdy Leete

WILEY

Wiley Publishing, Inc.

Macromedia Flash™ **MX 2004 For Dummies**®

Published by
Wiley Publishing, Inc.
111 River Street
Hoboken, NJ 07030-5774

www.wiley.com

For general information on our other products and services or to obtain technical support, please contact our Customer Care Department within the U.S. at 800-762-2974, outside the U.S. at 317-572-3993, or fax 317-572-4002.

Wiley also publishes its books in a variety of electronic formats. Some content that appears in print may not be available in electronic books.

Library of Congress Control Number: 2003112833

ISBN: 0-7645-4358-X

Manufactured in the United States of America

10 9 8 7 6 5 4 3 2

1O/QW/RQ/QT/IN

About the Authors

Ellen Finkelstein has written numerous best-selling computer books on AutoCAD, PowerPoint, and Flash. She also writes articles on these programs for Web sites, ezines and magazines. The four editions of her *AutoCad Bible* have sold more than 50,000 copies in the United States and abroad. As an Adjunct Instructor of Management she teaches eBusiness courses. She writes at home so that she can take the bread out of the oven on time.

Gurdy Leete has been working as a computer animator, computer animation software engineer, and teacher of computer animation since 1981. He has been teaching Flash and other computer animation programs for 11 years at Maharishi University of Management, where he is an Assistant Professor of Digital Media. You can see his art on the Web at www.infinityeverywhere.net.

Dedication

To MMY, for explaining that life is meant to be lived in happiness and teaching us how to realize that reality in daily life.

Authors' Acknowledgments

This book was very much a group effort. First, I'd like to thank my co-author, Gurdy Leete, without whom I could not have completed this book nor even thought of writing it. Gurdy was always a pleasure to work with, always in a good mood, and helpful. He's a brilliant artist and something of a programmer, too, while I am neither. I've been quite impressed.

At Wiley, I'd like to thank Steve Hayes, our acquisitions editor, for trusting us with this book. Great kudos go to Nicole Sholly, our project editor, for doing such a tremendous job.

Personally, I'd like to thank my husband, Evan, and my kids, Yeshayah and Eliyah, who helped out and managed without me as I wrote every day, evening, and weekend for months. I love you all.

Thanks to Macromedia, for creating Flash and supporting Flash authors during the beta period while we were learning all the new features of Flash MX 2004, testing Flash, and writing, all at the same time.

Finally, I'd like to thank the Flash community and specifically all the Flash designers who contributed Flash movies to make this book and its CD-ROM more valuable. Most computer books use dummy files, and we made up a few of our own to illustrate the point, but the real-world files we received for this book will help open up new vistas for our readers. And now, a few comments from Gurdy:

I'd like to echo all of Ellen's words and thank her for being such a great collaborator. She has such a talent for explaining things with the simplicity, precision, and humor that are so characteristic of the deeper workings of the cosmos. I'd also like to thank my intrepid research assistants, Nutthawut Chandhaketh, of Thailand; Radim Schreiber, of the Czech Republic; Burcu Cenberci, of Turkey; and Praveen Mishra, of Nepal, whose research activities on the Internet were so helpful in the writing of this book. Thanks to my omnitalented M.A. in Animation student Mike Zak, for the wonderful collection of clip art drawings he created in Flash for the CD-ROM. And thanks to my adorable wife, Mary, and my children, Porter and Jackie, for being so supportive during the many hours I spent working on this book.

Publisher's Acknowledgments

We're proud of this book; please send us your comments through our online registration form located at www.dummies.com/register/.

Some of the people who helped bring this book to market include the following:

Acquisitions, Editorial, and Media Development

Associate Project Editor: Nicole Sholly

Senior Acquisitions Editor: Steve Hayes

Senior Copy Editor: Teresa Artman

Technical Editor: Simon Allardice

Editorial Manager: Kevin Kirschner

Permissions Editor: Carmen Krikorian

Media Development Manager: Laura VanWinkle

Media Development Supervisor: Richard Graves

Editorial Assistant: Amanda Foxworth

Cartoons: Rich Tennant (www.the5thwave.com)

Production

Project Coordinator: Maridee Ennis

Layout and Graphics: LeAndra Hosier, Stephanie Jumper, Shae Lynn Wilson

Proofreaders: David Faust, John Greenough, Carl Pierce, TECHBOOKS Production Services

Indexer: TECHBOOKS Production Services

Publishing and Editorial for Technology Dummies

Richard Swadley, Vice President and Executive Group Publisher

Andy Cummings, Vice President and Publisher

Mary C. Corder, Editorial Director

Publishing for Consumer Dummies

Diane Graves Steele, Vice President and Publisher

Joyce Pepple, Acquisitions Director

Composition Services

Gerry Fahey, Vice President of Production Services

Debbie Stailey, Director of Composition Services

Contents at a Glance

Table of Contents

Introduction

Welcome to *Macromedia Flash MX 2004 For Dummies,* your friendly Web-animation companion. In this book, we explain in plain English how to make the most of Flash to create stunning Web site animations. *Macromedia Flash MX 2004 For Dummies* aims to give you all the information you need to start using Flash right away — with no hassle.

About This Book

As though you hadn't guessed, *Macromedia Flash MX 2004 For Dummies* covers the powerful animation product Flash MX 2004, from Macromedia. (The preceding version was Flash MX.) Flash MX 2004 is the latest version of the popular software used on some of the coolest Web sites on the Internet.

Flash now comes in two versions: Flash MX and Flash MX Pro. In addition to including all the features of Flash MX, the Pro version of Flash has powerful features for programmers and production teams, such as capabilities for project file management and version control of Flash files as well as for connecting Flash to live external data sources and to Web services.

In this book, we focus on the features of Flash MX rather than Flash MX Pro because they're much more interesting to people who are new to Flash. However, we do sometimes mention some of the Flash MX Pro 2004 features. We comprehensively explain the Flash features, including

- Working with the Flash screen, toolbars, and menus
- Creating graphics and text in Flash; adding sound and video
- Using layers to organize your animation
- Creating *symbols*, or objects that you save for repeated use
- Animating your graphics (the key to Flash)
- Creating interactive Web sites
- Publishing your Flash movies to your Web site

How to Use This Book

You don't have to read this book from cover to cover. *Macromedia Flash MX 2004 For Dummies* provides just the information you need, when you need it. Start with the first three chapters. Then play around with graphics until you create what you need for your Web site. You may want to check out Chapter 6, on layers, to help you organize it all. Then feel free to jump right to Chapter 9, on animation, to create your first real Flash movie. Chapter 13 tells you how to get your movie on your Web site. Then fire up your browser, sit back, and marvel.

Of course, you'll want to refer to other chapters when you need them so that you can create text and buttons, add sound and video, and create an interactive Web site. Chapter 12 provides some ideas for putting all the Flash features together for your best Web site ever.

Keep *Macromedia Flash MX 2004 For Dummies* by your computer while you work. You'll find it to be a loyal helper.

Foolish Assumptions

We assume that you're not already a master Flash developer. If you want to use Flash to create high-quality Web sites and you're not an expert animator already, you'll find this book to be a great reference. *Macromedia Flash MX 2004 For Dummies* is ideal for beginners who are just starting to use Flash or for current Flash users who want to further hone their skills.

Because Flash is generally added to Web sites, we also assume that you know some of the basics of Web site creation. You should know what HyperText Markup Language (HTML) is and understand the process of creating and structuring HTML pages as well as uploading them to a Web site.

If you need some help on the topic of Web sites, you may want to refer to *Web Design For Dummies,* by Lisa Lopuck (also by Wiley Publishing, Inc.).

Conventions Used in This Book

Sometimes it helps to know why some text is bold and other is italic so that you can figure out what we're talking about. (A typographic convention is *not* a convention of typographers meeting to discuss the latest typography techniques.)

New terms are in *italics* to let you know that they're new. When we suggest that you type something, what we want you to type is shown in **bold**. Messages and other text that come from Flash, including programming code, are in a `special typeface, like this`. When we say something like "Choose File⇨Save As," it means to click the File menu at the top of your screen and then choose Save As from the menu that opens. To distinguish between choosing a menu item or toolbar button from choosing an object, we generally say "Select the circle" or something similar to refer to the object. So you *choose* menu items but *select* objects on your screen. When we want you to use a toolbar or toolbox button (or tool), we tell you to click it. So now you know the difference between choose, select, and click.

How This Book Is Organized

We start by presenting an overview of the Flash universe and then continue in the general order that you would use to create a Flash animation. More basic material is at the beginning of the book, and more advanced material (but not too advanced!) comes later on. You may never use all the material in this book for one Flash movie.

To be more specific, this book is divided into seven parts (to represent the seven states of consciousness — okay, we don't have to get too cosmic here). Each part contains two or more chapters that relate to that part. Each chapter thoroughly covers one topic so that you don't have to go searching all over creation to get the information you need.

Part 1: A Blast of Flash

Part I contains important introductory information about Flash. In Chapter 1, we tell you what Flash is all about, show you what the Flash screen looks like, and explain how to get help when you need it most. You can also find instructions for starting Flash, starting a new movie, opening an existing movie, and a short tutorial. Chapter 2 explains in more detail the steps for creating a Flash movie. We also explain some basic concepts that all Flash users need to know.

Part 11: 1,000 Pictures and 1,000 Words

Part II explains all the tools available for creating graphics in Flash. Chapter 3 explains the unique drawing tools included in Flash. Of course, we also explain how to import graphics if you don't feel like creating your own. Chapter 4 shows you how to edit and manipulate graphic objects, and Chapter 5 is all about creating text. Chapter 6 explains *layers,* which help you organize your graphics so that they don't interfere with each other.

Part III: Getting Symbolic

Symbols are graphical objects that you save to use again and again. Whenever you want to place an object on a Web page more than once, you can save the object as a symbol. You can also group together many individual objects, making them useful when you want to manipulate, edit, or animate them all at one time. Chapter 7 explains creating and editing symbols. Chapter 8 describes how to create Web page buttons — not the kind that you sew but rather the kind that you click with your mouse. *Buttons* are a kind of symbol, but they execute an action when clicked.

Part IV: Total Flash-o-Rama

Part IV explains how to put all your graphics together and make them move. Chapter 9 covers animation in detail — from frame-by-frame animation to *tweening,* where Flash calculates the animation between your first and last frames. Tween movement to make your objects move or morph into new shapes. You can also tween color and transparency.

Chapter 10 shows how to create Web sites that react to your viewers. For example, when a viewer clicks a button, Flash can jump to a different part of a movie or go to a different Web page entirely. To create interactivity, you use *ActionScript,* Flash's JavaScript-like programming language. We tell you how to put ActionScript to work.

Chapter 11 is about adding multimedia — sound, music, and video — to your Flash movies and buttons.

Part V: The Movie and the Web

This part helps you put all your animated graphics and cool buttons together and publish your work on the Web. Chapter 12 outlines the various techniques that you can use to create a great Web site using only Flash.

Chapter 13 explains how to test your animation for speed and suitability for all browsers and systems. Then we cover all the details of publishing movies as well as the other available formats, such as HTML and GIF. You can also create *projectors* — movies that play themselves.

Part VI: The Part of Tens

What's a *For Dummies* book without The Part of Tens? Chapter 14 answers some frequently asked questions about Flash and introduces some fun techniques, such as creating drag-and-drop objects and simulating 3-D effects. Chapter 15 offers you the top ten Web-design tips, knowing that your Flash work must fit into the context of an entire Web site. Chapter 16 provides you with the ten best resources for learning about Flash (besides this book, of course). Chapter 17 lists our winners for ten great Flash Web sites, although new ones pop up every day.

Part VII: Appendixes

Last, but not least, we come to the appendixes. They add some valuable information to the end of this book, including instructions on setting preferences and options, illustrations of all the tools and panels in Flash MX 2004, definitions of obscure terms, and a listing of what's on the CD-ROM.

About the CD-ROM

The CD-ROM is stuffed with Flash movies you can play with and a library of graphics.

Icons Used in This Book

Icons help point out special information. Sometimes they tell you that you don't care about this information and can skip over it without fear.

This icon flags new features in Flash MX 2004. If you have been using Flash MX or even an earlier version, you may want to skim through this book and look for this icon to help you quickly get up to speed in the new version.

Look for this icon to find all the goodies on the CD included with this book.

This icon alerts you to information that you need to keep in mind to avoid wasting time or falling on your face.

Flash has some advanced features you may want to know about — or skip over entirely. This icon lets you know when we throw the heavier stuff at you.

Tips help you finish your work more easily, quickly, or effectively. Don't miss out on these.

Uh-oh! "Watch out here!" is what this icon is telling you, or else you never know what may happen.

Where to Go from Here

If you don't already have Flash installed, complete instructions for installing Flash are in Appendix A. Then open Flash, open this book, and plunge in.

We would love to hear your comments about this book. You can contact Gurdy Leete at gleete@mum.edu and Ellen Finkelstein at ellenfinkl@ bigfoot.com. Please note that we can't provide technical support on Flash. (If you need technical support, check out the resources listed in Chapter 16.) Enough of all this talk. Let's move into the real part of this book and start creating cool movies! Enjoy!

Part I
A Blast of Flash

In this part . . .

In this part, you discover what Flash can and can't do and start to make your way around the Flash world. In Chapter 1, we introduce you to Flash, show what it looks like, and explain how to use its toolbars and menus. You find out about the Stage and the Timeline, two of the central Flash concepts. Play your way through your first animation to get firsthand experience in the power of Flash.

In Chapter 2, you get an overview of the entire process of creating a Flash animated movie, from developing your concept to publishing your movie in the format a browser can display. We explain how to set properties that affect your movie as a whole and how Flash works with various kinds of graphics. We close with the steps for printing your movie on paper. This part provides the foundation for future success.

Chapter 1

Getting Acquainted with Flash MX 2004

*O*nce upon a time in a galaxy that seems far, far away by now, there was the Internet, which contained only plain, unformatted text. Then came the Web, and we gained text formatting and graphics. Then the Web grew up a little, and Web page graphics got fancier with things like small animations in banner ads. But people, being used to movies and TV, wanted an even more animated and interactive Web experience. Along came Flash.

Flash, created by Macromedia, Inc., is the software that runs some of the coolest Web sites around. When you surf the Web and see sites that contain animation across the entire page or buttons that do spectacular stunts when you click them, you're probably seeing some Flash magic. If you create a Web site, you can use Flash to rev up the basics so that your viewers will say, "Wow!"

In this chapter, you find out what Flash is all about, what the screen looks like, and how to use Help. Then you create your first, simple animation so that all the rest of this book makes sense.

Discovering Flash

Flash offers a powerful system for creating animation on the Web. In a nutshell, here's an overview of how you use the system:

1. **Create a Flash movie by creating graphics and animating them over the duration of the movie.**

2. **Use the Publish command within Flash to publish the movie into a Flash Player file that a browser can display.** At the same time, Flash creates the appropriate HyperText Markup Language (HTML) code that you need for your Web page.

3. **Insert HTML code into your HTML document that references the Flash Player file.** It's similar to adding a graphic to a Web page. Or, you can use the HTML code alone as a new Web page.

4. **Upload the new or edited HTML document and the Flash Player file to the location where you keep other files for your Web pages.**

5. **Open your browser, navigate to your Web page, and presto! — there's your cool animation on your Web page.**

You need the Flash Player to see the effects that Flash creates. These days, the Flash Player comes installed with most computer systems and browsers, so most people can view Flash-driven Web sites immediately without any special download or preparation. When you display a Web site that contains Flash effects, your system uses the Flash Player to play the animation. Users who don't have a Flash Player can download it for free from Macromedia at www.macromedia.com/shockwave/download/index.cgi?P1_Prod_Version= ShockwaveFlash.

Web sites are getting more and more sophisticated. By using animation and special effects, you can distinguish your Web site from the also-rans. Creating animation isn't hard, and you don't have to be a professional graphic artist, either. Anyone can create simple animations to enhance a Web site; it just takes a little time.

To find the most up-to-date Web sites that use Flash, check out the Macromedia site at www.macromedia.com/flash and choose Showcase⇨Case Studies. Don't get discouraged by seeing some of the truly professional results at these sites. You can start with a simple, animated site and go from there. (Chapter 17 lists ten great Web sites that use Flash.)

Understanding What You Can Create with Flash MX 2004

You can use Flash MX 2004 to create simple animation to add to your Web page. Or, you can create an entire Web page or site and incorporate text, graphics, interactive buttons, and animation. You can even program small applications in Flash.

This book helps you use Flash to create a simple or complex Web site. The following list describes some ways that you can manipulate text, graphics, and sound by using Flash MX 2004:

- **Create still or animated text on your Web page.** You can choose to stop the animation after a few seconds or repeat it while your viewers view the page.

- **Use Flash tools to create your own graphics for your Web page, or import graphics.** You can lay out an entire Web page graphically or add graphics to only a part of a Web page.

- **Animate graphics and make objects appear and disappear by using the transparency feature.** Objects can move, get bigger or smaller, or rotate. Flash also lets you *morph* — that is, transform — shapes into new shapes.

- **Fill shapes and text with *gradients*, which are colors that gradually change into new colors.** You can even fill shapes and text with bitmap images that you import into Flash. For example, you could fill the letters of your name with dozens of flowers. (You aren't a flower child any more?)

- **Create Web page buttons that not only lead your viewers wherever you want them to go but also change shape or color at the same time.** You can make buttons change when you pass your mouse over them. People who view your page can click a button to display a movie (animation) or start a small application.

- **Add sound or video to your movie.** You can control how long the sound or music plays and whether it loops to play continuously. You can play video files as well.

- **Create menus that viewers can use to navigate your site.** You can create navigation tools as well as forms, check boxes, and other interface elements.

As you can see, you can go far with Flash if you want. And why not? It's great fun!

Determining When Not to Use Flash MX 2004

If Flash MX 2004 is so wonderful, why doesn't every Web site designer use it? Why aren't most Web sites created completely with Flash?

Here's the other side of the story.

Although the vector graphics and animation of Flash load quickly, they don't load as quickly as plain text and simple graphics. Adding a movie to your Web page creates some overhead. There's no point in using Flash if you want simple pages consisting of mostly text and a few graphics that you want to stay put and not move.

You can create certain graphic effects much more easily by using bitmap graphics. Painted brushstroke and textured effects are examples. Graphic artists create these types of graphics by using graphics editing software, and the results are bitmaps. Similarly, to add photographs to your Web page, you need to scan the photographs as bitmaps. Flash creates *vector graphics* (defined mathematically), which are different from *bitmap graphics* (defined by lots of dots). You can find out more about bitmap and vector graphics in Chapter 2.

If you want simple animation, such as a few blinking dots or a marquee effect, animated *GIFs* (the animated bitmap graphics that you often see on the Web) are smaller than Flash movies, so they load faster. You can create animated GIFs by using animated GIF editing software.

Flash provides little in the way of 3-D graphics or animation. For those, you need to go to more sophisticated software, such as Poser or 3D Studio Max. (See Chapter 14 for more 3-D possibilities in Flash.)

Getting the Right Start

Well begun is half done, as the saying goes. The easiest way to begin using Flash MX 2004 is with a shortcut or alias right on your desktop. Double-click the Flash icon, and you're on your way. (See Appendix A for information on installing Flash.)

Starting Flash on a PC

Whether you installed Flash from the CD or by downloading it from the Macromedia Web site onto your PC, you may or may not have a shortcut

on your desktop. To create one, choose Start➪Programs➪Macromedia➪
Macromedia Flash MX 2004. Right-click the Macromedia Flash MX 2004 item
and choose Create Shortcut from the pop-up menu that appears. The new
shortcut appears on the menu. Drag that shortcut to your desktop.

To rename the shortcut, click the shortcut on your desktop. Then click the
text beneath the icon. Type **Flash MX 2004** (or whatever you want) and press
Enter. Just double-click the icon to open Flash.

Starting Flash on a Mac

Whether you installed Flash from the CD or by downloading from the
Macromedia Web site onto your Mac, you may or may not have an alias on
your desktop. To create one, open your drive and find the file named Flash
MX 2004 in the Macromedia Flash MX 2004 folder. Click the file to select it.
Then choose File➪Make Alias. This action creates the alias in the same
folder, named Flash MX 2004 Alias. Drag that alias to the desktop.

To rename the alias, click the alias on your desktop. Then click the text
beneath the icon. Type **Flash MX 2004** (or whatever you want) and press
Enter. Now you can just double-click the icon to open Flash.

Creating a new movie

Files that you create by using Flash are commonly called *movies*. When you
start Flash, you're immediately ready to create a new movie. The startup screen
appears (by default). In the Create New section, choose Flash Document. If you
have already opened a movie and have the menus available, choose File➪New.
In the New Document dialog box, choose Flash Document from the General tab
and then click OK. You usually start by creating or importing some graphics. (To
find out more about working with graphics, see Chapter 3.)

Opening an existing movie

If you want to work on a movie you've already created, when you first open
Flash, choose it from the Open a Recent Item section or choose Open to find
the file. If you've already opened a movie and have the menus available, press
Ctrl+O (Windows) or ⌘+O (Mac) or choose File➪Open; then double-click the
movie to open it. The first frame appears on your screen, and you can edit
the movie any way that you want.

Windows users can click Open on the Standard toolbar. If the Standard toolbar isn't displayed, choose Window➪Toolbars➪Main.

Taking a Look Around

If you've never created animation, the Flash screen is different from the screens in other programs that you may be used to, so take the time to get to know it. You can also customize the Flash screen. Figure 1-1 shows one possible display.

If your screen opens with several rectangular panels strewn about the screen or docked on various sides, don't worry about them now. We explain how to open and use these panels throughout this book, but you don't need them for this chapter. If they drive you crazy, right-click each panel's title bar and choose Close Panel from the menu that appears.

See Appendix B for a full layout of each panel and toolbar.

Tools panel

Layer list   Menu   Timeline   Zoom Control box

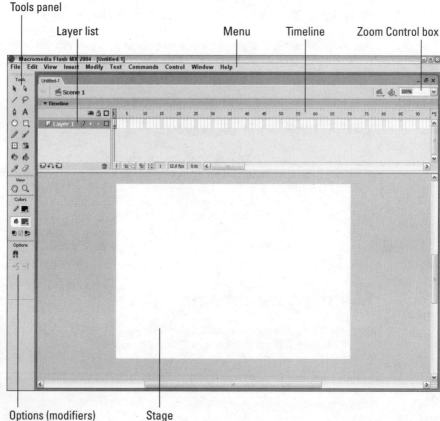

Figure 1-1:
The Flash
screen.

Options (modifiers)   Stage

Tooling around the toolbars

Flash contains two toolbars in the Mac version: the Tools panel and the Controller. To display or hide these toolbars, choose Window⇨Tools or Window⇨Controller. In Windows, Flash offers the four toolbars described in the following list. To display or hide the first three listed here, choose Window⇨Toolbars and click the toolbar that you want to display or hide. Here is a description of the toolbars:

- **Standard toolbar (Windows only):** Called the Main toolbar; contains commonly used commands. Many of these are familiar from other Windows programs. By default, Flash does *not* display the Standard toolbar.

- **Status toolbar (Windows only):** Contains a brief description of toolbar buttons and tells you when the Caps Lock and Num Lock buttons are on. By not displaying this mostly useless toolbar, you can reclaim some real estate on your screen. By default, Flash does not display the Status toolbar.

- **Controller:** Lets you control the playback of movies. For more information, see Chapter 9.

- **Tools panel:** Contains all the tools that you need to draw and edit objects. At the bottom of the Tools panel are options that modify how the tools function. (See Chapters 3 and 4 for a complete description of the features of the Tools panel.)

Using panels

Panels give you access to the many Flash settings. You access them from the Window menu. The specific panels are discussed throughout this book. In this section, we explain how to keep control over your panels.

Most panels are *dockable,* which means that they can sit at the side or bottom of your Flash window without covering up your work. You control panels by doing the following:

- **To dock a panel:** Drag it to the right or bottom of your screen.

- **To undock a panel:** Drag it from its grabber, at the left edge of its title bar.

- **To open or close a panel:** Choose it from the Window panel.

- **To close an undocked panel:** Click its Close button.

- **To close a docked panel:** Right-click (Windows)/Control+click (Mac) its title bar and choose Close Panel.

You can now stack panels just like you stack plastic containers in your refrigerator. Drag a panel by its grabber and drag it beneath another panel to stack it. You can also collapse or expand panels: A *collapsed* panel only displays its title bar, so it doesn't take up much space. Use the arrow on the left side of the title bar to collapse or expand a panel or click its title bar. Finally, on Windows only, there are new arrow buttons above panels that are docked at the bottom of your screen and to the left of panels docked at the right. Click an arrow to collapse the panels to just the tiny arrow button. Click the arrow again to expand the panels to their previous display.

The Property inspector is one of the most important panels. This panel displays information about selected objects, and you can modify objects in the Property inspector as well. It is *context-sensitive,* which means that its contents change according to what you're doing. For example, if you select a graphic object, the Property inspector provides settings relating to that object, and you can use the Property inspector to edit that object.

For the best in customization, you can save any layout of panels you like. Set up the panels and choose Window⇨Save Panel Layout. In the Save Panel Layout dialog box that opens, give the layout a name and click OK. To restore that layout at any time, choose Window⇨Panel Sets and choose your very own layout.

Discovering the Flash menus

Most drawing functions are available only in the Tools panel. Similarly, you often use the Timeline, as we discuss in "Following a timeline" later in this chapter, for creating animation. Almost every other function in Flash is on a menu somewhere. You just need to find it. In general, we discuss the specific menu functions where appropriate throughout this book. Table 1-1 offers a brief overview of the menus.

Table 1-1	Flash Menus
Menu	*What It Does*
Flash	(Mac only) Enables you to set preferences, create keyboard shortcuts, and quit Flash.
File	Enables you to open and close files; save files; import and export files; print; publish movies for the Web; send a movie as an e-mail attachment (Windows only); and quit Flash.
Edit	Provides commands that let you undo and redo actions; cut, copy, and paste to and from the Clipboard; delete, duplicate, select, and deselect objects; copy and paste entire frames; edit symbols (see Chapter 7 for the whole story on symbols); set preferences; and create keyboard shortcuts for commands.

Menu	What It Does
View	Helps you get a better view by letting you zoom in and out; show or hide various parts of the screen; and view a grid for easy layout.
Insert	Enables you to insert symbols (Chapter 7 explains this topic); insert and delete frames and keyframes (see Chapter 9 for more); insert layers (covered in Chapter 6); and create motion tweens (see Chapter 9).
Modify	Helps you modify symbols, frames, scenes, or the entire movie. Offers tools for transforming, aligning, grouping, ungrouping, and breaking objects apart.
Text	Enables you to format text.
Commands	Enables you to re-use and manage saved commands. You can save commands from the History panel. (See Chapter 4.)
Control	Provides options that let you control the playing of movies; test movies and scenes; engage certain interactive functions; and mute sounds.
Window	Enables you to open lots of things, including a new window; panels that help you control objects; the Library (more on the Library in Chapter 2); windows for creating interactive controls (explained in Chapter 10); and the Movie Explorer (to help manage your movie — see Chapter 12).
Help	Comes to the rescue when you need help.

The shortcuts are displayed on the menus, next to the command name. Here are some of the most commonly used keyboard shortcuts. (For more shortcuts, see the tear-out Cheat Sheet at the front of this book):

- **Ctrl+N (Windows) or ⌘+N (Mac):** Open the New Document dialog box so you can start a new movie.

- **Ctrl+O (Windows) or ⌘+O (Mac):** Open an existing movie.

- **Ctrl+S (Windows) or ⌘+S (Mac):** Save your movie. Don't forget to use this shortcut often!

- **Ctrl+X (Windows) or ⌘+X (Mac):** Cut to the Clipboard. Chapter 4 explains more about using the Clipboard.

- **Ctrl+C (Windows) or ⌘+C (Mac):** Copy to the Clipboard.

- **Ctrl+V (Windows) or ⌘+V (Mac):** Paste from the Clipboard.

✔ **Ctrl+Z (Windows) or ⌘+Z (Mac):** Undo. Would you believe that by default Flash remembers your last 100 actions and can undo them? What a relief! The only problem is that Flash doesn't provide a drop-down list of each action, so you're somewhat in the dark about what the next Undo will undo. Think of it as a journey into the long-forgotten past. (See Appendix A for details on customizing the number of Undos that Flash remembers.)

✔ **Ctrl+Y (Windows) or ⌘+Y (Mac):** Redo redoes actions that you undid by using the Undo button. (Got that?) This button remembers just as many actions as the Undo button. If you undo more actions than you want, click Redo (or press Ctrl+Y/⌘+Y) until you're back where you want to be. Using the Undo and Redo buttons is like traveling through Flash time — and it gives you lots of slack while you're working.

✔ **Ctrl+Q (Windows) or ⌘+Q (Mac):** Exit Flash.

We mention other keyboard shortcuts throughout this book when we discuss their corresponding commands.

You should note, although it's not a shortcut, that you can find the Zoom Control box in the upper-right corner of your screen. Click the arrow and choose a zoom factor to zoom in and out. Zooming doesn't change the actual size of objects — it just makes them look bigger or smaller.

You aren't limited to the choices on the Zoom drop-down list. Type a number in the Zoom Control box and press Enter to set your own zoom factor. For example, type **85** to set the zoom factor to 85 percent.

Staging your movies

The white box in the center of your screen is the *Stage*. Think of the Stage as a movie screen where you place objects. You can place graphics and text there and then animate them. Flash also plays back movies on the Stage.

Following a timeline

The Timeline window divides your movie into *frames*. Each frame represents a tiny stretch of time, such as $\frac{1}{12}$ of a second. Creating a movie is simply a matter of assembling frames, which are then quickly played in order.

Chapter 9 explains in detail how to make using the Timeline completely painless. For now, you should just understand the basics. See Figure 1-2 for the basic Timeline.

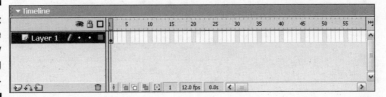

Figure 1-2:
The Timeline is your key to managing animation.

On the left side of the Timeline is the layer list. When you open a new movie, you see only one layer, unimaginatively named Layer 1. A *layer* is like a sheet of transparent acetate on which you draw objects. Layers help you keep objects from running into each other, causing unfortunate, messy results. You organize your entire movie by using layers. For example, if you want to keep some text constant throughout the movie but animate a bouncing dot, you would give the dot its own layer and animate it on that layer. The layer list has room for more layers, and you can add as many layers as you want. (Chapter 6 gives you the lowdown on layers.)

You can move the bottom edge of the Timeline to make room for displaying more layers. Hover the mouse cursor over the bottom line until you see the two-headed arrow and drag downward.

To the right of Layer 1, you see a bunch of rectangles, each representing a frame. (Actually, before you start using the Timeline, they're just potential frames, like unexposed frames on a roll of film.) By default, each frame lasts $\frac{1}{12}$ of a second. Each layer has its own row of frames because you can have different animations or objects on each layer.

A *keyframe* is a frame that defines some change in your animation. In some animations, every frame is a keyframe. Other animations need keyframes for only the first and last frames.

You don't use the Timeline until you're ready to animate. While you work, however, you should organize your objects on separate layers. Don't worry — you can always move an object from one layer to another.

Getting Help in a Flash

This book is all that you need to start creating great animations, but we would be remiss if we didn't tell you about the Flash Help system.

To use Flash Help, choose Help⇨Using Flash or Help⇨Help. Then click the Table of Contents button, as shown here. If you chose Help⇨Using Flash, you see a screen like the one shown in Figure 1-3.

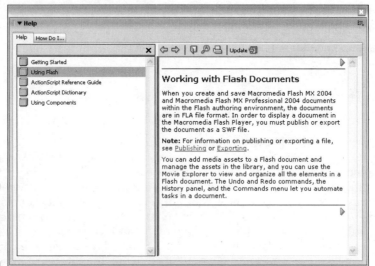

Figure 1-3:
The Using
Flash Help
screen.

Multiple Help manuals

Flash Help contains several sections:

- ✔ **Getting Started** contains a basic overview of Flash and creating a Flash movie.

- ✔ **Using Flash** is the main Help manual.

- ✔ **ActionScript Reference Guide** explains how to use *ActionScript*, which is the programming language that you use to create complex interactive movies. (See Chapter 10 to find out more.)

- ✔ **ActionScript Dictionary** is a thorough listing of all ActionScript terms.

- ✔ **Using Components** explains how to use components (did you guess?), which we explain in Chapter 10.

Click the How Do I tab in the Help panel to find some tutorials and brief explanations of common tasks in Flash.

 To search for a term, click the Search button. Then enter the term and click Search. You can then choose from the list of topics.

Finding more help on the Web

Macromedia offers some support on its Web site. To access it, choose Help➪ Flash Support Center, which takes you to www.macromedia.com/support/

flash/. There you can search the technical document and tutorials for answers to your questions.

Try It, You'll Like It

Perhaps by now you're getting impatient to try out Flash. Getting started is easy. You collect a few ideas, put together some art, add animation, save your movie, and publish it. Then you view it in a browser either online or offline. That's the gratifying part. In the following sections, you get to give Flash a try by working through a basic animation.

Conceiving your first animation

Suppose that you want to add an animated logo to a home page that you've already set up. You want the animation to run when the page loads and then stop. Figure 1-4 shows the Rainbow Resources company logo — unanimated, of course — that you can find on the CD that comes with this book.

Figure 1-4:
A company logo that could stand some animation.

Suppose that you want the word *Rainbow* to fly into your page from the right and the word *Resources* to fly in from the left. At the same time, you want the graphic to rotate 180 degrees. You find out in the following section how to create this animation.

Creating flashy drawings

You can use Flash to create a company logo, but importing one from this book's CD-ROM is simpler. Often, you import existing graphics (such as a company logo) from a file rather than create them from scratch. (Chapter 3 explains how to import and manipulate graphics.)

If you're going through the steps and make a mistake, choose Edit⇨Undo (or press Ctrl+Z/⌘+Z) and try again. You can use Undo repeatedly to undo several steps, if necessary.

To import the Rainbow Resources logo into Flash, follow these steps. (The steps may vary if you're importing some other graphic in a different format.)

1. **Start Flash.**

   See the instructions in "Starting Flash on a PC" or "Starting Flash on a Mac," earlier in this chapter, if you need help.

2. **Choose Flash Document from the Create New section of the Startup screen.**

   You see a spanking-new movie on your screen.

3. **Choose File⇨Import⇨Import to Stage.**

   The Import dialog box opens.

4. **Browse the dialog box until you find** `rainbow.gif` **in the Samples\Ch01 folder of the CD-ROM.**

5. **Click to select** `rainbow.gif` **and then click Open.**

   If you have difficulty importing the file, copy it to your hard drive and try Steps 3–5 again.

   You see the logo on your screen. You need to break the logo into pieces and make it a vector graphic so that you can animate it.

6. **Choose Modify⇨Bitmap⇨Trace Bitmap. In the Trace Bitmap dialog box, set the color threshold to 100, the minimum area to 1, the curve fit to Pixels, and the corner threshold to Many Corners. Click OK in the Trace Bitmap dialog box.**

   Flash creates a vector graphic and breaks up the graphic into individual components. The entire graphic, however, is selected.

7. **Click anywhere outside the graphic to deselect it.**

You've got your logo! Now you need to set it up for animation.

Turning your objects into symbols

In the logo that you imported in the preceding section, each letter is a separate object, which can get pretty confusing. Each line in the logo's design is also separate. But you want your words to stay together and the little design, too. So combining each word and the logo into a symbol is necessary.

To turn the words and the logo into symbols, follow these steps:

1. **Click the Zoom Control drop-down list box (at the upper-right corner of the Stage area) and choose 200%.**

   Use the scroll bar to scroll the words of the logo into view, if necessary.

2. **Click the Selection tool on the Tools panel if it's not already selected.**

3. **Click the upper-right corner of the word *Rainbow* (just above and to the right of the *w*) and drag to the lower-left corner of the *R*.**

   Dragging from right to left makes it easier to avoid selecting the logo at the same time. You should see the entire word selected. If not, click outside the word and try again.

4. **Choose Modify⇨Convert to Symbol. In the Convert to Symbol dialog box, click Graphic for the behavior and then click OK.**

   It is normally good practice to name the symbol, but not necessary for this exercise. When you click OK, Flash places a box around the word so that you can see that it's one object.

5. **Repeat the procedure outlined in Steps 3 and 4 with the word *Resources*.**

   In this case, you may want to start clicking and dragging from the upper-left area of the word; then choose Modify⇨Convert to Symbol again and click OK. Now all the letters of the word *Resources* are a single object.

6. **Click the Zoom Control drop-down list box and choose 100% so that you can see the entire logo.**

7. **Click above and to the left of the logo and drag to the lower right to select the entire logo.**

8. **Hold down the Shift key and click each word to remove both words from the selection.**

   Now the design portion of the logo is selected.

9. **Press F8 (the keyboard shortcut to create a symbol) and click OK in the Convert to Symbol dialog box.**

   Flash creates a symbol from the lines of the logo's design.

See Chapter 7 to find out more about symbols.

Putting your graphics on layers

Placing different components on different layers is required when you're animating. You need to use layers to organize your movie and keep shapes separate so that they don't bump into each other. (See Chapter 6 for the complete story on layers.)

To split your three symbols onto three separate layers, you can use a convenient feature of Flash MX 2004: Distribute to Layers. Follow these steps:

1. **Click the Selection tool on the Tools panel if it's not already selected.**

2. **Drag diagonally across the entire logo, including the two words, to select it.**

   You should see two rectangles inside one bigger rectangle. All three objects in the logo are selected.

3. **Choose Modify⇨Timeline⇨Distribute to Layers.**

   You now have three new layers, named from Symbol 1 through Symbol 3. The three objects of the logo have been distributed to Symbol 1 through 3 and removed from Layer 1.

4. **Click outside the Stage to deselect any objects.**

You're now ready for the animation process.

Making graphics move

We explain earlier in this chapter that your goal is to have the word *Rainbow* fly in from the right and the word *Resources* to fly in from the left. You also want the graphic to rotate 180 degrees at the same time. What you see now is how the animation will end — the last frame of the movie.

Follow these steps to create the last frame of the movie and save the file:

1. **For *each* of the three symbol layers, click frame 30 of the Timeline and choose Insert⇨Timeline⇨Keyframe.**

   You can find out more about keyframes in Chapter 9.

2. **Choose File⇨Save and pick a location where you save other documents that you create.**

   We don't recommend saving the file in the Flash MX 2004 program folder — it may get lost among your Flash program files.

3. **Give your movie a name, such as *Movie of the Year*, and click Save.**

   Flash creates a file named `Movie of the Year.fla`. Flash adds the `.fla` for you because that's the filename extension for Flash movies.

Go back and create the beginning of your movie. Flash can fill in all the blanks in between. Follow these steps to create the beginning of the movie and the animation:

1. **If the Properties panel is not already open, choose Window⇨ Properties to open it.**

   If the Properties panel is open but collapsed, click the arrow at the left end of its title bar to expand the panel.

2. **Select the word *Rainbow*. Click the first frame of the Timeline in the highlighted row.**

   When you select the word *Rainbow,* you can tell which layer it is on by looking at the highlighted layer.

3. **Press and hold down the Shift key while you drag the word to the right, just off the Stage into the gray area.**

   You may need to use the horizontal scroll bar to see the gray area. Pressing Shift keeps the object from moving up or down while you drag to the right.

4. **Click the word *Rainbow's* layer, anywhere between the first and the 30th frame.**

5. **On the Tween drop-down list of the Properties panel, choose Motion.**

   You now see a solid arrow and a light blue color on the Timeline between the first and 30th frames.

6. **Repeat Steps 2–4 for the word *Resources*. When you move the word *Resources,* hold down the Shift key and drag the word to the left, just off the Stage.**

7. **Select the logo design and click the first frame of the Timeline in the highlighted row.**

8. **Choose Modify⇨Transform⇨Rotate 90° CW to rotate the design 90 degrees clockwise.**

9. **Repeat the Modify⇨Transform⇨Rotate 90° CW command to rotate the design a total of 180 degrees.**

10. **Click the logo's highlighted layer, anywhere between the first and 30th frames, and choose Motion from the Tween drop-down list of the Properties panel.**

11. **If necessary, drag the horizontal scroll box until the Stage is in the center of your screen.**

    Otherwise, you won't be able to see the entire animation — and you don't want to miss this one!

12. **Click the first frame of any layer.**

    Your screen should look like the one shown in Figure 1-5.

13. **Press Enter (Return) and watch the animation. (Start writing your Academy Award acceptance speech.)**

14. **Save your movie again by choosing File⇨Save.**

Publishing your first animation for posterity

You can't watch the animation in a Web browser until you publish it and insert it into an HTML document. To do so, follow these steps:

1. **Click the Stage to change the display of the Property inspector.**

   You should see the Settings button next to the Publish label.

2. **Click Settings in the Property inspector.**

   The Publish Settings dialog box opens.

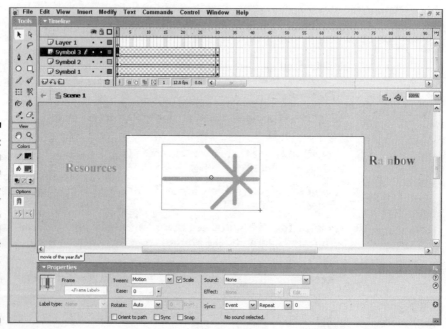

Figure 1-5:
Before you run the animation, *Rainbow* appears to the right and *Resources* to the left, and the line logo is rotated.

3. **Click the HTML tab.**

4. **Deselect the Loop check box in the Playback section to clear it.**

5. **Click Publish and then click OK to close the dialog box.**

   With scarcely a blip, Flash publishes your movie and creates two files, one named Movie of the Year.swf (assuming you used that name) and Movie of the Year.html. They're in the same folder as your .fla movie file. Movie of the Year.swf is the file that your browser reads to play the animation. Movie of the Year. html contains the HTML code required to display your movie on a Web page.

6. **Open your Web browser.**

7. **Choose File⇨Open and find** Movie of the Year.html **(or whatever you named your movie file).**

   You may need to click Browse and navigate to the file.

8. **Double-click the file.**

   Click OK to close the Open dialog box if necessary. Your browser opens the HTML document and reads its instructions to play the Flash movie.

9. **Sit back and watch it roll.**

   Don't blink or you'll miss it. (If you do miss it, click Refresh in your browser.) You can see the movie in Figure 1-6.

10. **When you finish watching the movie, close your browser.**

You can find the Movie of the Year files (.fla, .html, and .swf) in the Ch01 folder on the CD-ROM.

Exiting Flash

When you finish creating something in Flash, choose File⇨Exit (Windows) or choose Flash MX 2004⇨Quit (Mac).

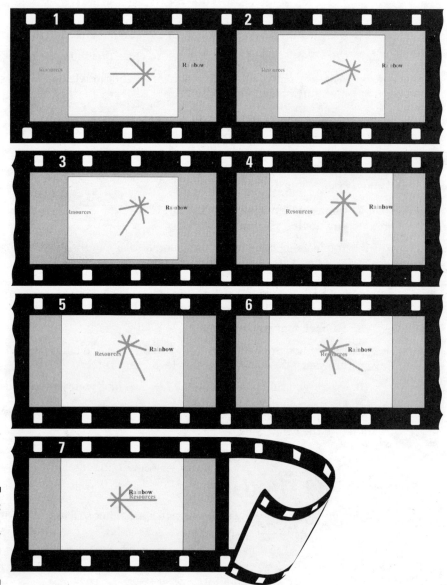

Figure 1-6:
The Movie
of the Year
animation
in detail.

Chapter 2

Your Basic Flash

This chapter starts with an overview of the process of creating animation in Flash. We then discuss some tools and features that are fundamental to using Flash efficiently.

As you find out in this chapter, you use movie properties to set the screen size and color, frame rate, and measurement units for the Flash movie as a whole. We also discuss the Library and how it's a storehouse for images, symbols, and sound. Templates enable you to create great movies without much work. Finally, near the end of this chapter, we explain how you can print a Flash movie.

Looking at the Big Picture

When you use Flash to create animation for your Web site, you generally go through several steps of construction. The steps may vary in their order, but in each case, the skills that you use are about the same. After you know the basics, you can start getting creative and make your Web site rock. Here's a typical path to add animation to an existing Web page:

1. **Think about it.** Noodle around, maybe make some doodles on a napkin, collect a few ideas, and choose one or all of them.

2. **Set up your movie.** Flash lets you choose the size and color of the Stage, the speed of animation (number of frames per second), and other general parameters that affect the entire Flash movie. See the next section of this chapter for details.

3. **Add some graphics.** You have to decide whether you want to create graphics in Flash, create them in another graphics software package, or import existing graphics. Your choice partly depends on how artistic you are, whether you have other software available to you, and whether you can find the right graphics elsewhere. You can also use a combination of sources, which is a common practice. (See Chapter 3 for some suggestions on great places to get graphics.)

4. **Lay out your graphics the way you want your animation to start.** Here's where you may want to scale, rotate, or otherwise fiddle with your graphics. (Chapter 4 has more on transforming your graphics.)

5. **Add some text.** Using Flash is a great way to get terrific text onto your Web site. Add text (also called type); then reshape it, make it transparent (if you don't want to be too obvious), add other effects, and place it where you want it. (Check out Chapter 5 for typography tips.)

6. **Organize your text and graphics by using layers.** Layers help you keep track of what each graphic and text object does while you organize everything into a powerful, coherent statement. Layers keep your animations from going bump in the night and getting entangled. Create as many layers as you need and transfer your existing graphics and text to those layers. (See Chapter 6 for further details on layers.)

7. **Turn a graphic into a symbol and multiply it all over the Stage.** Making objects into symbols is a way to keep from merging with other objects while they merrily animate. You also use symbols to keep the file size down and to enable animation, as well as for interactivity, especially buttons. (Turn to Chapter 7 for more info on symbols.)

8. **Design some buttons.** You know those buttons you click on Web sites all the time? The coolest ones are made in Flash. You can even use movie clips to create animated buttons. (Chapter 8 has more on buttons.)

9. **Animate!** You can create your animation frame by frame or let Flash fill in the animation between your first and last frames, which is called *tweening*. Flash can tween motion, shapes, colors, and transparency, which means that you can create some real magic. (See Chapter 9 for more on animation.)

10. **Get interactive.** You want to start a relationship with your Web viewers so that you can create buttons, frames, and symbols that respond to your viewers' actions. This is probably the most complex functionality of Flash, but we make most of it seem easy. (Turn to Chapter 10 for additional info on interactivity.)

11. **Make it louder! Make it move!** Who wants a quiet Web site? Add sound to your movies or your buttons. You can also add a video file. (Check out Chapter 11 for more on sound and video.)

12. **Publish your magnum opus.** Flash makes getting your movie to your Web site easy by creating both the Flash Player (.swf) file and the HyperText Transfer Language (HTML) code for your Web page. Flash has other options, too, so you can publish to other formats if you want. (Chapter 12 explains how to put it all together, and Chapter 13 is all about publishing your animation.)

Congratulations! You've completed your first Flash Web animation — in fantasy, at least. The following sections cover some details about how to get started.

Setting the Stage

Before you create graphics and animate them — all that fun stuff — you need to make some decisions about the structure of your entire movie. You should make these decisions before you start because changing midway can create problems.

The first step is to decide on the size and color of your Stage and other fundamental settings. Make sure that the Property inspector is open (choose Window⇨Properties). When the Stage is active (just click the Stage), the Property inspector looks like Figure 2-1.

Figure 2-1:
You can change movie properties in the Property inspector.

You can set the color of the Stage to create a colored background for your entire movie. Like with other settings, you need to consider the context of the Web page that will contain the Flash movie. For example, you may want to match the color of your Web page's background. If your Flash movie will constitute the entire Web page, set the Stage color to set the Web page background. You can also color the Stage to create a mood for your animation.

To set the Stage color, click the Background Color swatch in the Property inspector. Flash opens the Color palette. Click the color that you want.

In the Frame Rate text box, specify how many frames that a Flash movie plays each second and press Enter (Windows) or Return (Macintosh). A faster rate allows for smoother animation but may present a performance problem on slower computers. Chapter 9 explains more about this setting. The Flash default is 12 frames per second (fps), which is a good starting point. But changing the frame rate midstream in the creation process changes the rate of all the animation in your movie, which may not give you the results that you want.

The Size button displays the current size of the Stage. By default, Flash uses a Stage size of 550 pixels wide by 400 pixels high. To determine the proper setting, you need to know how your Flash movie will fit into your Web page or site. The default fits on almost everyone's browser screen. You may, however, want to fit your movie into a small corner of a Web page: for example, placing an animated logo in a top corner of a page. In that case, make the Stage smaller.

To change the Stage size, click the Size button to open the Document Properties dialog box, as shown in Figure 2-2. Type the dimensions that you want in the width and height text boxes.

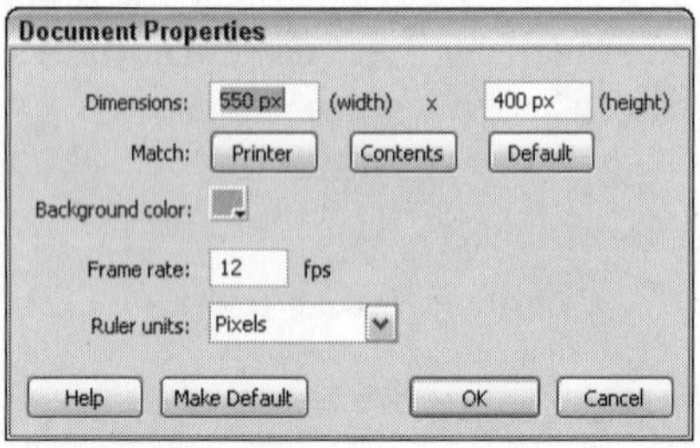

Figure 2-2:
The
Document
Properties
dialog box
sets the
movie's
overall
parameters.

```
Document Properties
   Dimensions:  550 px   (width)   x   400 px   (height)
        Match:  [ Printer ]   [ Contents ]   [ Default ]
Background color:  [  ]
   Frame rate:  12      fps
   Ruler units:  Pixels        [v]
[ Help ]  [ Make Default ]          [ OK ]   [ Cancel ]
```

Flash offers two shortcuts for setting the Stage size:

✔ Click Match Printer to set the Stage size according to the paper size set in the Page Setup dialog box (choose File⇨Page Setup). (For the Mac, the Print Margins dialog box, which you access by choosing File⇨Print Margins, also affects the paper size.) Flash sets the size of the Stage to the maximum possible area of the paper minus the margins. Later in this chapter, in the section "Printing Your Movie," we cover this dialog box in more detail.

✔ Click Match Contents to set the Stage size to the contents of the Stage. Of course, for this to work, you need some objects on the Stage. Flash creates a Stage size by placing equal space around all sides of the entire contents of the Stage. If you want to create the smallest possible Stage, place your objects in the upper-left corner and then click Match Contents.

To change the units used for measuring the screen and objects, choose a unit from the Ruler Units drop-down list.

Note that you can change the background color and frame rate in the Document Properties dialog box and in the Property inspector.

When you're done setting document properties, click OK to close the dialog box.

Grabbing a Graphic

The first step when creating animation for your Web site is usually to create or import graphics. First, you should know a little about the different kinds of graphics that you can use in a Flash movie.

Understanding vectors and bitmaps

If you know enough about graphics to understand the difference between bitmap and vector graphics, feel free to skip this section. (We hope you always feel free.)

Bitmaps are created with lots of dots. Put them all together, and you get a picture. On-screen, they're displayed as *pixels*. As you can imagine, it can take a large file to store the information about all the dots in a bitmap. Another problem with bitmaps is that they don't scale up well. If you try to enlarge a bitmap, it starts to look grainy because you see all those dots (as in the left example shown in Figure 2-3).

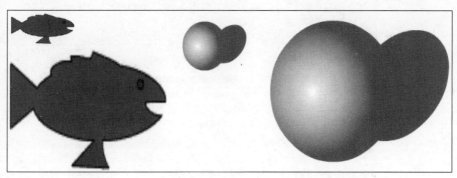

Figure 2-3:
Bitmaps
lose focus
when
enlarged;
vector
graphics
remain
sharp and
clear.

Vector graphics are defined with equations that specify lines, shapes, and locations. Blank space doesn't have to be recorded, and the equations are particularly efficient in storing information. As a result, file sizes are usually smaller.

Vector graphics are infinitely scalable, either up or down. No matter how big you make your graphic, it always looks perfect, as shown in the right example in Figure 2-3. In fact, your graphic may even look better when it's larger because the curves are smoother.

Flash creates vector-based graphics. The small size of the files means that Flash Player files load and play super fast on a Web page. As you undoubtedly know, fast file loading means that your Web page viewers don't have to wait a long time to see your effects. That's the advantage of Flash. (However, you can also import bitmaps. In Chapter 3, we discuss what you need to know about both bitmaps and vectors.)

Finding graphics

Okay, so you've doodled and played around with some ideas for your Flash animation and perhaps jotted down a few notes or maybe even made a few sketches. You're ready to start building your Flash animation. A logical place to start is to collect some of the graphics that will serve as building blocks in this process.

Where do you get them? You have several choices:

- ✔ Use the library of graphics that comes with Flash. You can use these graphics as is or as a springboard for your own, more customized, creations.
- ✔ Create your graphics from scratch (if you feel artistic) by using the Flash drawing tools that we describe in detail in Chapter 3.
- ✔ Create graphics in another graphics software package, such as Fireworks or FreeHand.
- ✔ Import graphics from archives of art available on this book's CD-ROM or the Web.
- ✔ Combine any or all of these approaches.

You can also import video files. If you want to add video to your Flash movies, see Chapter 11 for detailed instructions.

Going to the Library

Every graphic that you create in Flash is precious and deserves to be archived in style. Each movie file that you create has a Library. The Library saves the following types of objects so that they never get lost:

✔ Graphic, movie clip, and button symbols

✔ Sounds

✔ Imported bitmap graphics

✔ Imported video files

You'll find yourself going to the Library often. Figure 2-4 shows a Library containing several types of symbols plus a sound and a bitmap.

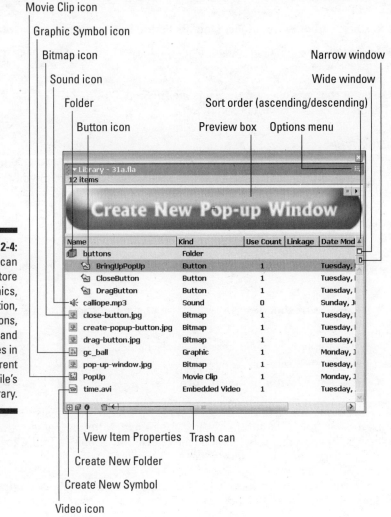

Movie Clip icon

Graphic Symbol icon

Bitmap icon

Sound icon

Folder

Button icon

Narrow window

Wide window

Sort order (ascending/descending)

Preview box   Options menu

Figure 2-4:
You can
store
graphics,
animation,
buttons,
sounds, and
video files in
your current
movie file's
Library.

View Item Properties   Trash can

Create New Folder

Create New Symbol

Video icon

To go to the Library, choose Window⇨Library. You can also press Ctrl+L (Windows)/⌘+L (Mac) or F11. When you open the Library, Flash creates a new window or adds the Library window to the set of panels that are already open.

To use any object in the Library, follow these steps:

1. **Select the layer on which you want to put the object or create a new layer for the object.**

2. **Click the point on the Timeline where you want the object to start or appear.**

3. **Click and drag the object from its listing in the Library to the Stage.**

   You can also select an object from the listing and drag its image from the preview box.

The point that you click on the Timeline (in Step 2) must be a keyframe. Chapter 9 explains keyframes in detail.

Using folders

A Flash movie can contain dozens or even hundreds of symbols, so you need to keep them organized. Flash provides several features to keep you from tearing out your hair.

You can, and should, organize your symbols into folders if you have more than a few. To create a new folder, follow these steps:

1. **Click the New Folder button at the bottom of the Library window.**

   Flash creates a new folder.

2. **Type a name that describes the type of symbols that you want to put into the folder.**

   For example, you could create a folder named Intro and another one named Conclusion.

3. **Press Enter (Windows) or Return (Mac).**

To put symbols into a folder, drag them to the folder. You can also move symbols from one folder to another — just drag them. Note that folders exist just to help keep you organized. You can move symbols from one folder to another without affecting your movie.

To keep your symbol list from getting unwieldy, you can collapse folders. A collapsed folder doesn't display its contents. As soon as you need to see what's inside, you can expand the folder. Double-click a folder to either collapse or expand it.

To quickly see the structure of your folders, click the Library's Options menu. Choose Collapse All Folders. You can also choose Expand All Folders to see everything in the Library.

More Library housekeeping

 By default, Flash alphabetizes items in the Library by name. You may, however, have different ideas. You can sort from A to Z (ascending) or from Z to A (descending). You can also sort by any of the columns in the Library. To change the direction of sorting (for any column in the Library), click the Sort Order button in the upper-right corner of the list. To sort, click the heading of the column that you want to sort by. (On the Mac, you can click the column heading again to change the sort order.)

You can resize the Library window by dragging its lower-right corner. Or you can click the Wide Window or Narrow Window button to grow or shrink its width, respectively (refer to Figure 2-4). You can resize any column by dragging the column heading's divider left or right.

To rename any Library item, double-click the item's name, type the new name, and press Enter or Return. Don't worry — the original filenames of imported files remain unchanged at their original location.

To delete an item, select the item and click the Trash can.

If you want to find out which items in the Library you aren't using, look in the third column (Use Count) for items with a zero use count. To make sure that the use count is accurate, click the Library's Options menu and choose Keep Use Counts Updated or Update Use Counts Now. After you know which items you aren't using, you should delete them to reduce the file size of your Flash movie.

You can keep imported bitmaps and sounds updated if the original files have changed. Select the file and choose Update from the Options menu of the Library window.

Using the Library of other movies

After you place objects in a file's Library, you can use those objects in any other Flash movie that you create. In your current movie, choose File⇨Open as Library, choose the movie file containing the symbols that you want, and then click Open. The new Library window is attached to the original window, but you can drag it off to its own window. Click the Expand/Collapse arrow to expand or collapse the Library window.

You can use the libraries of other open Flash movies in the same way. The Library of each open file has its own title bar in the Library window that you can expand or collapse as you wish.

You can copy symbols or anything else in a Library from one movie to another by simply dragging them from one Library to another. Expand the Libraries that you want to use, select an item, and drag it into the other Library. Easy!

To create a new symbol that goes directly into the Library (rather than on the Stage), choose Create New Symbol from the Library Options menu. You are transported to symbol-editing mode, where you can create your symbol as you normally would. To return to your main movie, choose Edit➪Edit Document. For more information on creating and editing symbols, see Chapter 7.

Exploring the Flash stock Library

Flash comes with four libraries that contain a basic assortment of sounds, ActionScript classes, learning interactions (structures for tests or polls), and button symbols. They are well done, so they're worth looking through. Choose Window➪Other Panels➪Common Libraries and choose one of the options to find the libraries.

Using a Template

To help you create Flash movies more easily, Flash MX 2004 comes with a few templates for common types of movies. Instructions are included on the templates themselves. To create a Flash movie from a template, choose File➪New and click the Templates tab. In the New from Template dialog box that appears (see Figure 2-5), choose a template category, choose one of the category items, and then click OK.

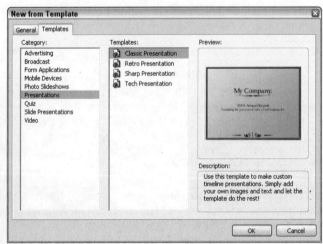

Figure 2-5:
Use the
New from
Template
dialog box
to create a
Flash movie
from a
template.

You can choose from the following template categories:

- ✔ **Advertising:** You can choose from a number of ad sizes. These templates simply contain a Stage of the ad size that you choose. Instructions are on a separate, nonprinting layer that you can hide.

- ✔ **Broadcast:** This creates movies that are the appropriate size for movies that you create for film, video, or television.

- ✔ **MobileDevices:** Three mobile devices are available, with brief instructions, a link for more information, and an appropriately sized Stage.

- ✔ **PhotoSlideshows:** This template creates a slide show of photos and explains how to prepare and name your photos.

- ✔ **Presentations:** Create your own presentation. Just follow the instructions and add the desired text and graphics to each frame.

- ✔ **Quiz:** Create a quiz, complete with several types of question formats and answer feedback. This template's instructions are fairly involved.

- ✔ **Slide Presentation:** Create slide presentations by using the new features of Flash MX 2004 Professional. (For more about slide presentations, see Chapter 12.)

- ✔ **Video:** Options for including video in your movies.

When you open a new movie from a template, you should save it as a movie. This way, the template is unchanged, and you are free to make any changes that you want.

You can also save movies as templates. If you create a movie that you want to reuse in many variations, choose File⇨Save as Template to open the Save as Template dialog box, as shown in Figure 2-6.

Figure 2-6:
The Save as Template dialog box saves your movies as templates.

Type a name, choose a category, and enter a description for your template. Then click Save. From now on, you can open your template just like any of the templates that come with Flash, just as we describe. Using templates can save you lots of work!

TIP

To create your own category for templates, type a category name in the Category text box instead of choosing one of the existing categories from the drop-down list.

Printing Your Movie

Usually, you don't print your movies — you publish them on the Web. But you may want to collaborate on a movie with others who don't have Flash (How unenlightened of them!). Or, you may just want to analyze a movie on paper, tack your animation frames on the wall, and rearrange their sequence. In this type of situation, you can print your animation frame by frame.

To print a movie, follow these steps:

1. **To set page margins, choose File⇨Page Setup (Windows) or File⇨ Print Margins (Mac).**

   The Page Setup (Windows) or Print Margins (Mac) dialog box appears, as shown in Figure 2-7.

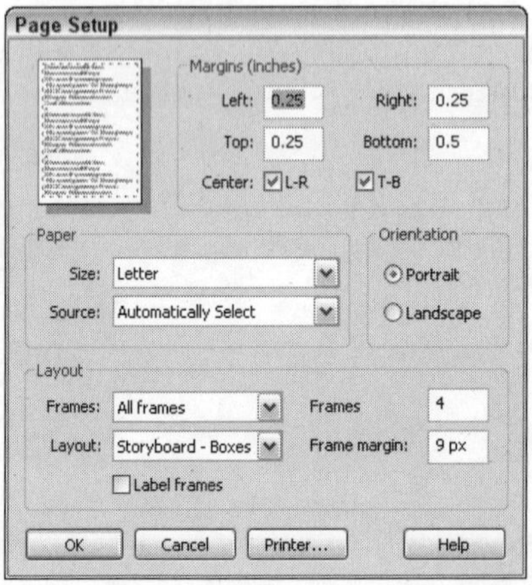

Figure 2-7:
Use the
Page Setup
dialog box
to specify
how to print
your Flash
movie.

```
Page Setup
┌─────────────────────────────────────────────┐
│  Margins (Inches)                            │
│         Left: [0.25]    Right: [0.25]        │
│         Top:  [0.25]    Bottom: [0.5]        │
│       Center: ☑ L-R     ☑ T-B                │
│                                              │
│  Paper                   Orientation         │
│    Size:   [Letter ▼]     ⊙ Portrait         │
│    Source: [Automatically Select ▼] ○ Landscape │
│                                              │
│  Layout                                      │
│   Frames: [All frames ▼]  Frames    [4]      │
│   Layout: [Storyboard - Boxes ▼] Frame margin: [9 px] │
│          ☐ Label frames                      │
│  [ OK ]  [ Cancel ]  [ Printer... ]  [ Help ]│
└─────────────────────────────────────────────┘
```

2. **In the Margins section, set the margins.**

   You can probably keep the default margins.

3. **Select the Center check boxes to center the printing horizontally (L–R) and vertically (T–B) on the page.**

4. **In the Layout section, click the Frames drop-down list and decide whether to print only the first frame or all frames.**

5. **Click the Layout drop-down list in the Layout section to choose from the following options:**

    • **Actual Size:** Lets you choose a scale. This option prints one frame to a page.

    • **Fit on One Page:** Fits one frame on a page, scaling it to fit the paper.

    • **Storyboard – Boxes:** Places several thumbnail sketches of your movie on a page. You can specify how many frames that you want in a row in the Frames box. You may need to experiment to get the right result. In the Frame/Story Margin text box, enter in pixels the space between the boxes. The Boxes option places each frame in a box.

    • **Storyboard – Grid:** Creates a grid of lines for your storyboard rather than individual boxes around the frames. This option is just a matter of aesthetics — don't get too hung up over these choices.

    • **Storyboard – Blank:** Leaves out the boxes or grid and just prints all your frames in the storyboard. You have the same Frames and Frame Story/Margin settings as for the other storyboard options.

6. **If you chose a Storyboard option, select the Label Frames check box (Windows) or Label (Mac) to give each frame a number.**

7. **On a Mac, when you finish setting your options, click OK; then choose File⇨Page Setup.**

    In Windows, you skip this step because you already opened the Page Setup dialog box in Step 1.

8. **Select the size of the paper; (Windows only) define the paper source in the Paper section.**

    Usually you can leave this section as is because it's based on your printer's default settings.

9. **In the Orientation section, select Portrait (taller rather than wider) or Landscape (wider rather than taller).**

10. **(Macintosh only) In the Format section, choose your printer from the pull-down list.**

11. **When you finish setting your options, click OK.**

12. **To print, choose File⇨Print.**

    Alternatively, you can press Ctrl+P (Windows) or ⌘+P (Mac).

Figure 2-8 shows an example of the storyboard with the grid option. The storyboard shows four frames across with a portrait orientation.

You can find out more about the Flash Player's special printing capabilities in Chapter 13.

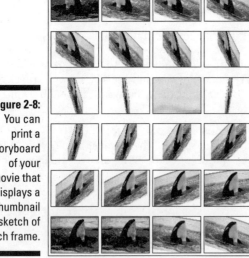

Figure 2-8:
You can print a storyboard of your movie that displays a thumbnail sketch of each frame.

Part II
1,000 Pictures and 1,000 Words

The 5th Wave   By Rich Tennant

In this part . . .

*G*raphics are the basis of animation. Before you can make anything move, you need to create the graphics that form the building blocks of your animation. Chapter 3 describes all the types of graphics that you can use, from basic shapes created in Flash to sophisticated imported bitmap graphics. The Flash tools are quite capable, and you can create exciting effects with gradient fills, softened edges, and transparency. The Flash editing features, as we describe in Chapter 4, offer more opportunities to create great-looking graphics — including skewing objects, using the Distort & Envelope options, and manipulating fills every which way.

In Chapter 5, you find ways to say great things with flexible text options and formatting. You can even break up text and animate it, letter by letter. To keep all the pieces of your animation from going completely out of control, you see how to use layers to organize your movie animation in Chapter 6. You can use special layers to guide animation along a path and hide objects behind a *mask*.

Chapter 3

Getting Graphic

• •

• •

*I*n this chapter, you get down to the details of creating your own graphics in Flash. The Flash graphics tools (found in the Tools panel) offer you the capability to easily create interesting and professional-looking shapes. Of course, you can also import graphics created in other programs.

After you master all the techniques for drawing and editing, you can create some very cool graphics. If you're new to Flash, take the time to try out all the tools and techniques until you feel comfortable with them.

For a handy reference to the Tools panel, which we refer to throughout this entire chapter, see the Cheat Sheet at the front of this book.

Sharpen Your Pencil

The Flash Pencil tool is designed to be used like a real pencil to create freehand shapes. Whenever you want to create a shape not available from other Flash tools (such as the circle and square), you can use the Pencil. But the Pencil tool goes beyond a regular pencil's capabilities by incorporating cool features that smooth or straighten what you draw. In addition to those features, the Pencil also includes the *shape-recognition* feature (perfect for those who are less artistic). Draw something that approximates a triangle, and Flash forgivingly perfects it for you. In this section, we explain exactly how to use this tool.

 To start, click the Pencil tool on the Tools panel. To draw without changing the Pencil modifier, move the cursor onto the Stage, click, and draw. After you release the mouse button, Flash modifies the shape according to the active modifier setting.

Setting the Pencil modifier

When you choose the Pencil tool, the Options area below the Tools panel changes to display the drawing mode modifier for the Pencil tool.

The Pencil modifier has three drawing modes:

- ✔ **Straighten:** Straightens lines and converts sloppy squares, rectangles, circles, ellipses, and triangles to perfect ones
- ✔ **Smooth:** Smoothes out curved lines, eliminating unsightly bumps and lumps
- ✔ **Ink:** Slightly smoothes and straightens your curves and lines but leaves them mostly the way that you drew them

In Figure 3-1, you see a right-pointing arrow. Suppose that you have already drawn the horizontal line and now want to create the arrow's point. See how the point looks before and after Flash modified it by using the Straighten drawing mode to create perfectly straight lines.

Figure 3-1:
Use
Straighten
mode of the
Pencil tool
to draw
straight lines.

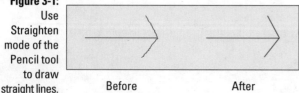

Before   After

Suppose that you want to animate some waves on your Web site. You start to draw the outline of the waves. Figure 3-2 shows how the waves look as drawn and after Flash smoothes them out by using Smooth mode.

Figure 3-2:
Smooth
mode
makes you
look like
a real
smoothie
when it
comes to
drawing
curves.

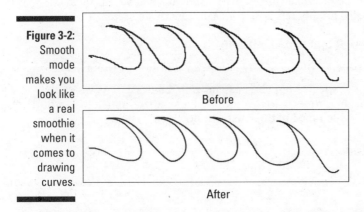

Before

After

For more complex shapes, Ink mode helps you look good without taking away too much of your own authorship.

How to set smoothing and shape-recognition preferences

You can tell Flash just how much you want it to smooth or straighten curved lines when you draw with the Pencil tool. Choose Edit⇨Preferences (Windows) or Flash MX 2004⇨Preferences (Mac) and click the Editing tab. From the Smooth Curves drop-down list, choose one of the following options:

- **Off:** Flash doesn't smooth or straighten at all.

- **Rough:** Flash smoothes or straightens only slightly, honoring your own work as much as possible.

- **Normal:** Flash smoothes or straightens a medium amount. Normal is the default setting.

- **Smooth:** Flash smoothes and straightens more so that you get fewer bumps and jolts.

In the same way, you can tell Flash how picky you want it to be in recognizing lines, circles, ovals, squares, rectangles, and arcs (90 degrees and 180 degrees). For lines, choose Off, Strict, Normal, or Tolerant from the Recognize Lines drop-down list. Normal is the default. Use Tolerant if you're a klutz; use Strict (or even Off) if you don't want Flash fiddling too much (or at all) with your work.

For other shapes and arcs, choose an option from the Recognize Shapes drop-down list. You have the same Off, Strict, Normal, and Tolerant options.

Setting the stroke type

While drawing with the Pencil (and any of the other drawing tools), you can also control the type of *stroke* (line style) as well as its *width* (also called *height* or *weight*). To modify stroke settings, follow these steps:

1. **Click the Pencil tool to make it active.**

2. **Open the Property inspector by choosing Window⇨Properties.**

   The Property inspector appears, as shown in Figure 3-3. As we explain in Chapter 1, the Property inspector changes depending on which tool is active and which part of the Flash window you're using.

Figure 3-3:
Use the
Property
inspector to
control line
type and
width.

3. **Click the Stroke style drop-down list to display the available line styles and choose a new line style from the list.**

4. **To change the line width, type a new value in the Stroke Height text box and press Enter or Return or drag the slider bar to the value that you want.**

The first available stroke width on the Stroke Style drop-down list is Hairline, which creates a hairline-width line. Flash measures *weights* of other line types in points. Any line that you create by using a tool will have the properties that you specify in the Property inspector.

A point equals ¹⁄₇₂ of an inch.

To create a custom weight, type a width in the Stroke Weight text box of the Property inspector and then press Enter or Return.

You can create custom line styles as well. In the Property inspector, choose Custom. In the Line Style dialog box that opens, you can create your own designer line styles.

Setting the color

 When using the Pencil, you can set the color of the stroke in the Property inspector or the Colors section of the Tools panel. In either location, click the Stroke Color box to open the Color palette and then choose a color.

We explain more about using colors in the section "A Rainbow of Colors," later in this chapter.

Creating Shapely Shapes

In the preceding section, we explain that you can draw shapes by using the Pencil tool. You can also draw lines, rectangles, squares, ovals, and circles by using the shape tools. Use these tools when you want more control over your shapes — for example, when you want to draw perfect circles, perfect squares, and straight lines.

Line up

 To draw a line, choose the Line tool from the Tools panel. Click the Stage at the desired starting point of the line and drag to the ending point. Then release the mouse button. To keep your lines at multiples of 45 degrees, press Shift while dragging. Flash creates the line at the 45-degree angle closest to your drag line.

When you use the Line tool, you can modify the line weight, style, and color in the same way as for the Pencil tool, as we discuss in the preceding section.

Be square

 To draw a rectangle, choose the Rectangle tool from the Tools panel. Click the Stage at one corner of the rectangle and drag to the opposite corner. Then release the mouse button. To create a square, press Shift as you drag.

When you click the Rectangle tool, you can modify the line weight, style, and color of the rectangle in the same way that you can modify a line when you use the Pencil tool. With rectangles, however, Flash creates *two* objects: the *fill* (the area inside the stroke) and the *stroke* (the outline of the rectangle).

Flash provides the following tools for adjusting the settings for rectangles:

- ✔ **Fill Color:** Determines the color that fills the inside of the rectangle. You can click the Fill Color box — either in the Property inspector or in the Colors section of the Tools panel — and choose one of the colors from the palette that opens. You can also choose from the gradients displayed at the bottom of the palette. (See the section "A Rainbow of Colors," later in this chapter, for details about customizing colors and gradients.)

- ✔ **Stroke Color:** Determines the color of the stroke (the outline) of the rectangle. Click the Stroke Color box — either in the Property inspector or in the Colors section of the Tools panel — and choose a color from the palette.

- ✔ **Black and White:** Sets the stroke color to black and the fill color to white. Click the Black and White button in the Colors section of the Tools panel.

- ✔ **No Color:** Sets either the stroke color or the fill color (whichever tool is pressed) to no color. You have to click either the Stroke Color box or the Fill Color box before you click the No Color box.

- ✔ **Swap Colors:** Switches the stroke and fill colors.

- ✔ **Round Rectangle Radius modifier:** Creates a rectangle with rounded corners. (It's located in the Options section of the Tools panel.) Click this tool to open the Rectangle Settings dialog box, where you can set the radius of corners in points; then click OK to close the dialog box. The rectangle that you draw will have nicely rounded corners.

If you want to create a rectangle with no fill, choose the Rectangle tool, open the Fill Color box, and click the box with the diagonal line in the upper-right corner of the Color palette. To create a rectangle with a fill but no outline, choose the Rectangle tool, click the Stroke Color tool, and choose the box with the diagonal line at the top of the palette.

Be an egg

To draw an oval, choose the Oval tool from the Tools panel. Click the Stage at one corner of the oval and drag to the opposite corner. (Ovals don't really have corners, but you get the idea after you try one or two.) Then release the mouse. To create a perfect circle, press and hold Shift while you drag.

After you click the Oval tool, you can change the line color, type, and weight in the same way as described in the "Setting the stroke type" section, earlier in this chapter, for the Pencil tool. You can set the colors as we describe in the preceding section on drawing rectangles.

Mixing and Matching Shapes

After you create shapes on the Stage, you need to understand what happens when two objects touch. It's a little weird, but you soon see how flexible the Flash drawing tools are. Two basic rules exist about objects that touch. We cover those rules in the following sections.

Cutting up shapes

The first rule is that when you use the Pencil or Line tool to draw a line that intersects any other shape or line, the line acts like a knife to cut the other shape or line. The line that you draw is also cut into segments. You don't see the effect until you try to select or move one of the objects. Suppose that you want to draw a broken heart. You can draw the breaking line by using the Pencil tool. You now have several objects, and you can easily move apart the two halves of the heart. In the second heart (see Figure 3-4), the line has been erased.

Figure 3-4:
Intersect any shape with a line, and the line splits the shape and is itself segmented.

Placing objects on top of each other

The second rule about objects that touch is that when you place one shape on top of another, the top shape replaces whatever is beneath it. Again, you can see the results only when you try to select or move the shapes. But now it gets a little complicated:

- If the two shapes are the same color, they merge together into one combined shape.
- If the two shapes are different colors, they remain separate.

Figure 3-5 shows a circle and a triangle on the left. They are the same color. On the right, you can see the result after moving the circle down over the triangle. Presto! It's an ice cream cone. If you try to select the shape, it's now one object.

Figure 3-5:
Build
complex
shapes by
combining
basic
shapes of
the same
color.

When you combine shapes of different colors, you create cutouts. Rather than add the shapes together, the top shape just replaces the area beneath it. Figure 3-6 shows how you can create a cutout. We've displayed a grid on the Stage (find more about that in Chapter 4) so that you can see that the image on the right is a cutout.

Figure 3-6:
Create
cutouts by
placing
different-
colored
shapes on
top of each
other.
There's a
hole in the
bucket!

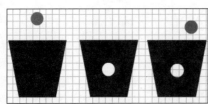

To create a cutout effect, follow these steps:

1. **Create two separate shapes of different colors.**

2. **Move one shape on top of another shape.**

3. **Deselect the shape that you moved by clicking anywhere off the shape.**

4. **Select the top shape again and drag it away from the bottom shape to create the cutout.**

See Chapter 4 for details on selecting and moving objects.

Creating Curves with the Pen

The Pen lets you draw *Bezier* curves, also called splines. Bezier curves are named after the French mathematician Pierre Bézier, who first described them. By using the Pen tool, you can create smooth curves that flow into each other. You can also create straight lines.

 You can set preferences for the Pen tool by choosing Edit⇨Preferences (Windows) or Flash⇨Preferences (Mac) and clicking the Editing tab. We suggest enabling Show Pen Preview to display a preview of the line or curve while you draw. This setting helps you get a better idea of what the result will be. Click OK when you finish setting your preferences.

To create a line or curve, choose the Pen tool from the Tools panel. What you do next depends on whether you want to draw a straight line or a curve. The following sections show you how to draw both.

Drawing straight lines

To draw a straight line with the Pen tool, follow these steps:

1. **To create a line segment, click the start point and then click the end point.**

2. **Continue to add line segments by clicking additional points.**

3. **Double-click to complete the process. You can also Ctrl+click (Windows) or ⌘+click (Mac) anywhere off the line.**

   Flash previews segments in blue. When you choose another tool, Flash displays Beziers in the current stroke color.

Close a figure by pointing near the start point. You see a small circle. Click the start point, and Flash closes the figure. Flash fills in the shape with the current fill color.

Drawing curves

Drawing curves with the Pen tool involves a couple of steps, depending on the complexity of the curve that you want to create. To draw a curve with the Pen tool, follow these steps:

1. **Click the start point and drag the mouse in the desired direction and distance for the start of the curve. Then release the mouse button.**

   You see a *tangent line* that defines both the direction and length, as shown in Figure 3-7.

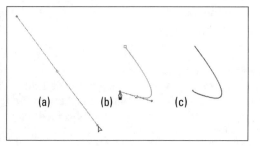

Figure 3-7: Drawing a curve with the Pen tool: 1, 2, 3 and you have a big nose!

(a)   (b)   (c)

2. **For one curve, move the mouse cursor to the desired end of the curve; then double-click to end the curve.**

   If you set preferences to show a preview of the curve (as we explain earlier in the section "Creating Curves with the Pen"), you also see a stretchy line attached to your mouse cursor that previews the shape.

3. **To continue to draw curves, again drag in the desired starting direction, release the mouse button, and move the mouse cursor to the end of the next curve. You can continue to draw curves this way until you double-click to end the curve.**

For both lines and curves, you can press and hold Shift to constrain the lines or curves (the tangent lines) to 45-degree angles.

Drawing curves with the Pen tool takes practice, but you soon get the hang of it.

Getting Artistic with the Brush

The Brush tool lets you create artistic effects that look like painting. You can adjust the size and shape of the brush, and if you have a pressure-sensitive pen and tablet, you can adjust the width of the stroke by changing the pressure on the pen.

To paint with the Brush tool, click the tool on the Tools panel and drag anywhere on the Stage. Press and hold Shift while you brush to keep your strokes either horizontal or vertical. The brush doesn't have a stroke (line) color. The brush creates only fills. Use the Fill Color drop-down list in the Property inspector or in the Colors section of the Tools panel to choose a fill color.

When you choose the Brush tool, the Brush modifiers appear in the Options section of the Tools panel, as shown in Figure 3-8.

Figure 3-8:
The brush modifiers control the size and shape of the brush as well as how the brush relates to existing images.

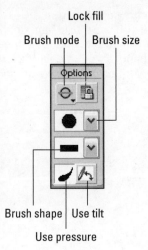

Lock fill

Brush mode | Brush size

Brush shape | Use tilt

Use pressure

Brush Mode

The Brush Mode modifier determines how the brush relates to existing objects on the Stage. Here are your choices for Brush mode. (Figure 3-9 shows some examples.)

- **Paint Normal:** You just paint away, oblivious to anything else. Use this setting when you don't need to worry about other objects.

- **Paint Fills:** You paint fills and empty areas of the Stage. The paint doesn't cover lines. Note that your lines seem to be covered while you paint, but when you release the mouse button, they reappear.

- **Paint Behind:** You paint behind existing objects, but only blank areas of the Stage. While you paint, the brush seems to cover everything, but when you release the mouse button, your existing objects reappear. You can messily paint over your objects, knowing that they won't be affected.

- **Paint Selection:** You paint only a filled-in area that you previously selected. While you paint, your existing objects are covered, but they reappear when you release the mouse button. You don't need to worry about painting within the lines because Flash fills only the selected area.

✔ **Paint Inside:** You paint inside lines. Only the fill where you start brushing is painted. Paint Inside also paints an empty area on the Stage if that's where you start brushing. Again, at first the paint seems to cover up everything, but when you release the mouse button, Flash keeps your paint nice and neat, inside the lines — like you learned in kindergarten.

Brush Size

Click the Brush Size drop-down list and choose a size from the list of circles. This list defines the width of the brush. If you use a brush mode that helps you draw neatly, such as Paint Selection, you don't need to be too concerned with the size of the brush. On the other hand, if you're creating an artistic effect by using Paint Normal mode, the width of the brush is important.

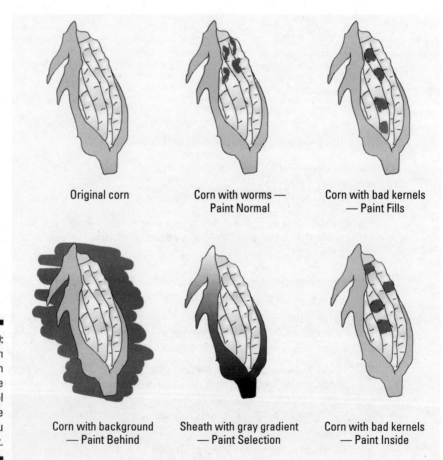

Original corn

Corn with worms —
Paint Normal

Corn with bad kernels
— Paint Fills

Corn with background
— Paint Behind

Sheath with gray gradient
— Paint Selection

Corn with bad kernels
— Paint Inside

Figure 3-9:
Set Brush
Mode when
using the
Brush tool
to get the
effect you
want.

Brush Shape

Flash offers several brush shapes you can choose from. Click the Brush Shape drop-down list and choose one of the shapes. Each shape produces a different effect, especially when you paint at an angle — you just need to try them out to see what works best. Figure 3-10 shows a honey jar drawn with various brush shapes.

Figure 3-10: Each brush shape creates a different effect — especially at the ends of the stroke.

Pressure and tilt modifiers

If you have a pressure-sensitive pen and tablet, Flash also displays a pressure modifier (refer to Figure 3-8) so that you can vary the width of your strokes according to the pressure that you put on your pen while you draw. Click the Use Pressure button to turn on this feature.

Flash fully supports pressure-sensitive pens and adds some unusual features, such as the ability to use the opposite end of the pen to erase — just like a real pencil. Figure 3-11 shows this type of pen and tablet.

A pressure-sensitive pen works together with a tablet to help you draw in Flash. The tablet tracks the movement and pressure of the pen while you draw. You can also use the pen as a mouse to choose menu and dialog box items. In other words, if you want, you can use the pen for all your Flash work. Alternatively, you can use the pen and tablet just for drawing and use the mouse when you want to work with menus and dialog boxes.

The Tilt modifier varies the angle of your brush stroke when you vary the angle of the stylus on the tablet. For example, holding the stylus straight up and down produces a different shape brush stroke from the one that you get if you hold the stylus at a 45-degree angle to the tablet.

Figure 3-11: This Wacom pen and tablet set is easier to draw with than a mouse and enables you to easily vary the brush width as you draw.

Use the Tilt modifier for fine control over your brush strokes. Click the Use Tilt button in the Options section of the Tools panel to turn on this feature. You see the effect most clearly with a large brush size and one of the narrow brush shapes. When you start to draw, change the angle of the stylus to the tablet. Watch the cursor shape turn, giving you a hint as to the shape of the brush stroke. Try brushing at a few angles to see how this works.

See the section "A Rainbow of Colors," later in this chapter, for an explanation of the Lock Fill modifier.

Smoothing your brush strokes

Smoothing brush strokes is similar to smoothing pencil strokes. You can finely adjust how much your brush strokes are smoothed after you finish drawing them.

Adjusting the smoothing of brush strokes is new for Flash MX 2004. In Flash MX, the smoothing was set at 50. Now you can set smoothing anywhere from 0.25 to 100.

To set brush smoothing, click the Brush tool and open the Property inspector (Window⇨Properties). Use the Smoothing text box or slider to set a new value. The default value is 50. The lower values change your strokes less. Therefore, if you set the Smoothing to 0.25, the brush stroke is closest to what you actually drew. The higher values smooth and simplify your strokes more. A setting of 100 creates strokes that are smoother. Lower values create more vectors, resulting in a larger file size for your movie.

Pouring on the Paint

The Paint Bucket creates fills that fill shapes with color. You may create fills when you use other tools, such as the Rectangle and Oval tools, or you may want to fill an enclosed area that you created with either the Line or Pencil tools. You can also fill enclosed shapes created with the Pen or Brush tools, as we explain earlier in this chapter.

The Paint Bucket is also handy for changing existing fills. You can change the color as well as fiddle around with gradient and bitmap fills. (See Chapter 4 for more on editing fills.)

 To use the Paint Bucket, choose the tool from the Tools panel. Set the color by clicking the Fill Color tool and choosing a color. Alternatively, you can use the Fill Color drop-down list in the Property inspector.

 Flash can fill areas that aren't completely closed. The Gap Size modifier, in the Options section of the Tools panel, determines how large of a gap that Flash will overlook to fill in an almost enclosed area. Choices range from Don't Close Gaps to Close Large Gaps. Because *small* and *large* are relative terms, you may have to experiment to get the result that you want. After you choose an option from the Gap Size modifier, click any enclosed or almost enclosed area to fill it, as shown in Figure 3-12.

Figure 3-12:
You can fill areas that are not completely closed by using the Gap Size modifier.

After you use the Paint Bucket to fill a shape created with another tool, you can erase the outline of the shape and keep just the fill.

Strokes, Ink

You use the Ink Bottle tool to create an outline on an existing shape. You can also use the Ink Bottle tool to change an existing line (also called a *stroke*).

To use the Ink Bottle tool, click it on the Tools panel. Click the Stroke Color tool to choose a color. Use the Property inspector, as we explain earlier in this chapter (in the discussion of the Pencil tool) to choose a line thickness and line style. Then click anywhere on the shape. If the shape has no existing line, Flash adds the line. If the shape has a line, Flash changes its color, width, or style to the settings that you created with the Property inspector.

A Rainbow of Colors

Flash offers you lots of color options. You can work with the solid colors that come with Flash. By default, Flash uses a palette of 216 colors that are Web-safe, which means that they look good on all Web browsers. Or, you can create your own colors.

Solid citizens

When you choose either the Stroke Color or Fill Color tool, Flash opens the *current Color palette,* which is the active set of colors that Flash uses. If you want to stick with Web-safe colors, you should choose one of these colors.

Creating new colors or editing existing colors

Flash provides two ways for you to specify your own colors. First, you can choose the Stroke Color or Fill Color tool from the Tools panel and click the Colors Window button in the upper-right corner of the palette to open the Color dialog box. Alternatively, you can choose Window⇨Design Panels⇨ Color Mixer to open the Color Mixer panel. These two methods duplicate each other; here, we explain how to use the Color Mixer panel, as shown in Figure 3-13. If you don't see the entire panel, click its Expand arrow in its lower-right corner.

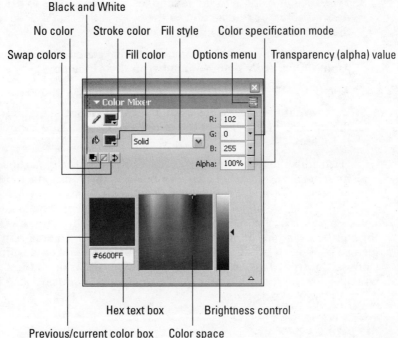

Black and White

No color Stroke color Fill style Color specification mode

Swap colors Fill color Options menu Transparency (alpha) value

Figure 3-13:
Use the
Color Mixer
panel to
create your
own colors.

Hex text box Brightness control

Previous/current color box Color space

If you select an object before you use the Color Mixer panel, the object's color changes immediately when you change the color in the Color Mixer panel.

To create a new color or edit an existing color, follow these steps:

1. **Click the menu icon in the upper-right corner of the Color Mixer panel to open the pop-up menu; then choose the color mode.**

   RGB specifies a color according to red, green, and blue components; *HSB* specifies a color by hue, saturation, and brightness. The pop-up menu automatically closes when you choose a color mode, returning you to the Color Mixer panel. You can also define a color by using *hexadecimal notation,* which is the system used on the Web: Just type the hexadecimal code in the Hex text box.

2. **Click the Stroke Color or Fill Color icon to specify which color you want to change — stroke or fill.**

   Click the icon to the left of the Stroke Color or Fill Color box — not the box itself — because if you click the box, you open the Color palette.

3. **Type the color specs in the text boxes, use the sliders to drag to the desired color, or find a color in the color space that's close to the one that you want and then click that color.**

4. **Set the level of opacity/transparency (also called *alpha*) by using the Alpha slider or by typing a number in the Alpha box.**

   A setting of 0% is completely transparent; 100% is opaque.

5. **If you want to create a new color swatch, click the menu icon in the upper-right corner of the panel and choose Add Swatch from the menu.**

   Flash adds the new color to the Color palette so that you can access it from the Stroke Color or Fill Color boxes in the Tools panel, the Property inspector, or the Color Swatches panel.

Look for openingmovie.fla in the Ch03 folder of this book's CD-ROM for a great example of the use of transparency. The transparent rectangles pass by each other, creating constantly changing color effects. Choose Control⇨Test Movie to see the movie run or open the .swf file, which is also on the CD-ROM. (*The Flash movie is courtesy of Jennie Sweo:* http://sweo.tripod.com.)

Managing colors

If you've added or changed colors, you can save this new palette. (A *palette* is a set of colors.) You can then save the palette for use in other Flash movies or import a Color palette from another Flash movie (so that you don't have to bother creating the colors again). Color palettes are saved as .clr files and are called *Flash Color Set* files.

Macromedia Fireworks and Adobe Photoshop use Color Table files (ACT files), and Flash can import and save these as well.

To import a Color palette, choose Window⇨Design Panels⇨Color Swatches to open the Color Swatches panel. Click the menu icon in the upper-right corner of the panel to open the menu. Choose Add Colors if you want to append this imported palette to an existing palette. Choose Replace Colors if you want the imported palette to replace an existing palette. Choose Save Colors to save a palette to a file for use in another movie or program.

You can use the same Color Swatches panel drop-down menu to manage your Color palettes. Choose from the following options:

✔ **Duplicate Swatch:** Creates a duplicate of a swatch. Do this when you want to create your own color and use an existing color as a basis.

✔ **Delete Swatch:** Deletes a color.

✓ **Load Default Colors:** Replaces the active Color palette with the Flash default palette of 216 Web-safe colors.

✓ **Save as Default:** Saves the active Color palette as the default palette for any new Flash movies that you create.

✓ **Clear Colors:** Clears all colors except black and white — for when you really want to start from scratch.

✓ **Web 216:** Loads the Web-safe, 216-color palette.

✓ **Sort by Color:** Sorts the display of colors by luminosity.

Gradient colors

So you're bored with solid colors and want something more interesting. *Gradients* are combinations of two or more colors that gradually blend from one to another. Flash can create gradients of as many as 16 colors — quite a feat. Gradients are always used as fills. The gradient can be linear or *radial* (concentric), as shown in Figure 3-14. Because the figure isn't in color, it can't begin to show you the glory of gradients.

Figure 3-14: Linear and radial gradients make your graphics much more interesting than plain solid colors.

Linear gradient   Radial gradient

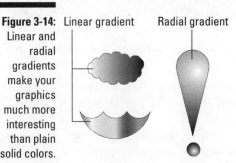

Flash offers a few standard gradients that you can find at the bottom of the Color palette. But you often need a more customized look, and Flash has the tools to create just about any gradient that you want.

Radial gradients look best on curved objects. A circle suddenly looks like a sphere when you fill it with a radial gradient. Radial gradients give the impression of light highlights if you put white at the center of the gradient. Linear gradients look best on straight objects.

To create your own gradient, follow these steps:

1. **Choose Window➪Design Panels➪Color Mixer to open the Color Mixer panel (refer to Figure 3-13). Then choose Linear Gradient or Radial Gradient from the Fill Style drop-down list.**

   If you select a fill before you use the Color Mixer panel, the object's fill color changes immediately when you change the gradient in the Color Mixer panel.

2. **To use an existing gradient as a starting point, click the Fill Color box in the Tools panel and choose a gradient from the bottom of the Color palette.**

   You can also choose Window➪Design Panel➪Color Swatches to open the Color Swatches panel and choose a gradient from the bottom of the Color palette there.

3. **To specify the color for each color pointer, click the pointer; then click the color space and choose a color.**

   You can click the color box and choose an existing color from the Color palette or specify a new color by using the methods that we describe in the earlier section, "Creating new colors or editing existing colors."

   Note that when you click a pointer, its point turns black to indicate that it's the active pointer. The square beneath the point displays the color pointer's current color.

4. **To change the number of colors in the gradient, add or delete color pointers.**

   To add a color pointer, click where you want the pointer to appear, just below the gradient bar. To delete a color pointer, drag it off the gradient bar.

5. **To save the gradient, click the menu icon in the upper-right corner of the Color Mixer panel and choose Add Swatch.**

The new gradient now appears in the Color palette of the Fill color box on the Tools panel and in the Color Swatch panel. Go ahead and fill something with it!

You can also move a gradient's center point, change its width and height, rotate it, scale it, skew it, and tile it. See Chapter 4 for more on editing gradients.

Bitmap fills

You can create the coolest, weirdest fills by importing a bitmap graphic and using the bitmap to fill any shape. For a hypothetical Web site protesting genetically engineered foods, for example, we could find a bitmap of a bug (representing the Bt bacteria genetically engineered into corn) and use it to fill a graphic of corn. Figure 3-15 shows the result.

Figure 3-15: You can fill any shape with a bitmap, repeated over and over and over. . . .

To use a bitmap graphic to fill a shape, follow these steps:

1. **Create the object or shape that you want to fill.**

2. **Choose File➪Import➪Import to Stage.**

   The Import dialog box opens.

3. **In the Import dialog box, choose the bitmap that you want to use as the fill and then click Open/Import.**

   The bitmap appears on the Stage. If necessary, move it away from any existing objects.

   We explain more about importing graphics in the section "The Import Business — Using Outside Graphics," at the end of this chapter.

4. **Choose Modify➪Break Apart.**

   Flash breaks the bitmap into separate areas of color.

5. **Click the Eyedropper tool on the Tools panel.**

6. **Click the bitmap on the Stage.**

   Notice that the Fill Color tool on the Tools panel now shows a tiny picture of your bitmap. Flash also automatically switches you to the Paint Bucket tool so that you can immediately fill an object.

7. **Click the object that you want to fill.**

   Flash fills it with the bitmap. The bitmap is repeated over and over, in an effect called *tiling.*

If you've already imported a bitmap, you can fill an object with the bitmap by opening the Color Mixer, choosing Bitmap from the Fill Style drop-down list, choosing the bitmap, and clicking inside a closed object. For either method of choosing a bitmap, you can switch to the Brush tool (instead of using the Paint Bucket tool) and then brush with the bitmap. Use a thick-enough brush size so that the bitmap shows clearly.

Locking a fill

Flash has another trick up its sleeve for gradient or bitmap fills. A *locked fill* looks as though the fill is behind your objects and the objects are just uncovering the fill. As a result, if you use the same fill for several objects, Flash locks the position of the fill across the entire drawing surface rather than fix the fill individually for each object. Figure 3-16 shows an example of a locked fill. In this figure, you see some windows and portholes filled with a locked bitmap of the sky. Doesn't it look as though the sky is really outside the windows?

Figure 3-16:
When you lock a fill, the fill's pattern across the Stage appears only where you use it.

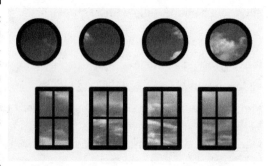

 To lock a fill, choose the Brush tool or the Paint Bucket tool with a gradient or bitmap fill, as we explain in the two preceding sections. Then click the Lock Fill modifier in the Options section of the Tools panel. Start painting where you want to place the center of the fill and continue to other areas.

Drawing Precisely

If drawing in Flash seems too loosey-goosey to you, you need to know about a few features that can help you draw more precisely. Other programs do offer more precise tools, but Flash may have the tools that you need.

The ruler rules

To help you get your bearings, you can choose View⇨Rulers to display the Flash ruler along the top and the left side of the Stage, as shown in Figure 3-17.

Figure 3-17: Display the ruler to help you draw more precisely; for more control, drag guides to the Stage.

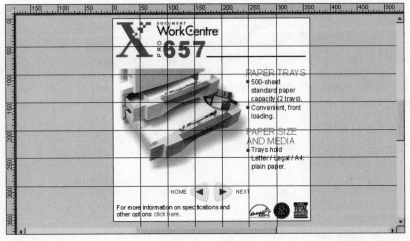

Figure courtesy of Phil Marinucci, Xerox.ca, and Julie Raymond, Xerox Canada.

To give yourself more room to work while you create drawing objects on the Stage, you can hide the Timeline by choosing Window⇨Timeline. Do the same to display the Timeline again when you need to work with layers or start animating your work.

By default, the ruler is measured in *pixels.* Computer screens are measured by how many pixels they display horizontally and vertically. Pixels are useful for Web site work because Web browsers work with only this unit. A pixel, however, is not a fixed physical size because it depends on the resolution capacity and settings of your screen. You may find it easier to think in inches or millimeters.

You can set the ruler to the unit of measurement that is most helpful to you. Choose Modify⇨Document to open the Document Properties dialog box. From the Ruler Units drop-down list, choose one of the units (pixels, inches, points, centimeters, or millimeters) and click OK.

When the ruler is displayed, lines appear on both the top and side rulers whenever you drag an object — either while creating it or editing it. For example, when you drag to create a square, you see a line on each ruler telling you where you started and where you end up.

If you're moving the square, Flash displays two lines on each ruler indicating the outside dimensions of the square. You can easily move the square one inch to the left by looking at the lines on the top ruler.

Using guides

Guides help you lay out the Stage more precisely. *Guides* (refer to Figure 3-17) are horizontal and vertical lines that you can use as drawing aids while you work. Don't worry — guides never appear in the published Flash Player file. To use the guides, you must display the rulers, as we describe in the preceding section. To display guides, choose View⇨Guides⇨Show Guides. But that action simply turns on the Guides feature; you still don't see anything!

To display the guides, you need to drag them from the rulers. Drag from the left ruler to create a vertical guide, and drag from the top ruler to create a horizontal guide.

To customize the guides, choose View⇨Guides⇨Edit Guides to open the Guides dialog box, where you can choose the guide color or clear all the guides. To force objects to *snap to* (attach themselves to) the guides, select the Guides check box in the Guides dialog box. You can use the Snap Accuracy drop-down list in the Guides dialog box to choose how precisely Flash snaps to the guides. To remove an individual guide, drag it back to its vertical or horizontal ruler. To lock the guides so that they don't move while you work, choose View⇨>Guides⇨Lock Guides.

Working with the grid

You can display a grid on the Stage to help you draw more accurately and to gauge distances. The grid exists only to guide you and never appears when the movie is printed or published on a Web site. Simply displaying the grid doesn't constrain your objects to points on the grid. Use the grid by itself when you want a visual guide for sizing, moving, and laying out the Stage.

To display the grid, choose View⇨Grid⇨Show Grid. Use the same command to hide the grid again. You can set the size of the grid squares. Choose View⇨Grid⇨Edit Grid to open the Grid dialog box. You can also change the color of the grid lines here.

You can change the units of measurement used for the grid by choosing Modify⇨Document. In the Modify Document dialog box, choose the unit that you want from the Ruler Units drop-down list and click OK.

Snapping turtle

When you want even more precision, you can turn on snapping. *Snapping* tells Flash to snap objects to the intersections on the grid or to other objects. Usually, you want the grid on when you use snapping so that you can see the snap points.

To turn on snapping, choose the Selection tool and click the Snap modifier in the Options section of the Tools panel or Choose View⇔Snapping⇔Snap to Objects. To snap to the grid, choose View⇔Snapping⇔Snap to Grid. Use the same method to turn snapping off again.

Snapping pulls your cursor to the grid points and to existing objects while you work. You can take advantage of snapping both while drawing new objects and editing existing objects. When you have snapping on and select an object, Flash displays a small, black circle and snaps that circle to the grid points.

Setting snap-to-grid preferences

You can get downright picky about how Flash snaps to grid points. Do you want the end of a line (for example) to always snap or only if it is close to a grid point or existing object? To set your preferences, choose View⇔Grid⇔Edit Grid. From the Snap Accuracy drop-down list, choose one of the options from Must Be Close to Always Snap.

Setting snap-to-objects preferences

Because snapping applies to objects as well as grid points, you can separately set how Flash snaps to objects. Choose Edit⇔Preferences (Windows) or Flash⇔Preferences (Mac) and click the Editing tab. Under Drawing Settings, click the Connect Lines drop-down list. Choose from Must Be Close, Normal, and Can Be Distant. Although Flash calls this the Connect Lines setting, it affects rectangles and ovals as well as lines drawn with the Line and Pencil tools.

This setting also affects how Flash recognizes horizontal and vertical lines and makes them perfectly horizontal or vertical. For example, the Can Be Distant setting adjusts a more angled line than the Must Be Close setting.

Pixel, pixel on the wall

If the grid isn't precise enough, you can snap to pixels. Choose View⇔Snapping⇔Snap to Pixels to toggle snapping to pixels on and off. If Snap to Pixels is on, when you zoom in to 400 percent or higher, Flash automatically displays the pixel grid. With Snap to Pixels on, all objects that you create or move snap to the pixel grid.

When Snap to Pixels is on, you can press the C key to temporarily turn off pixel snapping. In the same situation, you can press the X key to temporarily hide the pixel grid.

You can also precisely align existing objects. For more information, see Chapter 4.

The Import Business — Using Outside Graphics

So maybe you're the lazy type — or totally without artistic talent — and you really need help. Flash hasn't given up on you completely. Rather than create your own graphics, you can use the work of others. Although Flash creates vector-based graphics, it can import both bitmap and vector graphic files.

When using others' artwork, be careful about copyright issues. For example, some graphics available on the Web can be used for personal, but not commercial, purposes. Most Web sites offering graphics for downloading have a written statement explaining how you can use their graphics.

Importing graphics

To import a graphic file, follow these steps:

1. **Choose File⇨Import⇨Import to Stage.**

   The Import dialog box opens.

2. **In the dialog box, locate and choose the file that you want.**

3. **Click Open/Import to open the file.**

   The file appears on the Stage. If the file is a bitmap, it also goes into the Library. To import a graphic file directly into the Library without displaying it on the Stage, choose File⇨Import⇨Import to Library.

A cool feature of Flash is its ability to recognize and import sequences of images. If the image file that you choose in the Import dialog box ends with a number and other files in the same folder have the same name but end with consecutive numbers (for example, an1, an2, and so on), Flash asks whether you want to import the entire sequence of files. Click Yes to import the sequence. Flash imports the images as successive frames on the active layer so that you can use them as the basis for animation. (Chapter 9 explains more about frames and animation.) Table 3-1 provides a list of the types of files you can import into Flash.

Table 3-1	Files That Flash Can Import	
File Type	*Windows*	*Mac*
Adobe Illustrator (.eps, .ai); through Version 10	X	X
All PostScript (.eps, .pdf, .ai)	X	X
AutoCAD DXF (.dxf); 2-D only	X	
Bitmap (.bmp)	X	
Enhanced Metafile (.emf)	X	
Flash Player 6 (.swf)	X	X
FreeHand (.fh*); versions 7 to 10	X	X
FutureSplash Player (.spl)	X	X
GIF/animated GIF (.gif)	X	X
JPEG (.jpg)	X	X
MacPaint (.pntg)*	X	X
Photoshop (.psd)*	X	X
PICT (.pct, .pic)		X
PNG (.png)	X	X
QuickTime image (.qtif)*	X	X
Silicon Graphics Image (.sgi)*	X	X
Targa (.tga)*	X	X
TIFF (.tif)*	X	X
Windows Metafile (.wmf)	X	

*Only if QuickTime 4 or later is installed

Importing Adobe Acrobat's PDF format (listed under All PostScript in Table 3-1) is a new feature for Flash MX 2004.

You can also simply copy and paste graphics. From the other application, copy the graphic to the Clipboard; then return to Flash and choose Edit⇨Paste. However, in some cases, you may lose transparency when using this method. See Chapter 13 for details on exporting objects.

For a nice example of imported bitmap graphics, see `dc12_e_2.swf` and `Xerox 657e.swf` in the Ch03 folder of the CD-ROM. To view these movies, open the `.swf` file on the CD-ROM. (*Flash movies courtesy of Phil Marinucci and Julie Raymond, Xerox Canada.*)

Using imported graphics

Vector graphics from any drawing program become a grouped object that you can use like any other Flash object. The `.wmf` format, a Windows vector graphics format, also imports in this way. These formats work especially well when imported into Flash. You can sometimes find `.wmf` graphics in clip art collections and on the Web.

You can import text from a text editor, and Flash turns it into a Flash text object so that you can edit and format it within Flash. See Chapter 5 for more on text.

When you import a bitmap graphic, you often need to take some steps before you can use the graphic in your Flash file. You can manipulate your graphics in several ways to make them more Flash friendly:

✔ **Delete the background:** In many cases, Flash imports not only the shape you want but also a rectangular background that you don't want. To get rid of that background, deselect the imported object, select just the rectangular background, and press Delete. If that doesn't work, read on.

✔ **Ungroup the graphic:** Ungrouping separates grouped elements into individual elements. Ungrouping retains most of the features of your graphic. Select the graphic and choose Modify➪Ungroup. If you find that you still can't work with your graphic properly, read the next item.

✔ **Break apart the graphic:** Break imported graphics to separate them into ungrouped editable elements. Breaking apart is useful for reducing the file size of graphics that you import. Breaking apart converts bitmaps to fills, converts text to letters and outlines, and breaks the link between an Object Linking and Embedding (OLE) embedded object and its source application. In other words, the Break Apart command is a powerful tool. Select the graphic and choose Modify➪Break Apart.

✔ **Trace the bitmap:** Flash can work magic. If you want total control within Flash, convert a bitmap to a vector graphic.

To trace a bitmap, follow these steps:

1. **Import the bitmap — don't deselect it or perform any other action on it.**

2. **Choose Modify➪Trace Bitmap.**

   The Trace Bitmap dialog box opens.

3. **In the Color Threshold text box, type a number to represent the threshold.**

   The higher the number, the fewer colors you get in the final vector graphic. For close results, try a value of 10.

4. **In the Minimum Area text box, type a number to represent the number of nearby pixels that Flash considers when assigning a color to a pixel.**

   For greatest fidelity, try a value of 1.

5. **From the Curve Fit drop-down list, choose an option to represent how smoothly Flash draws the outlines.**

   For the most exact results, choose Pixel.

6. **On the Corner Threshold drop-down list, choose an option to represent how Flash reproduces sharp edges.**

   For sharpest results, choose Many Corners.

7. **Click OK to close the Trace Bitmap dialog box and then deselect the graphic to see the result.**

As we mention earlier in this chapter, when you import a bitmap graphic, Flash places the graphic in the current movie's Library. For best results, don't delete the original graphic from the Library, even if you have modified it. Flash continues to refer to the graphic after you have converted it to a symbol. (Chapter 2 explains all about the Library. See Chapter 7 for our total wisdom on symbols.)

If you're working in the Windows environment, you can also paste a graphic into Flash as an embedded object. To edit the object, double-click it to open the original application and use that application's tools.

To embed an object, follow these steps:

1. **From within the object's native application, select the graphic and choose Edit⇨Copy.**

2. **Close the other application and return to Flash.**

3. **Choose Edit⇨Paste Special.**

   The Paste Special dialog box opens.

4. **In the Paste Special dialog box, select the type of object that you want to embed, if you have a choice.**

5. **Select the Paste Link check box if you want to retain a link to the original file so that Flash updates the graphic if it changes.**

6. **Click OK to close the Paste Special dialog box.**

Whether you created your graphics in Flash or imported them, you probably need to edit them in many ways. Chapter 4 explains the details of editing objects.

Chapter 4

You Are the Object Editor

In This Chapter

- ▶ Selecting objects
- ▶ Manipulating objects (moving, copying, and deleting)
- ▶ Reshaping shapes
- ▶ Working with fills
- ▶ Transferring properties to other objects
- ▶ Using the Transform command (scaling, rotating, skewing, and flipping)
- ▶ Grouping and ungrouping
- ▶ Breaking apart objects
- ▶ Changing object order
- ▶ Reusing commands

This chapter tells you all you need to know about editing objects. You can manipulate objects in a zillion ways to suit your artistic fancy. The Flash editing tools can give you precisely the results that you want. Sometimes you need to edit because you made a mistake (rarely, of course), but often editing is just part of the creation process. You may also find that you have to alter imported graphics so that they fit into the scheme of things.

Selecting Objects

Before you can edit any object on the Stage, you need to select it. Flash offers many ways to select objects. After you get the hang of using the Flash selection tools, you'll find them efficient and easy to use.

Selecting with the Selection tool

 To select an object, click the black Selection tool and click the object. That sounds pretty basic. But just when you thought it was safe to skip the rest of this section, we add some ifs and buts, so read on.

What is an *object?* If you draw a shape with an outline (also called a *line* or a *stroke*) and a fill, such as a filled-in circle, you have two objects — the outline and the fill. Here are some pointers for selecting objects:

- ✔ If the object doesn't have an outline and is just a fill, you're home free. Click the object with the Selection tool, and it's selected.

- ✔ If the object has an outline and a fill, clicking the fill selects only the fill. The outline remains unselected. To select both the fill and the outline, double-click the object.

- ✔ You can also use the Selection tool to create a selection box. Click at one corner and drag to an opposite corner, making sure that the bounding box completely encloses the object or objects that you want to select, as shown in Figure 4-1.

Figure 4-1:
You can create a bounding box using the Selection tool to quickly select one or more objects.

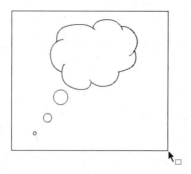

- ✔ To select just an outline, click the outline with the Selection tool. Still, you never know when an outline is really several objects, like the one in Figure 4-1. To select the entire outline, double-click it.

- ✔ To select several unconnected objects, select one object, press and hold the Shift key, and select additional objects. When you press Shift, you can add to already selected objects and select as many objects as you want.

To deselect selected objects, click any blank area.

So you're happily drawing away, using the various drawing tools. Then you want to select one of the objects, but you forget to change to the Selection tool. Oops! You draw another object by accident. Immediately, choose Edit⇨Undo. Then use one of the Flash arrow shortcuts:

✔ Press the V key to switch to the Selection tool.

✔ To temporarily switch to the Selection tool while you're using another tool, hold the Ctrl (Windows) or ⌘ (Mac) key while you select an object or objects.

Lassoing your objects

For you rodeo types, you can lasso your objects so that they can't escape. The Lasso tool creates a customized select area and selects everything inside. Use the Lasso tool when you want to select a number of objects that are near other objects that you want to remain free.

 To lasso objects, click the Lasso tool on the Tools panel.

To lasso freehand, make sure that the Polygon modifier is not selected. Click anywhere on the Stage and drag around the objects that you want to select. Flash creates a selection area while you drag. Release the mouse button close to where you started it to close the lasso's loop, as shown in Figure 4-2.

Figure 4-2:
Lasso
freehand to
select only
the objects
you want.

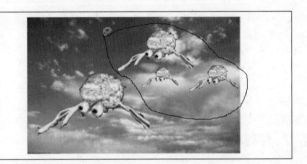

You may find that freehand lassoing is somewhat hard to control. If you find yourself inadvertently cutting across objects rather than around them, use the Polygon modifier to draw straight-line polygons instead — like a lasso with a very stiff rope.

To lasso by using straight lines, follow these steps:

1. **Click to choose the Lasso tool.**

2. **Click the Polygon modifier.**

3. **Click where you want the first line of the polygon to start.**

4. **Click again where you want the line to end.**

5. **Continue to click, creating line segments as you go.**

6. **Double-click when you finish lassoing the objects.**

Selecting everything in one fell swoop

Suppose that you want to select or deselect all objects at one time. Flash has some handy shortcuts to help you do that:

- **To select everything:** Press Ctrl+A (Windows) or ⌘+A (Mac). Or choose Edit➪Select All. Select All selects all objects on all layers except for objects on locked or hidden layers. (See Chapter 6 for an explanation of layers.)

- **To select everything on one layer:** Click the layer name.

- **To deselect everything:** Press Ctrl+Shift+A (Windows) or ⌘+Shift+A (Mac). Or choose Edit➪Deselect All. Deselect All deselects all objects on all layers. But the easiest method is to click off the Stage or on any blank area of the Stage.

- **To lock a group or symbol so that it can't be selected or edited:** Select the group or symbol and choose Modify➪Arrange➪Lock. To unlock a group or symbol, choose Modify➪Arrange➪Unlock All. (See the section "Getting Grouped," later in this chapter, to find out about groups. Chapter 7 is all about symbols.)

Moving, Copying, and Deleting

The most common changes that you make to objects are to move them, copy them, and delete them. Usually, moving, copying, and deleting are straightforward tasks, but Flash has a few tricks up its sleeve, so keep on truckin'.

Movin' on down the road

Before you can move, you have to select. After you select your object or objects, place the mouse cursor over any selected object until your cursor displays the dreaded four-headed arrow. (Okay, most people don't dread it at all.) Then click and drag to wherever you're going. Press Shift while you drag to constrain the movement to a 45-degree angle.

Moving precisely

When you drag an object, you immediately notice vertical and horizontal dashed lines when your object approaches existing objects.

The new Snap Align feature displays temporary dashed lines when you move objects to show you when the edges of objects are aligned, both vertically and horizontally, with existing objects.

Snap alignment is great for quickly aligning two objects without using the Align panel. While you drag a selected object, the dashed lines appear when you move an object in alignment with an existing object, as shown in Figure 4-3. You also see the lines when you drag an object close to any edge of the Stage.

To turn on snap alignment (although it is on by default), choose View➪Snapping➪Snap Align. You see a check next to the Snap Align item. Repeat the process to turn off snap alignment.

You can customize your snap alignment settings. Choose View➪Snapping➪ Edit Snap Align to open the Snap Align dialog box, as shown in Figure 4-4.

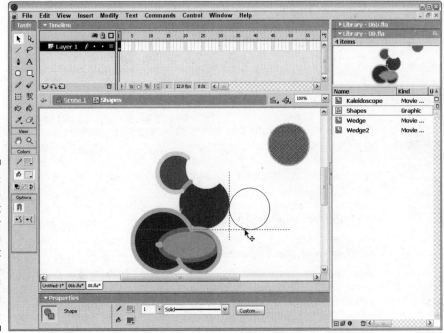

Figure 4-3: Snap alignment visually displays alignment between objects while you move them.

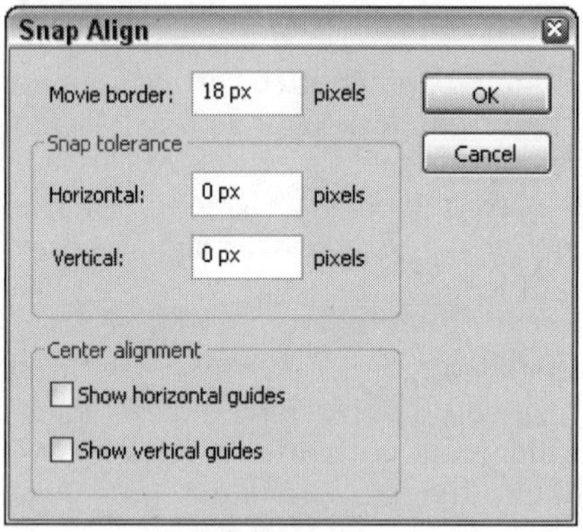

Figure 4-4:
The Snap
Align dialog
box makes
your snap
alignments
snap to your
orders.

In the Snap Align dialog box, you can also turn on snap alignment for the centers of objects, for easy centering of objects. Mark both check boxes in the Center Alignment section of the Snap Align dialog box.

You can control the accuracy of the snapping. To change the border of the Stage, type a different number in the Movie Border text box. To change the setting for alignment between objects, type a number in the Horizontal and Vertical text boxes in the Snap Tolerance section of the dialog box. Click OK when you are done to close the dialog box.

You can also use the grid and turn on the snapping feature for moving and copying objects. (See Chapter 3 to find out about the grid and snapping.) For example, you can attach one object to another by moving your first object until it snaps to the second, using the small black circle as a guide.

Snap align aligns objects by their edges. Object snapping aligns objects by their transformation point. See "Changing the transformation point" later in this chapter for more information.

You can also use the four arrow keys on your keyboard to move a selected object or objects. Each press of an arrow key moves the selection one screen pixel in the direction of the arrow. Press Shift plus an arrow key to move the selection by eight screen pixels.

Moving with the Clipboard

You can move an object by cutting to the Clipboard and pasting if you want to move the object to another layer, scene, file, or application. After you select the object or objects, choose Edit➪Cut. Alternatively, press Ctrl+X (Windows) or ⌘+X (Mac). Choose another layer or scene or open another file and do one of the following:

✔ **To paste the selection in the center of the display:** Choose Edit⇨Paste or press Ctrl+V (Windows)/⌘+V (Mac).

✔ **To paste the selection in the same position relative to the Stage:** Choose Edit⇨Paste in Place or press Ctrl+Shift+V (Windows)/⌘+Shift+V (Mac).

Moving with the Property inspector

If you want to place objects precisely, use the Property inspector. After you select an object or objects, choose Window⇨Properties and then click the Expand/Collapse arrow to display the expanded panel, as shown in Figure 4-5.

Figure 4-5: Use the expanded Property inspector to place objects precisely — down to the pixel, if necessary.

Use the X and Y text boxes to specify the location. The X setting specifies horizontal distance; the Y setting specifies vertical distance, both measured from the top-left corner of the Stage.

Moving with the Info panel

You can also use the Info panel to specify the X and Y positions of objects. Choose Window⇨Info to open the panel, as shown in Figure 4-6. You can use the grid next to the X and Y text boxes to measure either from the upper-left corner or the center of the selection — just click in the desired reference point on the grid. Flash uses the units that you specify in the Document Properties dialog box. (See the section in Chapter 3 on drawing precisely for information on setting the units.)

Figure 4-6: The Info panel.

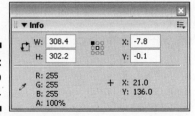

Remember that moving an object onto another existing object on the same layer either joins it (if the objects are the same color) or cuts it out (if they are different colors). See the section in Chapter 3 on mixing and matching shapes for more information.

Aligning objects with the Align panel

The new Snap Align feature, as we explain in the previous section of this chapter, is the quick way to align objects. However, for more options and precision, use the Align panel. The Align panel gives you the tools to line up two or more objects vertically or horizontally and also lets you put equal space between three or more objects. Align and space objects to make your Flash movie look professional, as opposed to something that you might create at 3 a.m. when your vision is too blurry for you to see straight.

To align objects, select the objects and choose Window⇨Design Panels⇨ Align to open the Align panel, as shown in Figure 4-7.

Choose the option that you want in the panel to align objects or distribute them. For example, you can align objects along their tops, their left sides, or any other direction. You can match the size of objects by using the Match Size buttons or make the spaces between objects the same with the Space buttons. Experiment with the options in this panel until you get the results that you want.

Figure 4-7:
Use the
Align panel
to line up
and evenly
distribute
objects.

To perfectly center one object on the Stage, select it and open the Align panel. Click the To Stage button. In both the Align Vertical and Align Horizontal sections, click the button that aligns objects through the middle. Flash centers the object on the Stage. A quicker way is to cut and paste the object because Flash automatically pastes objects at the center of the display (which is at the middle of the Stage if you haven't panned or scrolled the display).

Copying objects

After you spend loads of time creating a cool graphic, you may want to copy it all over the place. The easiest way is to clone it directly, by dragging. Just select the object and press Ctrl (Windows) or Option (Mac) while you drag. Flash makes a copy and moves it wherever you drag.

You can also copy objects to the Clipboard. Select an object or objects and choose Edit➪Copy or press Ctrl+C (Windows) or ⌘+C (Mac). You can paste the selection on the same layer or move it to another layer, scene, or file by using one of these techniques:

✔ **To paste the selection in the center of the display:** Choose Edit➪Paste or press Ctrl+V (Windows) or ⌘+V (Mac).

✔ **To paste the selection in the same position relative to the Stage:** Choose Edit➪Paste in Place. If you're on the same layer, scene, and file, you now have two copies, one on top of the other. The new object is selected, so you can immediately drag it to a new location.

Because Flash pastes objects from the Clipboard to the exact center of the display, cutting and pasting is a great technique to center objects on top of each other. For example, if you want to create two concentric circles, one on top of the other, create the circles in separate locations. Cut and paste the larger circle first, and then the smaller circle. You now have perfect concentric circles, and you can move them together to the desired location. This technique only works if the Stage is at the center of your display — if you haven't scrolled the display.

When you paste a new object, be sure to move the new object right away if it covers an existing object on the same layer. If you deselect the new object, it either joins the existing object (if the objects are the same color) or cuts it out (if they are different colors). Of course, that may be your intention. See the section in Chapter 3 on mixing and matching shapes for more information.

Makin' it go away

Making objects go away is easy. Just select them and press Delete or Backspace in Windows/Delete or Clear on the Mac.

Making Shapes More Shapely

Suppose that you created an object and now you want to tweak it a bit. Flash has many techniques to help you perfect your artwork, and you can modify both lines and fills.

Reshaping shapes and outlines

The Selection tool can do more than select objects — it can also reshape them. When you reshape with the Selection tool, you do *not* select the object.

To reshape an outline or a fill, choose the Selection tool and place the mouse cursor near the object or on the edge of the object:

- ✔ If you see a corner next to the cursor, you can move, lengthen, or shorten an end point, as shown on the left side of Figure 4-8.
- ✔ If you see a curve next to the cursor, you can reshape a curve, as shown on the right side of in Figure 4-8.

Figure 4-8:
The Selection tool modifies end points and curves.

Click and drag in the desired direction. Flash temporarily displays a black drag line to show you what the result will look like when you release the mouse button. If you don't like the result, choose Edit➪Undo — or press Ctrl+Z (Windows) or ⌘+Z (Mac) — and try again.

As with drawing, you may find it helpful to increase the zoom factor. Try editing at 200 percent or 400 percent.

Using the Subselect tool

You can use the Subselect tool to reshape strokes or fills created by using the Pen, Pencil, Brush, Line, Oval, or Rectangle tools. When you use the Subselect tool, you move *anchor points,* which are small squares that appear on the object. To use Subselect, follow these steps:

1. **Choose the Subselect tool (the white arrow in the Tools panel).**
2. **Click the stroke (outline) or fill shape to display the anchor points on the line or shape outlines.**
3. **Drag the anchor points to modify the shape.**

4. **To change the direction of a curve, click any anchor point to display tangent lines and drag the tangent line handles (the little dots at the ends of the tangent lines).**

The tangent lines indicate the direction of the curve. See the section in Chapter 3 on drawing curves with the Pen tool for information on anchor points and tangent lines.

If you click a graphic with the Subselect tool and points aren't displayed on its edges, maybe you grouped it as we describe later in this chapter (or maybe you didn't create it with the Pen, Pencil, Brush, Line, Oval, or Rectangle tool). In any case, try choosing Modify➪Ungroup or Modify➪Break Apart and then using the Subselect tool.

You can also delete anchor points. Flash reshapes the shape without that anchor point. Select the object with the Subselect tool, select an anchor point, and press Delete.

Freely transforming and distorting shapes

For way-cool distortions and reshapings, use the Free Transform tool, with its Distort & Envelope options. The Free Transform tool can work its magic on objects, groups, instances, or text blocks. In addition to its special ability to create distortions, it's flexible enough to move, rotate, scale, and skew objects. Flash also has other tools that rotate, scale, and skew — we cover them later in this chapter.

To use the Free Transform tool, select an object, symbol instance, group, or text block. (See Chapter 7 for more about symbols. We discuss groups later in this chapter.) Click the Free Transform tool in the Tools panel. The object displays a bounding box with handles and a *transformation point,* shown as a circle at the center of the bounding box, as shown in Figure 4-9.

Figure 4-9:
To free transform an object, you use a bounding box, handles, and a transforma-tion point.

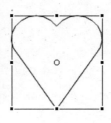

You can perform the following commonly used transformations on the selected object:

✔ **Move:** Place the cursor on the object itself; when you see the four-headed arrow, click and drag to move the selected object.

✔ **Set the center for rotation and scaling:** Place the cursor on the transformation point; when you see the small circle, you can drag the circle at the center of the bounding box to move the transformation point. The *transformation point* is the base point used for the current rotation or scaling operation.

✔ **Rotate:** Place the cursor just outside any corner handle; when you see the circular arrow, drag the object to rotate it around the transformation point.

Press Shift while you drag to constrain the rotation to 45-degree increments. Press Alt (Windows) or Option (Mac) while you drag to rotate around the diagonally opposite corner from your cursor.

✔ **Scale both dimensions:** Place the cursor on any corner handle; when you see the broken, two-headed arrow, drag inward or outward. Press Shift while you drag to ensure that the object is scaled proportionally without being distorted.

You can select as many objects as you want, and Flash scales them all. When you select more than one object, Flash places the handles around an imaginary bounding box that encompasses all the objects. Sometimes you may not get exactly the result you want using this method, so check carefully.

✔ **Scale one dimension:** Place the cursor on any side handle; when you see the two-headed arrow, drag inward or outward to scale in the direction that you are dragging.

✔ **Skew:** Place the cursor anywhere on the bounding box except on the handles; when you see the parallel lines, drag in any direction. (Skewing is covered in more detail in the "Getting skewy" section later in this chapter.)

Now for the more exciting transformations that you can create with the Free Transform tool.

Tapering objects

You can turn a square into a trapezoid by *tapering*. When you taper, you use the Free Transform tool to drag a corner handle. While you drag, the adjoining corner moves an equal distance in the opposite direction, as shown in Figure 4-10. You can taper other shapes, not just squares — but adjoining corners are always simultaneously stretched in opposite directions.

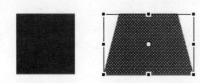

Figure 4-10:
Tapering
turns a
square into
a trapezoid.

 To taper, press Shift+Ctrl (Windows) or Shift+⌘ (Mac) while you drag on a corner handle of the bounding box. You can also use the Distort option of the Free Transform tool: Click the Distort button and press Shift while you drag any corner handle. (This technique is ideal for people who have trouble pressing both Shift and Ctrl or ⌘ at the same time.)

Distorting objects

For even weirder effects, you can *distort* shapes (objects) — but not symbols, symbol instances, text, or groups. When you distort an object, you change the shape of the bounding box, and the shape gets stretched in the same amount and direction as the bounding box, as shown in Figure 4-11.

Figure 4-11:
Drag the
bounding
box into a
new shape
and the
object
follows suit.

 To distort shapes with the Free Transform tool, press Ctrl (Window) or ⌘ (Mac) and drag either a corner or a side handle on the bounding box. You can also use the Distort option of the Free Transform tool — click the Distort button and drag the handle. To use the menu, choose Modify➪Transform➪ Distort.

Stretching the envelope

You can make even more refined changes in the shape of the Free Transform bounding box by using the Envelope option. With this option, the bounding box takes on editing points like you see when you use the Pen tool. As you drag the points, tangent lines appear, again like the Pen tool, as shown in Figure 4-12.

Figure 4-12:
The oval is like taffy when you push the envelope.

 To use the Envelope modifier, select an object — a shape — but not a symbol, instance, text, or group. Choose the Free Transform tool and the Envelope modifier. Drag any of the points in or out and then drag the end of any of the tangent lines to change the direction of the curve.

To end a free transformation, click anywhere off the selected object.

Straightening lines and curving curves

Just like you can straighten and smooth strokes by using the Straighten and Smooth modifiers of the Pencil tool, you can straighten and smooth strokes and fills of existing objects. (See Chapter 3 for more about the Pencil tool.)

You can activate the Straighten and Smooth modifiers repeatedly and watch while Flash slightly reshapes your strokes or fills each time. Eventually, Flash reaches a point where it can't smooth or straighten any more.

 Choose Edit⇨Preferences⇨Editing to adjust how Flash calculates the straightening and smoothing. Change the Smooth Curves and Recognize Shapes settings.

 To straighten a stroke, first select the object. With the Selection tool active, click the Straighten Modifier button in the Options section of the Tools panel. Flash straightens out curves and recognizes shapes, if appropriate.

 To smooth a curve, first select the object. With the Selection tool active, click the Smooth Modifier button in the Options section of the Tools panel. Smooth softens curves and reduces the number of segments that create a curve.

Optimizing curves

Flash offers a technique called *optimizing* for curves. Optimizing reduces the number of individual elements in a curve. Optimizing reduces the size of your file, resulting in faster download times on your Web site. You can optimize repeatedly, just as you can with smoothing and straightening. Optimizing works best for complex art created with many lines and curves. The visual result is somewhat like smoothing but may be even subtler.

To optimize, select the object or objects and choose Modify⇨Shape⇨ Optimize. Flash opens the Optimize Curves dialog box, as shown in Figure 4-13.

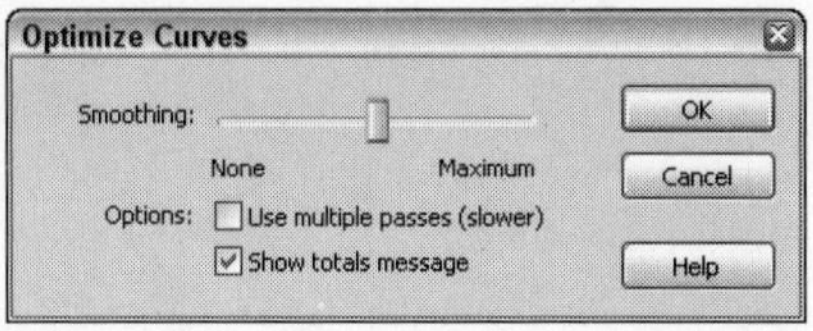

Figure 4-13:
Optimize to
reduce the
number of
curves.

As you can see in the dialog box, you can choose how much you want Flash to optimize curves. If you mangle your work too much on the first try, undo it and try again using a different setting. You can generally leave the other settings as they are. For a slower but more thorough optimization, mark the Use Multiple Passes (Slower) check box. And it's helpful to see the totals message that shows you how many curves Flash cut out and the percentage of optimization that number represents. Click OK to optimize.

Be careful to check the results after optimizing. Flash sometimes eliminates small objects that you may want to remain. If you don't like the results of optimizing, choose Edit⇨Undo.

Expanding and contracting filled shapes

You can expand and contract shapes. Expanding and contracting works best on shapes with no stroke (outline) because Flash deletes the outline when executing the command. If you want to expand or contract a shape with a stroke, scale it. We explain scaling later in this chapter in the "Scaling, scaling. . . ." section. The advantage of expanding and contracting is that you can specify a change in size in terms of pixels.

To expand or contract a shape, select it and choose Modify⇨Shape⇨ Expand Fill. The Expand Fill dialog box appears, as shown in Figure 4-14. Type a number in the Distance text box, using the units that you have set for the entire movie. By default, movies are measured in pixels. (See the section in Chapter 3 on drawing precisely for the details on setting movie units.)

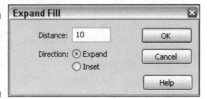

Figure 4-14: The Expand Fill dialog box.

To expand a shape, select the Expand radio button. To contract a shape, select the Inset radio button. Then click OK.

Softening edges

Softening edges is another shape-modification tool. You can soften edges of a shape to get a graphic to look like you created it in some high-end program, such as Photoshop. Figure 4-15 shows some text before and after its edges are softened. Note that adding softened edges can increase your file size.

Figure 4-15: Soften the edges of objects to create cool effects.

You can create this effect by breaking apart the text twice before softening the edges. We discuss breaking apart objects later in this chapter; Chapter 5 explains more specifically about breaking apart text into editable shapes.

To soften edges, select the object or objects and choose Modify⇨Shape⇨Soften Fill Edges. Flash opens the Soften Fill Edges dialog box, as shown in Figure 4-16.

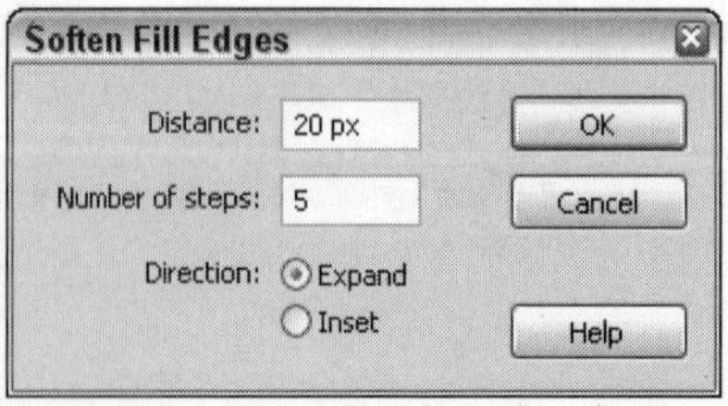

Figure 4-16: The Soften Fill Edges dialog box softens up your boss . . . uh, graphics.

To soften edges, follow these steps:

1. **Set the distance, which is the width of the softened edge.**

   The distance is measured in pixels unless you have changed the document units. (See the section in Chapter 3 on drawing precisely for information on setting the units in the Document Properties dialog box.)

2. **Choose the number of steps, which means the number of curves that Flash uses to create the softened edge.**

   Try the Flash default first and change it if you don't like the result. You can increase the number to get a smoother effect.

3. **Select either the Expand radio button to create the softened edge outside the shape or the Inset radio button to create the softened edge within the shape.**

4. **Click OK to return to your movie.**

   Your shape is still selected, so click anywhere outside it to see the result. If you don't like it, press Ctrl+Z (Windows) or ⌘+Z (Mac) and try again using different options.

You can also create soft edges by using gradients that blend into the Stage color or with partially transparent colors. Chapter 3 explains more about using colors.

Converting lines to fills

Flash offers lots of great ways to fill a shape — for example, with gradients and bitmap images. But what about those boring strokes or outlines? You can convert lines to fills and make them fun, fun, fun. (See Chapter 3 for an explanation of fills, including gradients and bitmap images.)

Mind you, there's not much point in converting a line to a fill if it's so thin that no one would ever see a fill in it. Figure 4-17 shows some waves created with a line (by using the Pencil tool) that is 10 points wide — the widest that Flash allows. We converted the line to a fill and then used the Paint Bucket tool to fill the line with a gradient.

To convert a line to a fill, select the line and choose Modify⇨Shape⇨ Convert Lines to Fills. You don't see any visible difference when you deselect the line, but now you can change the fill to anything that you want.

Figure 4-17:
Change the
line to a
fill and
then use
the Paint
Bucket tool
to change
the fill.

Transforming Fills

The Fill Transform tool offers a unique way to edit gradient and bitmap fills. You can perform the following changes to a fill:

- ✔ Move its center point.
- ✔ Change its width or height.
- ✔ Rotate it.
- ✔ Scale it.
- ✔ Tile it.
- ✔ Change the radius of a circular gradient.
- ✔ Skew (slant) it.

From this list, you can see that there's no point in fiddling with solid fills. They would look the same no matter what direction, size, or scale they were. (See the section in Chapter 3 on colors for colorful coverage of gradient and bitmap fills.)

 To edit a fill, choose the Fill Transform tool. Click any gradient or bitmap fill. Flash places an editing boundary and editing handles around the fill, as shown in Figure 4-18. The editing boundary is circular around a circular gradient fill but rectangular around a linear gradient or bitmap fill.

After you have a fill with an editing boundary, you're ready to go ahead and fiddle with the fills. Here's how to make changes:

- ✔ **Move the center of the fill:** Drag the center point, marked by a small circle at the center of the fill. You can move a center fill to change the apparent direction of light in a circular gradient or place a bitmap off-center.

Figure 4-18:
The Fill
Transform
tool places
an editing
boundary
around
the fill.

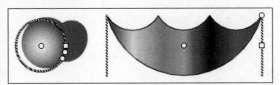

✔ **Change the width of a fill:** Drag the square handle on the side of the editing boundary. To change the height of a fill, drag the handle on the bottom of the editing boundary. If a fill doesn't have one of these handles, you can't edit the fill that way. Changing a linear fill perpendicular to its direction is the same as scaling the fill — the stripes get wider.

✔ **Rotate a fill:** Drag the rotation handle, a small circle at the corner of the editing boundary. Figure 4-19 shows a gradient rotated 45 degrees.

When rotating a fill, you can press and hold the Shift key while you drag to constrain the rotation of the fill to multiples of 45 degrees.

Figure 4-19:
Rotate a
linear fill
to create
diagonal
fills.

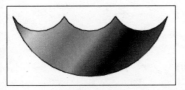

✔ **Scale a bitmap fill:** Drag the square handle at the corner of the editing boundary — inward to scale down and outward to scale up. To scale a circular gradient, drag the middle circular handle on the editing boundary. Figure 4-20 shows a bitmap gradient at original size and scaled down. Flash tiles the bitmap if you scale down significantly.

If you scale down a bitmap so that you see many tiles, the next time that you want to edit the bitmap, Flash places an editing boundary around each tile so that you have to edit each one individually. That could take a long time! If you want to edit a bitmap in several ways, save scaling down for last.

Figure 4-20:
You can scale a bitmap fill to make it larger or smaller.

✔ **To skew (slant) a fill:** Drag one of the circular handles on the top or right side of the editing boundary. You can only skew a bitmap. Skewing is different from rotating because the bitmap is distorted. Figure 4-21 shows an example of a skewed bitmap.

Figure 4-21:
You can skew a bitmap fill for really weird results.

Later in this chapter, we explain how to rotate, scale, and skew entire objects.

Transferring Properties

You can use the Eyedropper tool to copy outline and fill properties from one object to another. (See the section on bitmap fills in Chapter 3 for instructions on using the Eyedropper tool to create bitmap fills.)

To transfer properties, follow these steps:

1. **Choose the Eyedropper tool.**

2. **Select an outline or a fill.**

   If you select an outline, Flash activates the Ink Bottle tool. If you select a fill, Flash activates the Paint Bucket tool and turns on the Lock Fill modifier. (For more information, see the section in Chapter 3 that discusses locking a fill.)

3. **Click another outline or fill.**

   Flash transfers the properties of the original outline or fill to the new object.

Finding and Replacing Objects

One way to change an object is to change its properties. You can find graphics objects by color or bitmap and then replace the color or bitmap. For example, you can easily change every blue fill or stroke to red if your Web color scheme changes.

Find and Replace is a new feature in Flash MX 2004. You can find and replace according to color, bitmap, text, and font (Chapter 5); sound; or video (Chapter 11). You can also find and replace symbols (see Chapter 7).

To find and replace objects, choose Edit⇨Find and Replace to open the Find and Replace dialog box, shown in Figure 4-22.

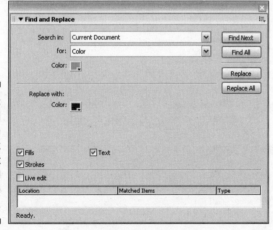

Figure 4-22:
The Find and Replace dialog box finds lost sheep and can change their color.

From the Search In drop-down list, choose to search in the entire Flash movie document or only in the current scene. (See Chapter 9 for a full explanation of scenes.)

From the For drop-down list, choose what you want to find from among the following: text, font, color, symbol, sound, video, and bitmap. The dialog box changes according to the choice that you make. For example, to find and replace a color, follow these steps:

1. **Click the top Color button and choose a color that exists in your document.**

2. **Click the Replace With Color button and choose the replacement color that you want.**

3. **Mark one or more of the three check boxes — Fills, Strokes, and Text — to define what type of objects you want to find.**

4. **To edit each object individually and one at a time, select the Live Edit check box.**

   When you enable Live Edit, you cannot make multiple changes.

5. **Click Find Next to find the next occurrence of the color or click Find All to find every object with that color.**

6. **To replace the color, click Replace to replace the currently selected object or click Replace All to replace the color of every object.**

Find and Replace is a very efficient way to make mass changes of fill, stroke, or text color.

Transforming Objects

Earlier in this chapter, in the "Freely transforming and distorting shapes" section, we explain how you can use the Free Transform tool to reshape objects. You can do many of the same tasks by using the Transform command.

To scale, rotate, and flip objects, choose Modify⇨Transform and choose one of the submenu commands. When you scale, rotate, or skew an object, Flash kindly remembers the object's qualities so that you can return the object to its original state before you fiddled around with it.

Scaling, scaling. . . .

Most of the time, scaling by using the Free Transform tool (as we describe earlier in this chapter) is the easiest, fastest way to go. Sometimes you may want more precision. You can scale any selected object in the Property inspector. (Choose Window⇨Properties. You may need to expand the Property inspector to its full size by clicking the Expand/Collapse arrow at the lower-right corner.) Change the value in the W (width) or H (height) box, or change both.

TIP

To make sure that the proportions of the object stay the same, click the padlock next to the W and H text boxes so that it looks locked. When you change either the W or the H text box, the other box automatically adjusts proportionally.

For yet more scaling options, select an object and choose Window⇨Design Panels⇨Transform to open the Transform panel, as shown in Figure 4-23.

TIP

The controls in the Transform window work only if an object is selected. If you forgot to select an object, you don't need to close the panel; just select an object.

Figure 4-23:
The
Transform
panel lets
you scale,
rotate,
and skew
objects
with great
precision.

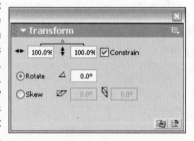

To scale the selected object or objects, type a scale value between 1–1000. Any value less than 100 reduces the size of the object, so a value of 10 creates a new object at 10 percent of the original object, and a value of 1000 multiplies the object's size by a factor of 10. Then press Enter or Return.

To make a copy of an object at a scaled size, click the Copy button (the left button in the lower-right corner of the panel). The copy appears on top of the original object but is selected so that you can immediately move it if you want. Figure 4-24 shows an example of how you can use scaling and copying together to create the impression of objects at varying distances. When you make the copy, just move it to a new location.

Figure 4-24:
The brain
creat-
ures are
attacking!

'Round and 'round and 'round we rotate

Most of the time, you can probably use the Free Transform tool to rotate objects, as we explain earlier in this chapter. If you want to rotate something exactly 20 degrees, use the Transform panel. Select the object and choose Window⇨Transform to open the Transform panel (refer to Figure 4-23).

To rotate the selected object or objects clockwise, type a value between 1–359. To rotate counterclockwise, type a value between –1 and –359. Then press Enter or Return.

If you don't like the results, click the Reset button in the lower-right corner of the panel and try again.

To make a copy of an object at a different rotation, click Copy (the left button in the lower-right corner of the panel). The copy appears on top of the original object but is selected so that you can immediately move it.

If you want to rotate a section by 90 degrees quickly by using the menu, follow these steps:

- **To rotate right (clockwise):** Choose Modify⇨Transform⇨Rotate 90° CW.

- **To rotate left (counterclockwise):** Choose Modify⇨Transform⇨ Rotate 90° CCW.

When you rotate, Flash rotates the object around its center. To rotate around a different point on the object, you can convert the object to a group or symbol and change its *registration point,* the point on an object that Flash references when rotating. See the section later in this chapter on changing the registration point.

You can create groovy circular patterns by using the rotate and copy functions, as shown in Figure 4-25. Unless the object you're working with is completely symmetrical, you need to change the registration point.

Getting skewy

Skewing is a variation of rotating. Rather than rotate an entire object, you slant it horizontally, vertically, or both. Skewing a square creates a rhombus (diamond). In Figure 4-26, you see a simple arrow before and after skewing.

Figure 4-25:
By rotating and copying an object at the same time, you can add flower power to your Web site.

The easiest way to skew objects is by using the Free Transform tool, as we explain earlier in this chapter.

Usually, you can eyeball the skewing process. If you want precision or to combine skewing with scaling, use the Transform panel. Select the object and choose Window➪Design Panels➪Transform to open the Transform panel. To skew the selected object or objects, click Skew.

Use the left box to skew horizontally. To skew clockwise, type a value between 1–89. To skew counterclockwise, type a value between –1 and –89. Then press Enter or Return.

To skew vertically, type a value in the right text box. Positive values skew clockwise, and negative values skew counterclockwise. If that sounds confusing, just try something out and see whether you like it. If you don't, click Undo (the right button in the lower-right corner of the panel) and try again.

To make a copy of an object at a skewed angle, click the Copy button (the left button in the lower-right corner of the panel). The copy appears on top of the original object but is selected so that you can immediately move it.

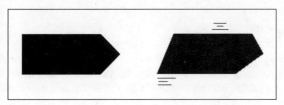

Figure 4-26:
After skewing, a boring arrow looks like it's in a hurry.

Flippety, floppety

Flipping reverses an object so that you have a mirror image of your original object. You can flip both horizontally (left to right or vice versa) and vertically (up to down or vice versa). Flash flips objects about their center so that they stay in their original position on the Stage.

Figure 4-27 shows a curlicue design in its original form, flipped horizontally and flipped vertically. If you flip an object horizontally and then vertically, you end up with an object that has been mirrored in both directions.

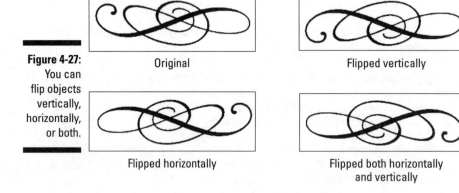

Figure 4-27:
You can
flip objects
vertically,
horizontally,
or both.

Original

Flipped vertically

Flipped horizontally

Flipped both horizontally
and vertically

To flip an object, select it and choose Modify⇨Transform⇨Flip Vertical or Flip Horizontal. To flip an object in both directions, flip it in one direction and then in the other.

To create symmetrical objects, you need to change the object's registration point from the center to one side or corner. Later in this chapter, in the section "Changing the transformation point," we explain how to use flipping to create symmetrical objects.

Getting Grouped

After you know how to create objects, you can get carried away and create so many objects on the Stage that they're hard to manage. You may want to move a number of objects at once. Although you can select them all and move them, that technique may not be enough. For example, you may inadvertently leave behind one piece and discover that it's hard to move that piece in the same way that you moved the rest. That's why Flash provides grouping. You select a group of objects and group them one time. From then on, you can select them with one click. If you move one, the rest come along for the ride.

In Flash, grouping has an additional advantage: If you put objects on top of each other, they merge if they're the same color or create cutouts if they're different colors. One way that you can avoid such friendly behavior and keep the integrity of objects is to group them. (You can also put them on different layers, as we explain in Chapter 6, or turn them into symbols, as we explain in Chapter 7.)

Grouping objects is easy. Select them and choose Modify⇨Group. You short-cut types can press Ctrl+G (Windows) or ⌘+G (Mac). When you group objects and select them, all the objects are surrounded by one blue selection border.

After you group objects, you can ungroup them at any time. Select the group and choose Modify⇨Ungroup. You can also break apart a group. See the discussion later in this chapter on breaking apart objects.

If you want to edit a component of the group without ungrouping first, Flash lets you do so. To edit without ungrouping, follow these steps:

1. **Using the Selection tool, double-click the group.**

   Flash dims other objects on the Stage and displays the Group symbol above the layer list.

2. **Edit any of the group components.**

3. **To return to regular editing mode, double-click any blank area on the Stage with the Selection tool, click the current scene symbol to the left of the group symbol, or click the Back arrow to the left of the scene symbol.**

   You can also choose Edit⇨Edit All.

Changing the transformation point

When Flash rotates or scales an object, it uses a *transformation point* as a reference. This point is generally the center of the object. For positioning and certain transformations of lines and shapes, Flash uses the upper-left corner. You may find that the point Flash uses isn't suitable for your needs. For example, you may want to rotate an object around its lower-left corner. For a single rotation or scaling of a simple graphic object, use the Free Transform tool and drag the transformation point — the little circle — to the desired location. If you deselect and reselect the object, you see that the circle has returned to its original central position.

Changing the transformation point is useful when you want to create symmetrical objects by flipping. To use flipping to create symmetrical objects, follow these steps:

1. **Select the object.**
2. **Choose Free Transform and drag the transformation point to one edge of the object, from where you want to mirror the object.**
3. **Choose Edit⇨Copy to copy the object to the Clipboard.**
4. **Choose Edit⇨Paste in Place to paste the copy on top of the original.**
5. **Choose Modify⇨Transform⇨Flip Vertical or Flip Horizontal.**

   You see your original and the copy. The copy has been flipped so that it's a mirror image of its original.

6. **To create a four-way symmetrical object, group the objects and change the transformation point to one side of the combined group; then repeat Steps 2 through 4, this time flipping in the other direction.**

Figure 4-28 shows a weird creature created by copying, changing the transformation point, and then flipping.

Figure 4-28:
Create
scary,
symmetrical
creatures by
manipu-
lating the
transformati
on point.

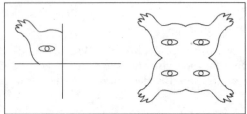

Groups, symbol instances, text, and bitmaps have a *registration point,* which Flash uses to animate and transform these objects. When you use the Free Transform tool to move the circle on these objects, the circle keeps its position even after you deselect and reselect it. To change an object's registration point for future operations, you can group the object. Follow these steps:

1. **Select a group, symbol instance, text object, or bitmap.**
2. **Choose the Free Transform tool.**

   Flash displays a small circle at the transformation point.

3. **Drag the circle to the desired location.**
4. **Click anywhere else on the Stage to hide the registration point.**

To return the registration point to its original position, double-click it.

Breaking Apart Objects

With the Break Apart command, you can break apart text, groups, instances of symbols, and bitmaps into separate objects that you can edit individually. To break apart one of these types of objects, select it and choose Modify⇨Break Apart.

What happens to your objects when you break them apart? Do they splatter all over the Stage? It's good to know:

- ✔ **Text:** When you break apart a block of text, Flash divides the words into individual letters, each one a separate object. If you use the Break Apart command a second time on one of the letters, the letter becomes a shape that you can modify like any other shape.

  Break apart blocks of text and then use the Distribute to Layers command to animate individual letters. For more information, see Chapter 5 about text and Chapter 6 about layers.

- ✔ **Groups:** Flash breaks up the group into its component parts. The result is that same as ungrouping.
- ✔ **Instances of symbols:** The symbol becomes a shape. (Symbols are covered fully in Chapter 7.)
- ✔ **Bitmaps:** Flash converts the bitmap to a fill.

Establishing Order on the Stage

Flash stacks objects in the order that you create them. If you draw a circle and then an overlapping square, the square looks like it is on top of the circle because you created it more recently.

If you place an object on top of another object, the objects become one if they're the same color. If they're different colors, the top object cuts out the underlying object.

One way to keep the integrity of objects is by grouping them. Symbols also maintain their integrity. (Symbols are covered in Chapter 7.) Groups and symbols are always stacked on top of regular objects. Therefore, ungrouped objects must be grouped or converted to a symbol to move them above existing groups or symbols. Some imported graphics may also need to be turned into a symbol or group before you can move them in the stack.

If you draw an object and it immediately disappears beneath another object, it's often because you tried to draw the object on top of a group or symbol. Group the object or change it to a symbol if it must be on top.

Another way to reorder objects is to put them on different layers. You can then reorder the objects by reordering their layers. (See Chapter 6 for the details.)

As long as you have objects that can maintain their integrity, you can change their stacking order. You can move them up or down in the stack or from the top or bottom of the stack. To change the stacking order of an object, select the object and choose Modify⇨Arrange. Then choose one of these options:

✔ **Bring to Front:** Brings the selected object to the tippy-top of the stack

✔ **Bring Forward:** Brings the selected object one level up

✔ **Send Backward:** Moves the selected object one level down

✔ **Send to Back:** Sends the selected object down, down, down to the bottom of the stack

Figure 4-29 shows an example of two objects stacked in two different ways.

Figure 4-29:
The big, old-fashioned bitmap star and the small, up-and-coming vector star vying to be in front.

Reusing Your History

If you make several changes to an object and would like to make the same changes to other objects, you can save time and increase accuracy by saving and reusing the steps for the operations that you performed. The steps are tracked in the History panel.

Using the History panel

The History panel lists every action that you perform in Flash during one session. When you save and close the file, the history list is not saved for next time. To open the History panel, choose Window⇨Other Panels⇨ History, as shown in Figure 4-30. The shortcut is Ctrl+F10 (Windows) or ⌘+F10 (Mac).

Figure 4-30: The History panel keeps track of everything you do.

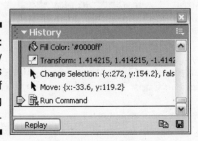

The History panel is new for Flash MX 2004. You can use this panel on its own to troubleshoot recent steps, repeat steps, undo steps, or save steps as commands for future use.

By default, Flash records up to 100 steps in the History panel. You can change the number of steps recorded by choosing Edit⇨Preferences (Windows) or Flash⇨Preferences (Mac). On the General tab, change the value for Undo levels. Valid settings are from 2–9,999. If you want to be able to go back and save earlier steps as commands, you probably need to record more than 100 steps.

Undoing steps

One of the simplest things that you can do in the History panel is to undo one or more operations. You can also undo operations by choosing Edit⇨Undo, but the description of the operation (such as Undo Move) is much more specific in the History panel, such as Move {x:0, y:-103.6}. As a result, when you use the History panel, you can more easily predict the result of undoing an operation.

You undo steps by using the slider on the left side of the History panel:

✔ **Undo the last operation that you performed:** Drag up the slider one step.

✔ **Undo several steps:** Drag the slider to the step above the first step that you want to undo.

   For example, if you want to undo three steps, drag the slider up three steps — it's now next to the step previous to the one that you undid. This is the last step that has still been executed. You can also click to the left of a step. The slider scrolls up to that step and undoes all the later steps.

When you undo a step, the History panel displays the step as dimmed.

Replaying steps

You can repeat any command from any time during a Flash session. For example, if you filled an object with a specific color, you can fill another object with the same color, even if you have done other operations in the meantime.

To replay a step, click the step itself (not the left side of the step above the slider). Then click the Replay button. If you want to replay the step on a different object, first select that object.

Copying steps

You may want to keep a list of certain steps or use them in a different movie. Select one or more steps and click the Copy Selected Steps to the Clipboard button.

Flash copies the step or steps as JavaScript code. Therefore, when you paste the step or steps into a word processor or text editor, you see the JavaScript code, which looks more complex than the step listing in the History panel. Usually, you can figure out what it means, even if you don't know JavaScript. For example, `Fill Color: '#0000ff'` appears as `fl.getDocumentDOM().setFillColor('#0000ff');`.

Saving commands

If you want to save a step or set of steps to use the next time that you open the movie, save a command. Saving a command is even useful if you want to re-execute some steps several times later on in the same session because scrolling back to find the exact steps that you want to reuse can be time-consuming.

To save a command, follow these steps:

1. **In the History panel, select the steps that you want to save.**

   You can drag along the step names (not along the left side, where the slider is). You can also use the usual methods of selecting multiple objects in a list — click the first, press Shift and click the last, or press Ctrl (Windows)/⌘ (Mac) and click each step that you want to select.

2. **Click the Save Selected Steps as a Command button.**

   This button is at the lower-right corner of the History panel. The Save As Command dialog box opens.

3. **In the Save As Command dialog box, enter a name for the command.**

   You can simply summarize the steps. An example might be Fill Blue Rotate 45.

4. **Click OK to close the dialog box.**

See the next section for instructions on using the commands that you save.

Clearing the History panel

If you don't like the History panel recording everything that you do —
perhaps it makes you feel as if you don't have any privacy left any more —
you can clear the history list. Clearing the history list doesn't undo any steps.
To clear the History panel, click the options menu and choose Clear History.
Click Yes to do so.

The menu in Figure 4-31 shows the command `Fill blue, rotate 45` that
fills any selected shape with blue and rotates the shape 45 degrees. To use
that command, you simply select a shape and then choose Commands⇨Fill
Blue, Rotate 45. Presto! It's all done. As you can imagine, you can combine
complex commands and save them to automate the authoring process of
creating Flash movies.

Figure 4-31:
When you
save a
command in
the History
panel, it
appears
on the
Commands
menu.

For good Commands menu housekeeping, choose Commands⇨Manage Saved
Commands to open the Manage Saved Commands dialog box. In this dialog
box, you can delete or rename a command. When you're done, click OK to
close the Manage Saved Commands dialog box.

You can get more commands from the Flash Exchange hosted online by
Macromedia. The Flash Exchange contains commands that other Flash users
have posted. Choose Commands⇨Get More Commands.

Chapter 5

What's Your Type?

In This Chapter

▶ Creating, editing, and formatting text

▶ Using cool text effects

*W*e assume that occasionally you want to say something on your Web site, so this chapter covers text in all its forms and formats. You can use Flash to create the text for your Web pages if you want (you don't have to). But if you want flashy text effects, Flash is definitely the way to go.

Typography is the art or process of arranging text on a page, and basically that's what this chapter is all about. Many graphics programs call text *type*. We use the words interchangeably here — we don't care what you call it.

Presenting Your Text

The majority of text on most Web sites is formatted by using HyperText Markup Language (HTML) coding that sets the font, size, and color of the text. Using HTML code is ideal for larger amounts of text because the HTML is simple to code and loads fast.

For smaller amounts of text that you want to have special formatting or effects, Flash offers more options than HTML. Of course, if you want to animate your text, you can use Flash. For example, an animated logo usually includes not only the graphic art but also the name of the organization, which is, of course, text.

Here are some innovative things that you can do with text:

- ✔ Rotate, scale, skew, or flip text without losing the ability to edit the text.
- ✔ Turn text into shapes and modify them any way that you want. However, after you turn text into shapes, you can't edit the text characters by simply typing. Figure 5-1 shows some text that was modified in this way.
- ✔ Create transparent type.
- ✔ Create hyperlinked text that links users to other Web pages when they click the text.
- ✔ Enable viewers to control some aspect of the movie by entering text in a text box or load text, such as sports scores or current weather, dynamically from a server.

Figure 5-1:
You can turn
text into a
shape and
edit it to
your heart's
content.

Spring

Creating text

Creating text in Flash is simple. Follow these steps:

1. **Click the Text tool on the Tools panel.**

2. **Specify the text starting point on the Stage.**

   - To specify the width of the text, click the Stage in the upper-left corner where you want your text to start and drag to the right until you have the width that you want. Flash places a square block handle in the upper-right corner of the text block.

   - To create a text block that expands while you type, just click the Stage at the desired starting point. Flash places a round block handle in the upper-right corner of the text block.

3. **Start typing; to force a return to the left margin, press Enter or Return.**

4. **After you finish typing, click anywhere off the Stage to deselect the text.**

Congratulations! — you've just said something. We hope it was worthwhile!

Editing text

After you type text, it never fails that you want to change it. Editing text is easy in Flash, but first you have to select it. Here are the selection techniques:

- ✔ **To edit an entire text block:** Choose the Selection tool and click the text. Flash places a selection border around the text. You can move, rotate, and scale all the text in a text block this way.

- ✔ **To edit the content of text itself:** Double-click the text by using the Selection tool. (Or choose the Text tool and click the text.) Flash switches you to the Text tool automatically and places the text cursor where you clicked or double-clicked the text, more or less.

- ✔ **To select a character or characters individually:** Choose the Text tool and drag across one or more characters. Do this when you want to edit only those characters.

- ✔ **To select a word:** Choose the Text tool and double-click any word to select it.

- ✔ **To select a string of words or block of text:** Choose the Text tool, click at the beginning of the text that you want to select, and then Shift+click at the end of the desired selection.

- ✔ **To select all the text in a text block:** Choose the Text tool, click in a text block, and then press Ctrl+A (Windows) or ⌘+A (Mac).

To change the content of the text, select the characters or words that you want to change, as we explain in the preceding list. Type to replace the selected text. Other text-editing techniques are the same as in your word processor. For example, you can press the Delete key to delete characters to the right of the text cursor (Windows only) or press the Backspace key (Windows) or Delete key (Mac) to delete characters to the left of the cursor.

Checking spelling

You should certainly check your spelling and correct any mistakes that you find. Nothing spells unprofessional like misspellings. The same is true for grammar and punctuation, but for those, you're on your own.

Spell checking is a new feature of Flash MX 2004. It works like the spell check in your word processor, so you'll probably find it easy to use. This feature shows Macromedia's commitment to reducing typos on the Web!

The first step is to set up the parameters for spell checking. Choose Text⇨ Spelling Setup to open the Spelling Setup dialog box, as shown in Figure 5-2. In fact, you can't check your spelling until you have opened this dialog box and closed it again; then the Check Spelling item becomes available on the Text menu.

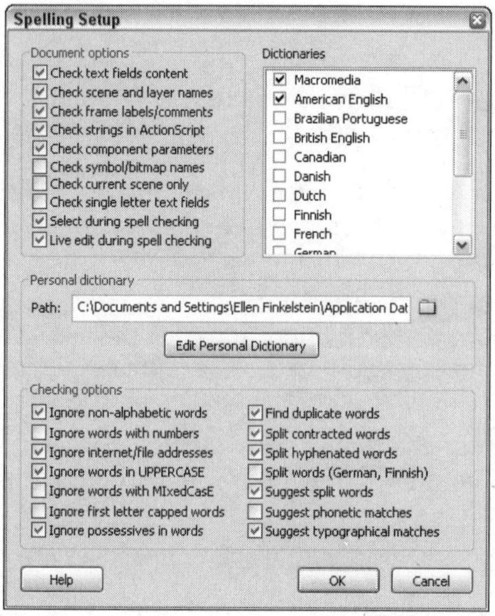

Figure 5-2:
Use the
Spelling
Setup
dialog box
to specify
how spell
checking
works.

The Spelling Setup dialog box has three sections:

- **Document Options:** Choose which parts of a movie that you want to check. You can also specify whether you want each misspelled word to be highlighted.

- **Personal Dictionary:** You can change the location of the file that holds words that you add to the dictionary. Click the Edit Personal Dictionary button to add words directly. Otherwise, you add words when you are checking spelling of specific text.

- **Checking Options:** Set options that define how spell checking works. For example, you can choose to ignore words in uppercase or with numbers.

When you're done, click OK to return to your movie. You are now ready to check spelling.

To check spelling, you can select text if you want to check just that text or leave all the text unselected to check the entire movie. Choose Text➪Check Spelling to open the Check Spelling dialog box, as shown in Figure 5-3.

If you selected text, Flash checks that text first and then asks you whether you want to check the rest of the document. Click Yes to continue or No to end the spell check. For each misspelled word, you can do one of the following:

- Choose one of the suggestions and click Change to change that instance of the word.

- Choose one of the suggestions and click Change All to change all instances of the word.

✔ Click Ignore to go to the next misspelled word.

✔ Click Ignore All to ignore all instances of that word and go to the next misspelled word.

✔ Click Delete to delete the word.

✔ Click Add to Personal to add the word to the Personal Dictionary so that it won't appear as misspelled in the future.

Figure 5-3:
The Check
Spelling
dialog box.

When you check spelling, the Movie Explorer opens so you can spell check text inside symbols or imported text.

To finish spell checking, click Close. You may see a message asking whether you want to start from the beginning of the document. Click Yes to do so. When spell checking is complete, you see a Spelling Check Completed message. Click OK to return to your movie.

Finding and replacing text

If you need to change all instances of the word *big* to *large,* you're in luck. The new Find and Replace feature comes to the rescue. For more information about this feature, see Chapter 4. In that chapter, we discuss this feature in detail and specifically how to find and replace color. Here we explain the steps (which are very similar) for finding and replacing text:

1. **Choose Edit⇨Find and Replace.**

2. **In the For drop-down list, choose Text.**

3. **In the Search in Text text box, enter the text that you want to find.**

4. **In the Replace with Text text box, enter the replacement text.**

5. **If you want, enable one or more of the left three check boxes to define what type of text you want to find: Whole Word, Match Case, and Regular Expressions.**

6. **If you want, mark one or more of the right check boxes to define where you want Flash to look for text.**

   • **Text Field Contents** searches text objects.

   • **Frames/Layers/Parameters** looks for frame labels and scene names (see Chapter 9), layer names (see Chapter 6), and component parameters (see Chapter 10).

   • **Strings in ActionScript** looks for strings in ActionScript.

7. **To edit each object individually and one at a time, check Live Edit.**

   When you use Live Edit, you cannot make multiple changes at one time and you return to the Stage to directly edit each object.

8. **Click Find Next to find the next occurrence of the text or click Find All to find all occurrences.**

9. **To replace the text, click Replace to replace the currently selected object or click Replace All to replace all instances of that text.**

When Flash finds the specified text, the box at the bottom of the dialog box displays its location, and type, along with the entire text so that you can see the context of the text that you're replacing. You can resize the Find and Replace dialog box as well as the columns in the list of found items.

When you're done, click the Find and Replace dialog box Close button to return to your movie.

Setting character attributes

Of course, you don't always want to use the Flash default font and size for your Web site. Boring! You can set the attributes before you start typing or edit the attributes of existing text. To edit existing text, double-click the text block and then select the characters or words that you want to format. To either set or edit attributes of text, choose Window⇨Properties to open the Property inspector. Figure 5-4 shows the expanded Property inspector when some static text is selected. The Property inspector changes slightly depending on which type of text you select. See "Creating input and dynamic text" later in this chapter for more information about the various types of text.

Setting the font, font size, and font style

Usually, the first step in formatting text is selecting a font. To select a font for your text, simply choose one from the Font drop-down list of the Character panel. Flash changes the font of the selected text.

You can change the font characteristics that control specific properties of the font, such as size and style:

✔ **To choose a font size:** Type a font size in the text box or drag the slider to the desired value.

✔ **To choose a font style:** Click Bold, Italic, or both. Flash applies the style to selected text.

You can also choose fonts, font sizes, and font styles directly from the Text menu. This menu is devoted entirely to helping you format your text.

You can create vertical text, like the text on the spine of a book. Okay, so the purpose is mostly for languages, such as Chinese, that are often written that way. Vertical text must be static and can go from either left to right or right to left. (We explain static, input, and dynamic text later in this chapter.) Figure 5-5 shows some vertical text.

To create vertical text, follow the instructions for creating normal text, but before clicking on the Stage to place the text, choose either the Left-to-Right or Right-to-Left option from the Change Direction of Text button on the Property inspector (refer to Figure 5-4).

Specifying text color

Black is the Flash default color, but you have lots of additional options. The first concern is that the text is legible against its background. Yellow text looks great in front of black, but it's almost invisible against white. Also consider that text is often unreadable in front of complex graphic images, no matter what the color.

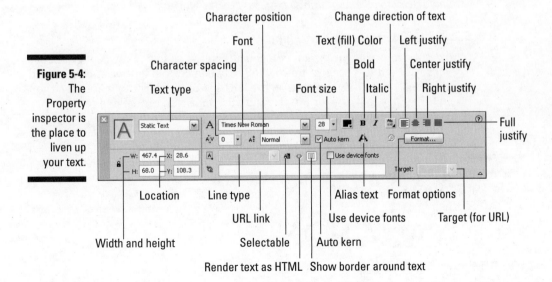

Figure 5-4: The Property inspector is the place to liven up your text.

D
o
w
n

w
e

g
o

Figure 5-5:
Try vertical
text for a
change of
direction.

To set text color, select the text that you want to change. In the Property inspector, click the Text Color button (refer to Figure 5-4) to open the Color palette. Choose a color. (For more information on colors, see Chapter 3.)

To create transparent (or semitransparent) text, select the text and choose Window➪Color Mixer to open the Color Mixer panel. Type a new Alpha percentage and press Enter. A 100 percent alpha setting results in opaque text. Text with a 0 percent alpha setting is completely transparent. A setting of 50 percent results in text that looks somewhat transparent but is still visible. To see the results, deselect the text by choosing the Selection tool and clicking outside the text.

For a nice example of text animation, open `time.fla` from the Ch05 folder of the CD-ROM. Then choose Control➪Test Movie from within Flash. *(Thanks to the animation's creator, Stefano Gramantieri, [gramants@libero.it] for this movie.)*

Adjusting kerning and tracking

To get the look that you want, you can adjust the spacing between letters of your text. *Kerning* reduces the spacing between certain letters, such as V and A. Because of the diagonal line on the left side of the A, without kerning, the V and the A may look too far apart. Figure 5-6 shows an example of text with and without kerning.

Figure 5-6:
The first
line uses
kerning; the
second line
doesn't.

VACATION

VACATION

By default, Flash uses a font's kerning information, which is embedded in the font definition. Sometimes with smaller font sizes, kerning can make text hard to read, so you can turn it off. Without kerning, text takes up slightly more space. To turn off kerning, select the characters that you want to adjust and clear the Auto Kern check box in the Property inspector.

You can adjust the spacing between all the letters, called *tracking*. Perhaps you need the text to fit into a tight space or you want to stretch it out without changing the font size. Figure 5-7 shows some text two letter spacing settings. To change tracking, open the Property inspector as we explain earlier and type a value in the Character Spacing text box or drag the slider bar to the desired value.

Figure 5-7: Stretched and condensed text.

Split the scene and leave it clean

Split the scene and leave it clean

Split the scene and leave it clean

Split the scene and leave it clean

Hyperlinking text

You can create text that links users to other Web pages when they click the text. Flash underlines linked text, following the universal convention on Web sites. To create text with a hyperlink, follow these steps:

1. **Select the text.**

2. **Choose Window⇨Properties to display the Property inspector.**

3. **In the URL text box, type the URL (Uniform Resource Locator, or Web address) of the Web page that you want to use.**

   The URL text box is on the expanded Property inspector. If necessary, click the Expand arrow in the lower-right corner of the Property inspector to display the URL text box. When your Flash movie appears on a Web site, clicking the hyperlinked text sends users to the URL that you specified.

4. **In the Target drop-down list, choose one of the window targets for the URL. The two most common are:**

   • _blank opens the URL in a new browser window.

   • _self opens the URL in the same window and is the default.

Getting the best text appearance

Flash usually stores outlines of the text in your movie when you publish or export it, so your audience will see your fonts in your movie even if they're not installed on your audience's computer. However, not all fonts displayed in Flash can be stored as outlines when you publish or export your movie.

To test whether a font can be exported with a movie, choose View⇨ Preview Mode⇨Antialias Text. You should see the text become smoother and less jagged. If the text remains jagged, Flash cannot export the text with the movie.

The way that your type looks on the Stage is only an approximation of how it looks when you publish or export your movie. To see a more accurate rendering of how your type looks when you publish or export it, view your movie by choosing Control⇨Test Movie.

The Property inspector has an Alias Text button that helps to make small text look smoother. Select some text and click Alias Text. Click the button again to turn off aliasing for the selected text.

If you want to use type in a font that can't be exported, you can break apart the type into shapes, as we describe at the end of this chapter, but this increases the size of your movie file, and you cannot edit the text any more.

If you'd like a space-saving alternative to storing your text as outlines in your Flash movie, you can use Flash's three *device fonts* that the Flash Player always converts to the closest available font on the local computer:

- ✔ _sans: A sans serif font similar to Arial (Windows) and Helvetica (Mac)

- ✔ _serif: A serif font similar to Times New Roman (Windows) and Times (Mac)

- ✔ _typewriter: A font that looks like it has been typed on a typewriter. (Are you old enough to remember what that is?) It's similar to Courier New (Windows) and Courier (Mac).

When you use device fonts, your resulting published movies are smaller, so download time is shorter. With device fonts, your text also may be more legible in text sizes below 10 point. To use device fonts, select the text and enable the Use Device Fonts check box in the Property inspector. This setting only applies to horizontal static text.

If you choose the Use Device Fonts setting in the Property inspector, when you publish your movie, you should use the Device Font setting in the HTML tab (Windows only). Chapter 13 tells more about publishing settings.

Setting up paragraph formats

You can set paragraph attributes such as alignment, margins, indents, and line spacing. Use these settings whenever you type more than one line of text.

Setting text alignment

You can align text along the left margin *(left justification)* or right margin *(right justification)* of the text block. You can also center text. You can create an even edge along both margins, called *full justification* or *justified text.* By default, text is left justified.

To align text, select it and choose Window⇨Properties to open the Property inspector, as shown earlier in this chapter, in Figure 5-4. Then click Align Left, Align Center, Align Right, or Justify.

Setting margins and indents

The *margin* is the space between the text block border and your text. By default, the margin is 0 pixels. You can increase the margin to guarantee some space around the text. You can set only the left and right margins (not the top or bottom ones).

To set the left margin, select the paragraph and click Format in the Property inspector to open the Format Options dialog box, as shown in Figure 5-8. Type a value in the Left Margin text box or click the arrow and use the slider to specify a value. Then press Tab or Enter (Windows) or Return (Mac). To set the right margin, use the Right Margin text box.

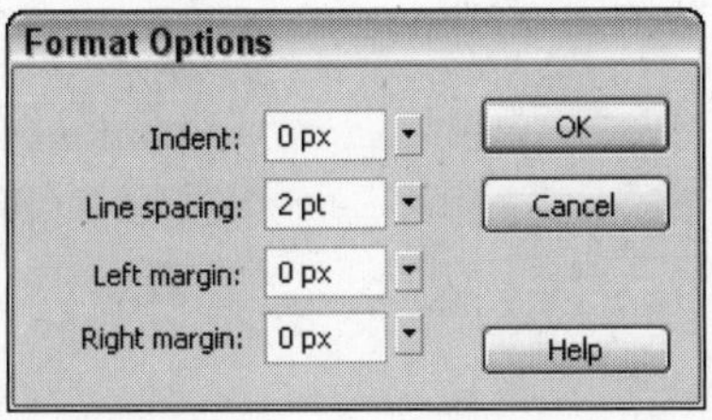

Figure 5-8:
Use the
Format
Options
dialog box
to whip your
paragraphs
into shape.

Format Options		
Indent: 0 px ▾	OK	
Line spacing: 2 pt ▾	Cancel	
Left margin: 0 px ▾		
Right margin: 0 px ▾	Help	

Indentation creates an indented first line. It's equivalent to placing a tab at the beginning of a paragraph. (Remember your sixth grade teacher who told you to always start each paragraph with an indent?) To indent the first line, select the paragraph and type a value in the Indent box or click the arrow and drag the slider bar. Press Tab or Enter (Windows) or Return (Mac).

Specifying line spacing

Line spacing determines the space between lines. Flash measures line spacing in points (1/72 of an inch) because font size is measured in points. For example, if your text is 18 points high and you want to double-space the lines, use a line spacing of 18 points so that a space exactly one line high exists between each line of text. To set line spacing in the Format Options dialog box, select the paragraph and type a value in the Line Spacing box or click the arrow and drag the slider bar. Press Tab or Enter (Windows) or Return (Mac).

Flash remembers paragraph properties from movie to movie. When you change paragraph properties for one movie, they rear their ugly heads in your next movie. If your text automatically indents at the beginning of paragraphs, or comes out double-spaced, check out the Format Options dialog box. Click OK when you're done with the Format Options dialog box.

Creating input and dynamic text

You can create three kinds of text in Flash:

- ✔ **Static text:** Regular text that doesn't change or do anything, although you can animate it

- ✔ **Input text:** Text that viewers can enter, as in a text box — used for forms and surveys or to interactively create values that affect the movie

- ✔ **Dynamic text:** Text that changes based on data coming from an external source (such as a Web server) or an internal source (such as ActionScript or input text in the movie) — often used for data like sports scores, current weather, and stock prices

To choose the type of text (or the type of type), choose it from the Text Type drop-down list in the Property inspector. (It's a good thing they didn't call it the Type Type drop-down list.) For an example of input text, see Chapter 8.

Several of the text settings in the Property inspector apply only to input or dynamic text:

- ✔ **Instance Name:** This box appears under the Text Type drop-down list when you choose Input or Dynamic text. You can refer to the instance name in ActionScript. This is handy because with Input or Dynamic text, the contents of the text field can change while your Flash movie is playing; but if you give your text field an instance name, you can always refer to it by using ActionScript, even though you don't know the contents of the text field ahead of time.

✔ **Line Type:** Defines how text is displayed.

- **Multiline** displays the text in multiple lines.

- **Single Line** displays the text as one line.

- **Multiline No Wrap** displays text in multiple lines that break only if the last character is a breaking character, such as Enter (Windows) or Return (Macintosh).

- **Password** displays asterisks.

✔ **Render Text as HTML:** Preserves formatting, such as fonts and hyper-links, with certain HTML tags. You need to create the formatting by using ActionScript.

✔ **Show Border:** Displays a black border and white background for the text field. This border helps users know where to enter text in an input text block.

✔ **Selectable:** Enables users to select dynamic text by dragging across it with the mouse. They can then copy it to the Clipboard. Deselect this button to prevent users from selecting dynamic text.

✔ **Variable:** Type a variable name for the text field. Variable names are used similarly to instance names, but your options are more limited.

✔ **Character:** Opens the Character Options dialog box, where you can select options for embedding font outlines. Choose No Characters or Specify Ranges. If you choose Specify Ranges, choose the types of charac-ters that you want to embed and click OK. These font outlines are then exported when you publish the movie to ensure a smooth appearance. Limiting the font outlines you export helps to make the file size smaller.

Creating Cool Text Effects

Flash wouldn't be worth its salt if you couldn't create some flashy effects with text. You can manipulate text in two ways:

✔ **Transform text just like other objects.** In other words, you can scale, rotate, skew, and flip type. Figure 5-9 shows an example of skewed text.

✔ **Convert type to shapes by breaking it apart.** Select the text and choose Modify⇨Break Apart. The first time that you use the Break Apart com-mand, words are broken up into individual letters. Use this command again, and letters are turned into shapes so that you can then edit the text in the same way that you edit shapes. However, you can no longer edit the text as text so check your words before converting them! Refer to Figure 5-1 for an example of text turned into a shape.

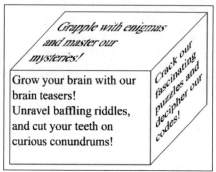

Figure 5-9:
This text is
skewed to
match the
angles of
the skewed
rectangles,
creating a
3-D effect.

To animate text, you usually break it apart so that you can move letters individually. You can then use the Modify⇔Timeline⇔Distribute to Layers command to put each letter on a separate layer. After that, you can animate each letter. (See Chapter 9 for the details on animation.)

Chapter 6

Layer It On

• •

In This Chapter

▶ Creating layers

▶ Modifying layers

▶ Using guide layers

▶ Creating holes with mask layers

• •

*F*lash lets you organize objects on the Stage in layers. *Layers* keep objects separated from each other. Remember that Flash either combines or creates cutouts when two objects overlap. By placing the two objects on different layers, you can avoid this behavior yet retain the appearance of overlapping objects.

Layers are also necessary for error-free animation. To move one object across the Stage in front of other objects, such as a background, you need to put the object on its own layer. If you want to animate several objects across the Stage, put each object on a separate layer.

You can hide layers. Flash doesn't display objects on hidden layers. Hidden layers are great for hiding some objects temporarily while you figure out what to do with all the rest of the stuff on the Stage. In other words, hiding layers helps unclutter the Stage so that you can work more easily.

Finally, layers are great places to put sounds and ActionScript code. For example, you can name a layer *Music* and put your music there. Then you can easily find the music if you want to change it. Layers provide a great way to keep the various components of your movie organized. (See Chapter 10 to find out more about ActionScript.)

In this chapter, you get all the information that you need to use layers effectively.

Creating Layers

Flash lists layers in the upper-left area of the Stage. New movies start out with one layer, creatively named Layer 1. You can, and should, change the name of this layer and new layers to something more descriptive, as shown in Figure 6-1.

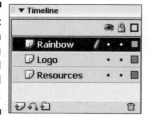

Figure 6-1:
Flash
keeps you
organized
by listing all
your layers.

If you're the organized type, you should think about your animation in advance and decide which layers you need. For some reason, it doesn't often work that way, and you may find yourself creating layers after you've created objects. Either way, you create the layer in the same way.

To create a layer, click the Insert Layer button at the bottom of the layer list (or choose Insert⇨Timeline⇨Layer). Flash displays the new layer above the active layer and makes the new layer active.

To name the layer, double-click its name, type something meaningful, and then press Enter (Windows) or Return (Mac).

Using layers

Any object that you create goes on the active layer. You can tell which layer is active because it's highlighted in black and has a pencil icon next to its name (refer to the Rainbow layer in Figure 6-1). To change the active layer, just click any inactive layer on its name. You can also click anywhere in the layer's row on the Timeline.

To help make your work easier, Flash automatically changes the active layer to match any object that you select. So, if you're working on a layer that you named *Text* and select a shape on a layer that you named *Shapes,* Flash automatically switches you to the Shapes layer. Any new objects that you create are now on the Shapes layer. Of course, if that's not the layer that you want, you can switch to any other layer at any time by clicking its name.

If you click a layer to make it active, Flash selects all the objects on that layer that exist in the current frame. (Even if a layer is already active, you can click its name to select all its objects.) This feature is helpful for working with all the objects on a layer and discovering which objects a layer contains. If you don't want all the objects selected, click anywhere not on an object.

Because each animated object needs to be on its own layer, you often need to distribute objects to their own layers. Select the objects and choose Modify⇨Timeline⇨Distribute to Layers. This command saves lots of work!

Changing layer states

Besides being active or inactive, layers have three states that determine how objects on that layer function or look. Use these states to help you organize how you work. The more objects and more layers that you have, the more you need to use these layer states.

To the right of the layer name, you see an eye, a lock, and a box. These aren't mystical symbols. The following sections explain how to use them.

Show/Hide

 Use Show/Hide (as shown at the left) to hide all objects on a layer (also called *hiding a layer*). Hide a layer to reduce clutter while you work. To hide a layer, click beneath the eye icon on that layer's row. Flash places a red X under the eye icon. All the objects on that layer disappear. Click the X to get them back again. To hide (or show) all the objects on the Stage, click the eye icon itself; but keep in mind that you can't work on a hidden layer.

 But don't forget hidden layers because they do appear in your published movies.

To show or hide all layers *except* one, Alt+click (Windows) or Option+click (Mac) beneath the eye icon of that layer's row. You can also right-click (Windows) or Control+click (Mac) on a layer and choose Hide Others from the shortcut menu.

Lock/Unlock

 Use Lock/Unlock to prevent objects from being edited by locking their layers. Lock a layer when you want to avoid changing objects by mistake. To lock a layer, click beneath the lock icon on that layer's row. Flash places a lock in the layer's row. Click the lock to unlock the layer again. The lock disappears, and you can now edit objects on that layer. You can lock *all* layers by clicking the lock icon directly. Click the lock icon again to unlock all the layers — but remember that you can't work on a locked layer.

To lock or unlock all layers *except* one layer, Alt+click (Windows) or Option+click (Mac) beneath the lock icon on that layer's row. You can also right-click (Windows) or Control+click (Mac) a layer and choose Lock Others from the shortcut menu.

Outlines

Use Outlines to display objects as outlines of different colors. *Outlines* help you see which layers objects are on because each layer uses a different color, as shown in Figure 6-2. (Okay, you can't *really* see the colors in a black-and-white book, but you can probably tell by the variations in gray that the objects aren't all the same color.) To display outlines, click beneath the Outlines (box) icon on that layer's row. Flash puts a colored box in the layer's row, and all objects on that layer are now shown as outlines in that color. (Text is still filled in, however.) Click the box to display objects on that layer normally. To display *all* layers as outlines, click the Outlines icon directly. Click it again to see your objects as normal. You can work on outlined layers, but all new objects appear as outlines, so telling how they appear when displayed normally is difficult.

In Figure 6-2, some text has been broken apart for animation and is therefore outlined like other objects.

To display all layers as outlines except for one layer, Alt+click (Windows) or Option+click (Mac) beneath the outline icon on that layer's row.

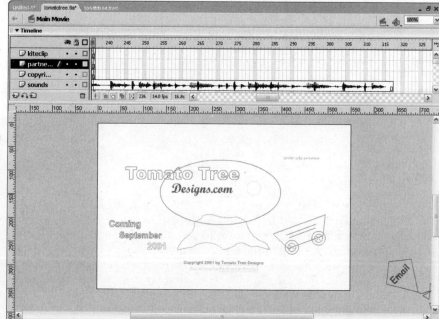

Figure 6-2:
All the objects on the Stage are shown as outlines except for text that hasn't been broken apart.

Getting Those Layers Right

Good layer housekeeping can help keep you sane. Delete layers that you no longer need. You can rename layers when their content changes; you can copy layers with their entire contents (rather than re-create them from scratch). Here we explain how to keep control over layers.

You can select more than one layer at a time. To select a contiguous group, click the first layer, hold down the Shift key, and click the last layer in the group. To select more than one layer when they're not all together in a group, click the first layer, press and hold the Ctrl key (Windows) or ⌘ key (Mac), and click any additional layers that you want to select.

Deleting layers

When you work, you may find that a layer no longer has any objects. It's a layer without a purpose in life, so delete it. Select the layer and click the Trash can at the bottom of the layer list. You can also drag the layer to the Trash can; those of you who use Macs are accustomed to dragging items to the Trash can.

When you delete a layer, you delete everything on the layer. Not everything on a layer may be visible. You see only what exists on the Stage in the current frame. For example, if you introduce a circle in Frame 15 of a layer named *Circle* but you're in Frame 1, you don't see that circle. Deleting the Circle layer, however, deletes the circle, although you can't see it.

To check for objects on a layer, right-click the layer and choose Hide Others from the contextual menu. Click the first frame on the Timeline and press Enter (Windows) or Return (Mac) to run any existing animation. Objects on that layer appear during the animation if they exist. To properly see the animation, you may need to choose Control⇨Test Movie to run the movie in the Flash Player — especially if you used ActionScript to control the animation. (Chapter 10 explains how to use ActionScript to control animation.)

Copying layers

You can copy a layer, along with its entire contents, throughout all frames. If you've created a great bouncing ball and now want two balls, copy the layer. You can then modify the position of the second ball throughout the Timeline without having to re-create the ball itself. Now you have two bouncing balls.

To copy a layer, follow these steps:

1. **Click the layer name to select the layer.**

2. **Choose Edit➪Timeline➪Copy Frames.**

3. **Click the Insert Layer button to create a new layer.**

4. **Choose the new layer to make it active.**

5. **Choose Edit➪Timeline➪Paste Frames.**

Renaming layers

Rename a layer whenever you want. By default, Flash names layers *Layer 1, Layer 2,* and so on. When you use a layer, rename it to reflect its contents. To rename a layer, double-click the layer name and type a new name. Then press Enter (Windows) or Return (Mac).

You can rename a layer as many times as you want.

Reordering layers

In Chapter 4, we explain how to change the order of objects on the Stage when they're on the same layer. When objects are on different layers, a new rule applies.

The order of the layers indicates the display order of objects on the Stage. Therefore, objects on the first layer on the list are always on top, objects on the second layer appear one level down, and so on. Objects on the last layer on the list appear on the bottom level of the Stage, behind everything else.

In fact, a simple and effective way to control object stacking is to put objects on different layers and then move the layers higher or lower on the layer list.

To move a layer, just click and drag it to the desired location. Figure 6-3 shows an example before and after moving a layer. The ball and the oval are on different layers. The left image looks a little odd, but when you reorder the layers, their objects are reordered as well, and you can then see a ball and its shadow.

Changing the layer order can help you more easily select and edit objects that are covered up by other objects. Simply drag the layer to the top of the list, and the objects on that list then appear on top. When you finish editing the objects, drag the layer back to its original location.

Figure 6-3:
By changing
the order of
the layers,
you change
the order of
the objects
on those
layers.

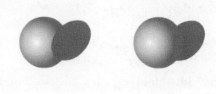

Organizing layers

Sometimes layers can get out of hand. You may have many layers with actions on them or several layers for each animation. Tame those layers by putting them into *folders*. A folder holds layers. Instant organization! For example, you can create an Actions folder and folders for each animation group.

 To create a folder, click the Insert Layer Folder icon below the layer list. You see a new folder just above the active layer. Name the folder in the same way that you name a layer: Double-click it, type the name, and press Enter (Windows) or Return (Mac). You can distinguish a folder from a layer by its folder icon.

After you have a folder, you fill it up with layers by dragging layers into it. Click and drag a layer onto the folder's row until the folder icon darkens. At the same time, the layer's name is indented so that you can easily tell that it's in a folder, as shown in Figure 6-4.

Figure 6-4:
Put your
layers into
folders
to keep
yourself
organized.

You can even put folders in folders. Just drag one folder into another. Here are some other things that you can do with folders:

- **Remove a folder from a folder:** Drag the nested folder above its parent folder.

- **Remove a layer from a folder:** Drag the layer above the folder name or to another location where it doesn't darken a folder.

- **Collapse and expand individual folders:** Click the folder's arrow at the left of its icon.

- **Expand and collapse all folders:** Right-click (Windows) or Ctrl+click (Mac) and choose Expand All Folders or Collapse All Folders from the shortcut menu.

- **Hide or lock an entire folder and its layers:** You can hide or lock a folder just like you hide or lock a layer. (See "Changing layer states," earlier in this chapter.) Click beneath the eye (Show/Hide) or lock (Lock/Unlock) icon on the folder's row.

- **Reorder folders:** You can change the order of folders, which automatically changes the order of the layers that it contains. Just drag any folder up or down. For more information, see "Reordering layers," a little earlier in this chapter.

- **Copy the contents of a folder to another folder:** To make a quick shortcut for copying layers and their contents, you can copy folders. Collapse the folder and click the folder name. Choose Edit⇨Timeline⇨Copy Frames. Create a new folder. With the new folder active, choose Edit⇨Timeline⇨Paste Frames.

- **Delete folders:** You can delete folders in the same way you delete layers. Select the folder and click the Trash can icon.

Deleting a folder deletes all layers in the folder and everything on those layers. Luckily, Flash warns you before you take the plunge.

Modifying layer properties

You can use the Layer Properties dialog box, as shown in Figure 6-5, to change certain layer properties, such as the color used for the layer's outlines and the layer height. Most settings, however, are easily accessible from the layer list. Choose Modify⇨Timeline⇨Layer Properties to open the Layer Properties dialog box.

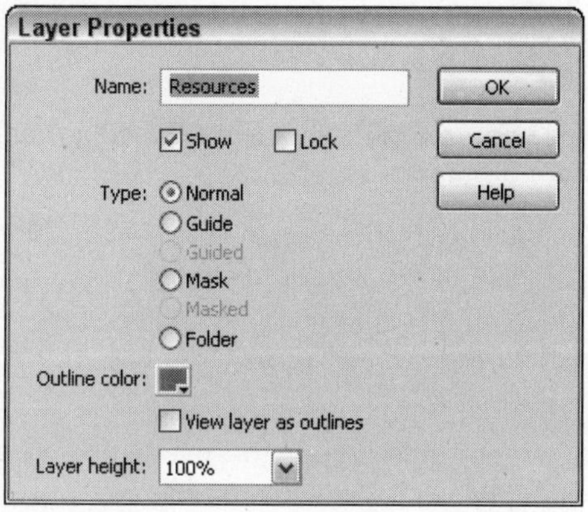

Figure 6-5:
The Layer
Properties
dialog box
lets you
fine-tune
layer
settings.

Here's how to use this dialog box to get the most from your layers:

- **The Name text box displays the current name of the layer.** You can rename the layer here if you want.

- **Change the Show/Hide and Lock/Unlock layer states by marking (or clearing) the appropriate check boxes.** Usually, you change these states directly on the layer list, as we explain earlier in this chapter, in the "Changing layer states" section.

- **You can change the type of layer by choosing from the list of layer types.** Guide and mask layers are covered later in this chapter.

- **You can change the color that Flash uses when the layer is displayed as outlines.** Click the Outline Color swatch and choose another color from the Color palette.

- **Mark the View Layer as Outlines check box to turn on outlines.** As we explain earlier in this section, you can accomplish this task easily from the layer listing.

- **You can change the layer height to two or three times normal.** One reason to change the height of a layer is to more easily view sound waves on a layer containing a sound. Another is to see larger previews of your keyframes in the Timeline — you can turn these on by clicking the Frame View button in the upper-right corner of the Timeline and choosing a size from the pop-up menu.

After you finish using the Layer Properties dialog box, click OK.

Creating Guide Layers

A *guide layer* is a layer that's invisible in the final, published animation. You can use guide layers for several purposes:

- ✔ **Layout:** Although Flash MX 2004 lets you display guides on the screen to help you draw precisely (as we describe in Chapter 3), you can also place gridlines on guide layers to help you lay out the Stage. Graphic designers use these types of gridlines to figure out how to create a balanced, pleasing effect in their art.

- ✔ **Drawing:** You can import a bitmap graphic onto a guide layer and draw over the graphic on a regular layer by using the Flash drawing tools. This technique of drawing over a graphic can be a big help when creating your artwork.

    Of course, you could use a regular layer and then erase whatever you don't want to appear in the final movie. But if you need to go back and make changes, you would have to create the guide layer over again. Using a guide layer gives you the flexibility of keeping the layer in the movie file, knowing that it will never appear in the published animation.

    Layers that are hidden appear in the published .swf file.

- ✔ **Animation:** You can place a path on a guide layer to control the motion of an object during animation. Figure 6-6 shows a guide layer that contains a motion guide for the skateboarder. When animated, the skateboard does two flips, following the motion guide. (Read through Chapter 9 for the lowdown on how to create a motion guide.)

Figure 6-6:
A guide layer controls the motion of an object during animation.

To create a guide layer, create a new layer. Then right-click (Windows) or Control+click (Mac) and choose Guide from the contextual menu. The layer is now a guide layer.

Use the same procedure to convert a guide layer back to a regular layer. The Guide item on the menu is a toggle, so when you click it again, Flash removes the guide status of the layer.

When you use a guide layer as a motion guide, Flash links the guide layer to a layer that contains the objects that you want to guide. The layer with the guided objects is called a *guided layer*. In Figure 6-6, the loops are on a guide layer, and the skateboarder is on a guided layer. All objects on a guided layer automatically snap to the path of the motion guide on the guide layer. To link a layer to a guide layer, creating a guided layer, you can do any of the following:

- ✔ Create a new layer under the guide layer.
- ✔ Drag an existing layer under the guide layer.
- ✔ Alt+click (Windows) or Option+click (Mac) the layer.
- ✔ Choose Modify➪Layer and choose Guided in the Layer Properties dialog box.

Flash indents the guided layer beneath the guide layer to help you see that they're linked.

If you want to unlink a guided layer, drag the layer above the guide layer or choose Modify➪Timeline➪Layer Properties and choose Normal in the Layer Properties dialog box.

Opening Windows with Mask Layers

A *mask layer* hides every object on its related layers except inside a filled shape or text object. You can use mask layers to create peepholes or spotlight effects. Figure 6-7 shows a keyhole shape on a mask layer that hides the entire garden scene except for the part within the keyhole. The garden scene is a rectangle much larger than the section displayed through the keyhole.

Figure 6-7:
You can use a mask layer to create a hole through which you can see the layer or layers beneath.

Creating a mask layer

To create a mask layer, including the object on the mask layer and the objects behind the mask layer, follow these steps:

1. **Create the objects that you want to show through the hole in the mask layer.**

   These objects can be on one or more layers. Place all the layers that you want to be masked next to each other and at the top of the layer list.

2. **Select the topmost layer on the layer list and click the Insert Layer button to create a new layer at the top of the list.**

   This layer will become the mask layer.

3. **Create, insert, or import one filled shape, text, or an instance of a symbol on the new layer. (See Chapter 7 for more about symbols.)**

   The filled part of the shape, text, or instance becomes the hole — in other words, it's transparent. Unfilled portions of the objects become opaque, so everything becomes the opposite of its current state.

4. **Right-click (Windows) or Control+click (Mac) the layer's name and click Mask from the contextual menu.**

   Flash turns the layer into a mask layer and locks the mask layer as well as the layer just beneath it on the layer list. The masked layer is indented. You see the mask effect displayed. (To link more than one layer to the mask layer, see the next section on editing mask layers.)

Editing mask layers

Because Flash locks both the mask layer as well as the layer or layers that are masked, you cannot edit them. To edit them, click the lock icon above the layer list. Flash unlocks the layers and removes the mask effect.

After you finish editing the layers, lock them again to redisplay the mask effect.

When you create a mask layer, Flash links only the layer directly beneath it to the mask layer. A layer linked to a mask layer is masked. If you place objects that you want to be masked on several layers, you need to change the property of all those layers from normal to masked.

All the layers that you want to be masked must be directly under the mask layer.

You can link a layer to a mask layer in several ways:

- ✔ If you drag a normal layer directly beneath a mask layer, Flash links it to the mask layer in addition to existing masked layers.

- ✔ Alt+click (Windows) or Option+click (Mac) the layer that you want to be masked.

- ✔ Right-click (Windows) or Control+click (Mac) the layer and choose Properties. Choose Masked in the Layer Properties dialog box.

Similarly, you can unlink a layer from its mask layer by using one of these methods:

- ✔ Drag the linked layer above the mask layer.

- ✔ Right-click (Windows) Control+click (Mac) the layer and choose Properties. Choose Normal in the Layer Properties dialog box.

Animating mask layers

Mask layers are more fun when you animate them. You can move them, change their size, and change their shape. If you create a keyhole like the one shown in Figure 6-7, you can move the keyhole past the masked layers, revealing what lies beneath while the keyhole moves. You can use the same technique to create an effect of a spotlight moving around a stage, revealing whatever it lights up. The only thing that you can't do is to animate the mask layer objects along motion paths. (Chapter 9 explains how to animate masks along with other objects.) You can create more complex mask animations by using ActionScript. See the section on creating animated masks with movie clips in Chapter 10 for the steps.

Look for di.swf in the Ch06 folder of the CD-ROM. This movie from Dennis Interactive, at www.dennisinteractive.com, starts with a good example of a mask. This is a Flash Player file, so you can view it by double-clicking the file. *(Thanks to Leslie Allen-Kickham for this file.)*

Part III
Getting Symbolic

VISUAL WEB DEVELOPMENT TEAM

"Give him air! Give him air! He'll be okay. He's just been exposed to some raw HTML code. It must have accidently flashed across his screen from the server."

In this part . . .

Symbols teach us about the deeper levels of life, and Flash symbols let you get down deep into the mechanics of animation. In this part, you discover the three kinds of symbols — graphic, button, and movie clip symbols — and how to use them.

Manipulating symbols is a critical feature of Flash. Symbols enable you to easily place duplicate graphics in your movie without significantly increasing the movie's size, and you use symbols when you start to animate. This part also gives you the lowdown on buttons, which are so central to the Web lifestyle in the 21st century. Flash lets you create buttons that change when you pass the mouse cursor over them and again when you click them. You can even make animated buttons. Part III provides you with the basis for creating great animations.

Chapter 7

Heavy Symbolism

Flash offers a way to simplify your work, called symbols. A *symbol* can be any object or combination of objects, animation, or a Web button. When you create a symbol, the objects (or animation) become one symbol. Sounds like grouping, yes? (If you've already read Chapter 4, you know what we mean.) The difference is that Flash stores the definition of the symbol in the Library. From the Library, you can now effortlessly insert multiple copies of the symbol into your movie. Each copy is called an *instance*.

Besides making your life easier when you want to use a set of objects more than once, symbols have another advantage: They significantly reduce the size of your files. Rather than store each instance that you use, Flash stores one definition for the symbol and only refers to the definition each time that you display an instance of the symbol. You can place symbols inside other symbols. Used this way, symbols are the building blocks for complex graphics and animation. Motion-tweened animation requires symbols, groups, or text, so you often create symbols when preparing to animate. (Chapter 9 explains tweened animation.)

So, symbols are all-around good guys, and you should use them as much as possible.

Understanding Symbol Types

Flash offers four types of symbols: graphic, movie clip, button, and font. Each type is made up of a group of objects or animation, but each type has a different purpose. Understanding these types is very important to understanding symbols and Flash animation in general.

Using graphic symbols

Graphic symbols are the simplest and most obvious type of symbol. When you create a Flash movie, you create objects on the Stage. Some objects may remain still, such as backgrounds. You animate other objects — after all, what is Flash for? Use graphic symbols for collections of static objects or for animation. Figure 7-1 shows a graphic symbol.

Figure 7-1:
A graphic symbol, created from several objects, has a single selection border.

You create graphic symbols to reduce the size of your file and to make it easier to add multiple copies of a graphic to your movie. Symbols are stored in the Library and are available to not only the movie in which you created them but also any other movie. Therefore, using symbols is a good way to store graphic images for use in Flash movies. You don't have to re-create the wheel.

Flash ignores sounds or actions inside graphic symbols. ActionScript code (which we explain in detail in Chapter 10) is the key to creating interactive movies. For that reason, turn animation into graphic symbols only when the animation is simple.

Using movie clip symbols

A *movie clip* is like a movie within a movie that you can manipulate by using interactive controls (created with ActionScript, which you can read about in Chapter 10). Movie clips are crucial for complex animation and especially interactive animation. A movie clip has its own Timeline independent of the movie's main Timeline. For example, you can go to a movie clip at any time, play it, and then return to where you left off on the Timeline. You can also attach movie clips to buttons. We explain how to create movie clips in this chapter; Chapter 8 discusses using movie clips with buttons. Chapter 9 covers using movie clips in animation, and Chapter 10 explains how to use and control movie clips by using interactive controls.

Flash comes with several *components,* which are special movie clips that allow you to add user interface elements — such as radio buttons, check boxes, and scroll bars — to your movies. Choose Window➪Development Panels➪Components and drag one of your choices to the Stage. Then choose Window➪Development Panels➪Component Inspector to set the parameters of the component. For example, you can insert a list box and then add all the items (called *labels* on the Component Parameters panel) that you want on the list. For more information on components, see Chapter 12.

Using button symbols

Button symbols create *buttons* — those little graphics that you click in Web sites to take you to other places on the site or the Internet. In Flash, you can use buttons in the same way, but you can also use buttons to let viewers decide whether they want to see a movie — when they click the button, the movie starts. You can also use advanced scripting to create buttons that control interactive games and other viewer activities. However you want to use buttons, button symbols are the way to start. You can add movie clips and interactive controls to buttons. Find out all about buttons in Chapter 8.

Using font symbols

Font symbols are used to export a font for use in multiple Flash movies. This is great whenever you use the same font in more than one Flash movie on a Web site: Your audience needs to download the font information only once instead of every time for every single Flash movie. This makes your Flash movies smaller and their loading time faster. We show you how to use font symbols in Chapter 12.

Creating Symbols

For graphic symbols and button symbols, usually you create the objects that you need and then turn them into a symbol. However, creating a movie clip symbol is different because it's a type of animation. Either create an animation on the Stage and then convert it to a movie clip symbol; or create the movie clip symbol, create the initial objects, and then create the animation.

To create a symbol from objects you've already created, follow these steps:

1. **On the Stage, select the objects that you want to convert to a symbol.**

2. **Choose Modify➪Convert to Symbol or press F8.**

   The Convert to Symbol dialog box opens, as shown in Figure 7-2.

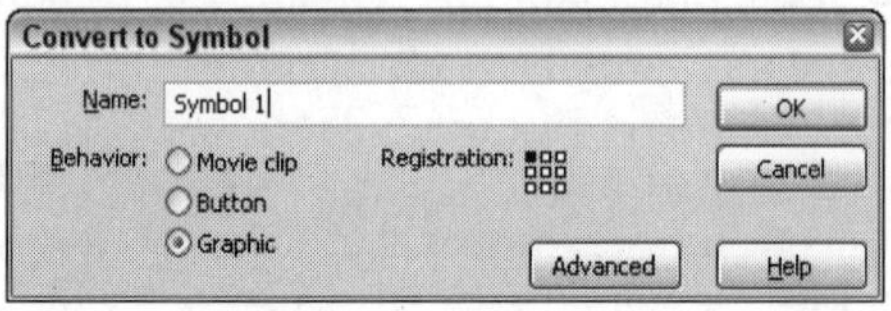

Figure 7-2:
The Convert
to Symbol
dialog box.

3. In the Name text box, type a name for the symbol.

A common convention is to name the symbol in a way that's unique
and also indicates the symbol type. For example, `btn_Help` could be the
name for a button symbol that will become a Help button on a Web site.

**4. From the Behavior list, choose the type of symbol that you want to
create: graphic, button, or movie clip.**

**5. Click OK to create the symbol and close the Convert to Symbol
dialog box.**

The objects that you selected become one object, indicated by a single
selection border around all the objects. Flash also stores the symbol in
the Library. (Chapter 2 explains how to use the Library.)

Each type of symbol has its own icon that's used in the Library. The following
table shows what type of symbol each icon represents:

Symbol	*What It Represents*
	Movie clip
	Button
	Graphic

Another type of symbol, the *font* symbol, exports a font so that you can use it
in other Flash movies. For more information, see Chapter 12.

Rather than create a symbol from existing objects, you can create an empty
symbol and then create the objects for the symbol. If you know in advance
that you want to create a symbol, you can use this method.

To create an empty symbol, follow these steps:

1. With no objects selected, choose Insert↪New Symbol.

The Create New Symbol dialog box opens.

2. In the Name text box, type a name for the symbol.

3. **From the Behavior list, choose the type of symbol you want to create — graphic, button, or movie clip — and then click OK.**

   Flash switches to symbol-editing mode, which we describe in the section "Editing symbols," later in this chapter.

4. **Create the objects or animation for the symbol in the same way that you do in regular movie-editing mode.**

5. **Choose Edit⇨Edit Document to leave symbol-editing mode and return to your movie.**

   Your new symbol disappears! Don't worry — Flash saved the symbol in the Library. To insert the symbol on the Stage, see the section "Inserting instances," later in this chapter.

You can create a movie clip symbol by converting regular animation to a movie clip. Use this method when you already have the animation created on the Timeline.

To convert an animation on the Stage to a movie clip symbol, follow these steps:

1. **On the layer listing, select all frames in all layers containing the animation by clicking the first layer and pressing Shift while you click the last layer in the group.**

   Alternatively, you can press Ctrl (Windows) or ⌘ (Mac) and click additional layers.

2. **On the Timeline, right-click (Windows) or Control+click (Mac) and choose Copy Frames to copy all the frames of the animation to the Clipboard.**

   Alternatively, you can choose Edit⇨Timeline⇨Copy Frames.

3. **With no objects selected (click off the Stage to be sure that no objects are selected), choose Insert⇨New Symbol.**

   The Create New Symbol dialog box opens.

4. **In the Name text box, type a name for the movie clip.**

5. **From the Behavior list, choose Movie Clip as the type of symbol.**

6. **Click OK to close the Create New Symbol dialog box.**

   Flash switches to symbol-editing mode so that you can edit the symbol.

7. **Click the first frame of the Timeline to set the start of the movie clip symbol.**

8. **Choose Edit⇨Timeline⇨Paste Frames to paste the animation into the Timeline and create the symbol.**

9. **To return to the main movie and Timeline, choose Edit⇨Edit Document.**

10. **To delete the animation from the main movie (now that you've saved it in a movie clip), select all layers as you did in Step 1 and choose Edit⇨Timeline⇨Remove Frames.**

    You can delete the animation from the main movie because you now have a movie clip in your Library containing that animation.

One more way to create a graphic, button, or movie symbol is to duplicate an existing symbol. To duplicate a symbol, follow these steps:

1. **Open the Library (choose Window⇨Library).**

2. **Select the symbol that you want to duplicate.**

3. **Click the Options menu in the upper-right corner of the Library window and choose Duplicate.**

    Flash opens the Duplicate Symbol dialog box.

4. **In the Name text box, type a name for the duplicate and choose the type of symbol that you want to create if you want a different kind from the original.**

5. **Click OK to close the dialog box and create the duplicate symbol.**

Changing the properties of a symbol

You may need to change a symbol's properties. For example, you may create a graphic symbol and then realize that you need it to be a movie clip. Or you may want to change the font used by a font symbol. No problem!

To change the properties of a symbol, follow these steps:

1. **Choose Window⇨Library to open the Library.**

2. **Right-click (Windows) or Control+click (Mac) the symbol's icon (not its name) and choose Properties from the menu.**

    The Symbol Properties dialog box opens.

3. **If the symbol is a graphic, button, or movie clip, from the Behavior list choose the type of symbol that you want and click OK. If the symbol is a font, change the font or its size or style as you desire and click OK.**

Look in the Ch07 folder on the CD-ROM for `invent.fla` and `invent.swf` for a good example of a short movie with lots of different types of symbols. This movie is taken from the beginning of the `www.omm.ch` Web site, with a humorous twist (press the Enter button). *(The Flash movie is courtesy of Stephan Oppliger, of OMM Oppliger Multimedia.)*

Editing symbols

Part of the power of symbols lies in their control over instances. An *instance* is a copy of a symbol that you insert into your movie. If you edit a symbol, Flash updates all instances of that symbol in the movie. You can change a symbol once and save yourself the time of creating the same change for every instance of that symbol. For that reason, it's worthwhile to make a symbol every time that you want to use a certain shape or group of shapes more than once.

You can edit a symbol in three different modes:

- ✔ **Edit in Place:** Lets you edit a symbol while still viewing other objects on the Stage. Other objects are dimmed while you edit the symbol.

- ✔ **Edit in Symbol-Editing Mode:** Switches you to symbol-editing mode. You see only the symbol.

- ✔ **Edit in a New Window:** Opens a new window where you can edit your symbol. You see only the symbol.

The value of editing in place is that you can see how your change works with the rest of the objects that you have on the Stage. For example, if you want to make your symbol bigger, you need to make sure that it doesn't obscure some nearby text. If you have lots of stuff on the Stage, however, editing in symbol-editing mode or in a new window can help you focus more easily on the symbol itself.

To edit a symbol, follow these steps:

1. **Select any instance of the symbol on the Stage.**

2. **Right-click (Windows) or Control+click (Mac) and choose Edit in Place, Edit in New Window, or Edit. (Choosing Edit puts you into symbol-editing mode.)**

   Flash displays the symbol name (Tomato, in the example) above the Timeline. Other objects are dimmed in Edit in Place mode, as shown in Figure 7-3.

   (Thanks to Polly Wickstrom, www.tomatotreedesigns.com, *for this movie,* tomatotree.fla. *We use it again in Chapter 11, so you can find it on the CD-ROM in the Ch11 folder.)*

3. **Edit the symbol in any way you want.**

4. **After you finish editing (from Edit or Edit in Place), click the scene name to the left of the symbol name or choose Edit⇨Edit Document; from a new window, click the Close button.**

   You are now back in your main Movie.

Figure 7-3:
The "tomato," the red circle on the tree, is being edited. The other objects are dimmed because Flash is in Edit in Place mode.

Using symbols from other movies

After you create a symbol and store it in the Library, you can use that Library in any other movie. You can also open the Library from any other movie and use its symbols in your current movie.

If the other movie is open and its Library is open, you can access that movie's Library from within your current movie. Libraries of any open movie are available from any other open movie.

To use a symbol from the Library of another movie that is not open, follow these steps:

1. **Choose File⇨Import⇨Open External Library.**

   The Open as Library dialog box opens.

2. **Select the movie file.**

3. **Click Open.**

   Flash displays the Library of the other movie in a new Library window.

The new Library may hide your current movie's Library. Just drag it by its grabber in the upper-left corner of the panel window under the current library until it docks there. In the new Library, many Option menu items and icons are disabled to prevent you from making changes in the other movie's file.

When you have more than one Library open, the background of the listing in Library of your current movie is white. The background of Libraries from other movies is gray. So you can look at the background to quickly see which Library is which.

To use a symbol from the other Library, drag it onto the Stage. When you do this, Flash places a copy of the symbol in the current movie's Library. (See Chapter 2 for more information about the Library.)

You can also update or replace any graphic, button, or movie clip symbol in your movie's library with the content of a symbol from any other library on your hard drive or network. Accessing a symbol in this way is called *author-time sharing* of symbols or assets. Compare it with symbols or assets that you share at runtime, after your movie has been uploaded. A *font symbol* is a special type of symbol that you use at runtime. Runtime shared libraries (which can include sounds) are explained in Chapter 12.

When you share a symbol while you're creating a movie (during *authoring*), the symbol in your current movie keeps its original name, but the contents take on the properties of the symbol that you're sharing. If you have already replaced a symbol and the outside symbol changes (because it has been edited), use author-time sharing to update the symbol in your current drawing to match the symbol's new properties.

To update or replace a graphic, button, or movie clip symbol in your movie with the properties of another symbol, follow these steps:

1. **Open the Library (choose Window⇨Library) and select the symbol that you want to update or replace.**

2. **From the Library menu, choose Properties.**

   The Symbol Properties dialog box opens.

3. **Click Advanced, if necessary, to see the expanded dialog box. In the Source section, click Browse.**

   The Locate Macromedia Flash Document File dialog box opens.

4. **Navigate to the movie (.fla) file that contains the symbol that you want to use. Select it and click Open.**

   The Select Source dialog box opens. You see a list of the symbols in the movie that you selected.

5. **Choose a symbol and click OK.**

   When you choose a symbol, you see a preview in the preview box, so you can easily find the symbol you want. When you click OK, you're back in the Symbol Properties dialog box.

6. **In the Source section of the Symbol Properties dialog box, select the Always Update Before Publishing check box if you want to automatically update the symbol if the original has changed.**

Enable this check box to create a link between the source symbol and the symbol in your current movie.

7. **Click OK.**

You now have a symbol in your Library that has its original name but looks like the symbol that you chose from the other movie.

Using the Flash Library

Flash comes with several libraries that you can use. To access these libraries, choose Window➪Other Panels➪Common Libraries and then select one of the libraries. Flash includes buttons and sounds. These libraries are also a good place to pick up ideas and see what you can create in Flash.

Using the Flash For Dummies Library

The Flash libraries contain some good examples, but they miss many basic shapes and simple objects. We decided to fill in the gaps! We created a library of art, geometric shapes, and fun shapes that you can use in your movies. The *Flash For Dummies* Library is named `Flash For Dummies Library.fla`. You can find it in the Library folder of the CD-ROM.

To use this library in Windows, copy `Flash For Dummies Library.fla` from the `Samples\Library` folder of the CD-ROM to the `Documents and Settings\[username]\Local Settings\Application Data\Macromedia\Flash MX 2004\ en\Configuration\ Libraries` folder on your hard drive. On the Mac, copy `Flash For Dummies Library.fla` from the `Samples\Library` folder of the CD-ROM to the `Applications/Macromedia Flash MX 2004/Configuration/Libraries` folder on your hard drive.

After that, you can always open this library the same way you open other common libraries: Choose Window➪Other Panels➪Common Libraries➪Flash For Dummies Library.fla. We hope you enjoy it!

Working with Instances

After you create a symbol, you can use it in many ways. You can insert it in your movie or inside other symbols or even in other movies. Each copy of the symbol is called an *instance*. You can change the properties of an instance so that the symbol differs from its parent symbol. For example, you can change the color of an instance — the original symbol remains unchanged.

Inserting instances

To insert an instance of a symbol, follow these steps:

1. **Choose Window⇨Library (Ctrl+L or F11 for Windows or ⌘+L or F11 for the Mac) to open the Library, as shown in Figure 7-4.**

2. **Choose the layer where you want the instance to be placed.**

3. **Click a keyframe on the Timeline where you want the instance to be placed.**

   Flash places instances only in keyframes. If you don't select a keyframe, Flash puts the instance in the first keyframe to the left of the current frame. (See Chapter 9 for more about keyframes.)

4. **Drag the symbol from the Library to the Stage.**

Figure 7-4: Insert an instance of a symbol by dragging it from the Library.

When you insert a graphic instance, you need to consider how it fits within your entire animation. For example, the instance may be the starting point for some animation, or it may be part of the background that remains static throughout the animation. Perhaps you want the instance to suddenly appear at some point in the animation. If the instance contains animation, you need to insert it at its proper starting point. (Chapter 9 explains how to copy graphics across any number of frames to create a static background and covers the entire topic of animation in detail.)

A movie clip instance, on the other hand, takes up only one frame on the Timeline. It plays and loops automatically unless you create ActionScript code to control it. (Chapter 10 talks about ActionScript.)

Editing instances

A symbol's *children* don't have to be carbon copies of their parents, thank goodness. Instances of a symbol can differ from their parent symbol by color, type, and play mode. You can also rotate, scale, or skew an instance, leaving the parent symbol unchanged.

When you edit an instance, Flash remembers the changes. If you go back and edit the symbol, Flash doesn't forget. Suppose that you create a red circle graphic symbol and change an instance to pink. Then you edit the circle symbol to change it to an oval. The instance is now a pink oval. Its shape has been updated, but the color remains.

No matter what change you want to make to an instance, you do it in the Property inspector. (Choose Window⇨Properties.)

You can change an instance's color (or tint), brightness, or transparency, giving you some very useful control over the appearance of your instances. To change an instance's color, brightness, or transparency, follow these steps:

1. **Select the instance.**

2. **Choose Window⇨Properties to open the Property inspector.**

3. **From the Color drop-down list, choose one of these options:**

    • **None:** Adds no color effect

    • **Brightness:** Changes the lightness or darkness of the instance

    • **Tint:** Changes the color of the instance

    • **Alpha:** Changes the opacity/transparency of the instance

    • **Advanced:** Changes both the color and the alpha at one time

4. Make the desired changes, as we explain in the next few sections.

You see the changes that you make in the Property inspector immediately in your selected instance.

Changing brightness

When you choose Brightness from the drop-down list, a slider and a text box appear. Type a brightness percentage or drag the slider and see the result immediately in the symbol instance. High brightness makes the image light, and 100 percent brightness makes the instance disappear. Low brightness makes the image dark so that 0 percent brightness turns the instance black.

Changing tint

When you choose Tint from the drop-down list, you can pick the color and then the amount of the color (the tint), by percentage, that you want to apply. Figure 7-5 shows the controls for this option. You can pick a color by clicking the Tint Color button and choosing from the color swatches or type red, green, and blue values (if you know them).

Figure 7-5:
Changing
color and
tint used on
a symbol
instance.

Specify the percentage of the color that you want to apply by typing a value in the percent text box or by clicking the drop-down arrow and dragging the slider to choose a percentage. When the percentage is set to 100%, the instance completely changes to the color that you specified. If the percentage is set to 0%, Flash leaves the instance unchanged.

The Flash method of specifying a color gives you great flexibility and precision. You can choose a color and use the tint control to create a meld of the current color and your chosen color.

If you want to stick to Web-safe colors, just choose a color swatch from the ones displayed when you click the Tint Color button and then slide the tint control all the way up to 100%.

Changing transparency

Choose Alpha from the Color Effect drop-down menu to change the transparency of an instance. (*Alpha* enables levels of transparency, and you can think of the term as somewhat synonymous to *opaqueness*.) Use the slider or type a value in the text box. A value of 0 (zero) means that your instance becomes completely transparent — in that case, when you return to the Stage, all you see is the selection border and the small plus sign that marks the symbol's registration point. When you deselect the instance, you see absolutely nothing! (Chapter 4 explains more about a symbol's registration point, including how to move it. See the section on groups.)

Partial transparency lets your background show through. A partially transparent instance blends in with your background, creating a softer effect.

Changing color and transparency at the same time

Choose Advanced from the Color Effect drop-down menu to change both the color and the transparency at the same time, by using red, green, and blue values. The Settings button appears on the Property inspector. Click Settings to open the Advanced Effect dialog box. Figure 7-6 shows the controls, which are complex.

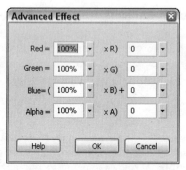

Figure 7-6:
The
Advanced
Effect
dialog box.

Use the controls on the left to reduce the color or transparency by a specific percentage compared with the current values. Use the controls on the right to change the color or transparency to a specific, absolute amount. Flash then calculates the new color value by multiplying the current value by the percentage that you specified and then adding the value from the right side. As you can see, this method provides lots of control — but it may make you crazy first.

To simply change both the color and the transparency of an instance, use the Tint controls to change the color and then just change the left Alpha setting in the Advanced Effect dialog box.

Changing an instance's type

The instance type — the graphic, movie clip, or button — comes from the symbol type, but you may want to change it. For example, if you created some animation and saved it as a graphic symbol, you may want to use it as a movie clip. Rather than change the symbol type, you can change only the type of the instance that you have inserted.

To change the instance type, follow these steps:

1. **Select the instance.**

2. **Choose Window⇨Properties to open the Property inspector.**

3. **From the Symbol Behavior drop-down list, choose one of the following types:**

   • **Graphic:** If the graphic contains animation, choose Graphic in the Behavior box and then determine how the animation will run in the Play Type drop-down list on the Property inspector. You have three choices:

   Loop plays the animation contained in the instance over and over during the frames occupied by the instance.

   Play Once plays the animation one time from the frame that you specify.

   Single Frame displays any one frame of the animation. In other words, the animation doesn't play; you specify which frame the movie displays.

   • **Button:** Choose the Button option to determine how the button is tracked in the Tracking Options section. From the Options drop-down list, choose Track as Button when you're creating single buttons. Choose Track as Menu if you're creating pop-up menus.

   • **Movie Clip:** Choose the Movie Clip option and specify an Instance name in the Name text box. You use this name with certain ActionScript controls so that you can refer to and control the instance. (For more information about ActionScript, see Chapter 10.)

Replacing an instance

Suppose that you create a complex animation with bouncing bunnies all over the Stage. Suddenly your boss decides that some of the bouncing bunnies should be bouncing squirrels instead. Meanwhile, you had already edited all the bunnies to make them different sizes and colors. You need a way to replace some of the bunnies with squirrels without losing their sizes and colors.

To replace an instance, follow these steps:

1. **Create the squirrel symbol (or whichever new symbol you need).**

   Flash stores the new symbol in the Library.

2. **Select an instance of the bunny — that is, your original instance — on the Stage.**

3. **Choose Window⇨Properties to open the Property inspector.**

4. **Click the Swap Symbol button to open the Swap Symbol dialog box.**

5. **In the dialog box, select the squirrel or any other symbol.**

6. **Click OK to swap the symbols and close the Swap Symbol dialog box.**

   Flash retains your color effects and size changes but changes the symbol.

Unfortunately, you must repeat this process for all the bunnies that you want to change on the Stage, but it's better than reinserting all your instances and re-creating the instance changes.

If your boss actually wants you to change ALL the bunnies to squirrels, your job is much simpler. Just edit the bunny symbol (as we describe in the "Editing symbols" section earlier in this chapter) to replace the bunny image with a squirrel. Then all the instances of that symbol instantly change to squirrels yet retain the color effects and size changes that you gave them while they were still bunnies.

Duplicate a symbol when you want to use one symbol as a springboard for creating a new symbol. Follow the instructions earlier in this chapter in the "Creating Symbols" section. Make any changes that you want to the new symbol and place instances on the Stage.

Breaking apart an instance

You can break apart an instance into its component objects. The original symbol remains in the movie's Library. You may want to use the instance as a starting point for creating a completely new symbol or you may want to animate the components of the symbol so that they move separately. Other instances remain unchanged.

To break apart an instance, select it and choose Modify⇨Break Apart. If an instance contains symbols or grouped objects within it, you can use the Break Apart command again to break apart those internal objects as well.

Chapter 8

Pushing Buttons

. . . .

. . . .

When you view a Web page, you see buttons that you can click to move to other pages or sites. These buttons are graphical images, but they're hyperlinks as well. If you start to pay attention to these buttons, you see that some of them change when you pass your mouse cursor over them. They change again when you click them. Sometimes they make a sound when you click them.

Flash can create these types of buttons and more. You can animate Flash buttons, for example, so that they move or rotate when viewers pass over or click them. You can add interactive controls (actions) to buttons so that passing over or clicking them starts other movies or creates other effects.

In this chapter, you find out how to create buttons that look the way you want. You also discover how to make more complex buttons that include sounds, movie clips, and simple ActionScript. To discover more about ActionScript and interactivity, see Chapter 10.

Creating Simple Buttons

Before you create a button, stop and think about what you want the button to accomplish on a Web page and how you want it to look. Web page designers often create a series of buttons that look similar and lead to various Web pages. Buttons often include some text to identify the button's purpose.

But you can use buttons for lots of other more advanced purposes than navigating to Web pages. A button can stop music, indicate a choice in a survey or game, or be dragged around on a puzzle or game Web page.

A *button* is a symbol. (See Chapter 7 for the lowdown on how to create and edit symbols.) In this chapter, we cover the entire process of creating buttons.

Understanding button states

A button has four states that define characteristics of the button:

- ✔ **Up:** Defines what the button looks like when the mouse pointer is not over the button. The viewer initially sees the Up state of a button.

- ✔ **Over:** Defines what the button looks like when the pointer is over the button (but it hasn't been clicked).

- ✔ **Down:** Defines what the button looks like when the button is clicked.

- ✔ **Hit:** Defines the area of the button that responds to the mouse. The user doesn't see this area — it's invisible. When you pass the pointer over the hit area, the pointer is considered over the button. When you click anywhere in the hit area, the button works.

Figure 8-1 shows a button in its four states. A typical, simple button may show a lit-up effect for the Over state and an indented look (as though the button is pressed in) for the Down state. In this example, the Down state moves the highlight to the right, giving the impression of movement when the button is clicked.

Figure 8-1:
The four states of a button: Up, Over, Down, and Hit.

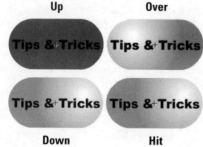

Up · Over · Down · Hit

Radial gradients are useful for creating a lit-up or pushed-in look. Use a light color or white to create the appearance of a highlight. Use a dark color or black to create an indented look. Just changing the color of the fill (often to a lighter color) is often enough to make it seem lit up.

The button shown in Figure 8-1 is on the CD-ROM. Look for `capsule.fla` in the Ch08 folder. To try out the buttons in this movie, choose Control⇨Test Movie.

Making a basic button

To create a simple button, follow these steps:

1. **Choose Insert⇨New Symbol to open the Create New Symbol dialog box.**

2. **In the Name text box, type a name for the button.**

3. **In the Behavior section, choose Button and click OK.**

   You're now in symbol-editing mode. Flash displays the special Timeline for buttons, with four frames: Up, Over, Down, and Hit, as shown in Figure 8-2. Note the dot in the Up frame, indicating that the frame is a keyframe. (For more information about keyframes, see Chapter 9.) The word *Up* is highlighted, indicating that the Up frame is active.

Figure 8-2:
The Flash symbol-editing mode for buttons displays a Timeline with four frames.

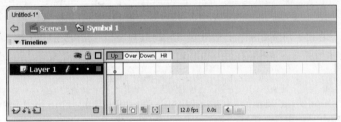

4. **Create the graphic for the Up state.**

   You can use the Flash drawing tools, an imported graphic, or an instance of a symbol. You can create as many layers as you want for the button. For an animated button, use a movie clip symbol. We explain how to create an animated button in the "Adding a movie clip to a button" section, later in this chapter.

   If you want the button image for the four states to be in the same place, place the graphic in the center of the display and build the other states in the center as well. To do this, cut and paste the graphic. (See Chapter 4 for more about centering objects on the display.) If the button images aren't in the same place, the button appears to shift when the viewer passes the cursor over or clicks the button.

5. **Right-click (Windows) or Control+click (Mac) the Over frame and choose Insert Keyframe from the pop-up menu.**

   Flash inserts a keyframe in the Over frame of the button. You can also choose Insert⇨Timeline⇨Keyframe or press F6. (F6 is actually a shortcut for Modify⇨Timeline⇨Convert to Keyframes, but in this case you can use either command.) The graphic for the Up state remains on the Stage.

6. **Create the graphic for the Over state.**

   You can use the graphic for the Up state as a starting point and change it (or leave it the same if you don't want the button to change when the mouse pointer passes over the button). You can also delete the graphic and put a new one in its place. If you have more than one layer, place a keyframe on each layer before creating the artwork for that layer.

7. **Right-click (Windows) or Control+click (Mac) the Down frame and choose Insert Keyframe from the pop-up menu.**

8. **Create the graphic for the Down frame.**

   Repeat as in Step 6.

9. **Right-click (Windows) or Control+click (Mac) the Hit frame and choose Insert Keyframe from the pop-up menu.**

10. **Create the shape that defines the active area of the button.**

    This shape should completely cover all the graphics of the other state. Usually, a rectangle or circle is effective. If you ignore the Hit frame, Flash uses the boundary of the objects in the Up frame.

    If you use text for the button, viewers have to hit the letters precisely unless you create a rectangular hit area around the text. To cover an area of text, create a filled-in shape on a new layer.

11. **Click the scene name above the layer list (or the Back arrow to the left of the scene name) to return to the regular Timeline and leave symbol-editing mode.**

12. **If the Library isn't open, choose Window⇨Library and drag the button symbol that you just created to wherever you want it on the Stage.**

    You just created a button!

A button is a symbol, but when you want to place a button on the Stage, you must drag the button from the Library to create an instance of the symbol. See Chapter 7 for a full explanation of symbols and instances.

Putting Buttons to the Test

After you create a button, you need to test it. You can choose from a couple of methods.

The fastest way to test a button is to enable it. An enabled button responds to your mouse as you would expect — it changes as you specified when you pass the mouse over it and click it. To enable the buttons on the Stage, choose Control⇨Enable Simple Buttons. All the buttons on the Stage are now enabled.

Have fun with your button! Pass the mouse over it, click it, and watch it change.

After you test your button, suppose that you want to select the button to move it. You try to click it to select it, and it only glows at you, according to the Down frame's definition. Choose Control⇨Enable Buttons again to disable the buttons. Now you can select a button like any other object. In general, enable buttons only to test them.

However, if you really want to select an enabled button, you can do so with the Selection tool by dragging a selection box around it. You can use the arrow keys to move the button. If you want to edit the button further, choose Window⇨Properties to open the Property inspector and edit the button's properties as we explain in Chapter 7.

If you have other animations on the Stage, you can play an animation with the buttons enabled. Choose Control⇨Play or press Enter (Windows) or Return (Mac). By playing the animation, you can see how the buttons fit in with the rest of your movie.

Another way to test a button is to test the entire movie. Choose Control⇨Test Movie. Flash creates an .swf file just as it would if you were publishing the movie — except that this .swf file is temporary. Any animation plays, and you can test your buttons as well. When you're done, click the Close box of the window.

If your button contains movie clips, you must use this method of testing the button because the animation doesn't play on the Stage.

Creating Complex Buttons

Buttons can do more than just change color or shape. You can enhance a button in three ways:

- **Add a sound:** For example, you can add a clicking sound to the Down frame of a button so that users hear that sound when they click the button.

- **Add a movie clip:** To animate a button, you add a movie clip to it. You can animate the Up, Over, and Down frames, if you want.

- **Add an action (interactive control):** To make a button do something, you need to add an action to it by using ActionScript. Actions are covered in Chapter 10, but we discuss some of the basic concepts here.

Adding a sound to a button

For fun, you can add a sound to a button. Usually, sounds are added to the Over or Down frame — or both, if you want. Chapter 11 explains lots more about sound, but in this section, we explain how to add a simple sound to a button.

Look in the Ch08 folder for `click.wav`. You can add this sound to the Down frame of a button.

To add a sound to a button, follow these steps:

1. **Create the button symbol.**

2. **Choose File⇨Import⇨Import to Library to open the Import dialog box.**

3. **Select the sound file (in `.wav`, `.aiff`, or `.mp3` format) and click Open.**

   Flash stores the file in the Library.

4. **Choose Window⇨Library to open the Library.**

5. **If you aren't in symbol-editing mode, double-click the button's icon in the Library to enter symbol-editing mode.**

6. **Click the plus sign at the bottom of the layer list to add a new layer.**

   See Chapter 6 for a full explanation of layers.

7. **Name the new layer *Sound* or something similar.**

8. **In the new layer, right-click (Windows) or Control+click (Mac) the frame where you want to place the sound — for example, the Down frame — and choose Insert Keyframe from the contextual menu.**

9. **Choose Window⇨Properties to open the Property inspector.**

10. **From the Sound drop-down list, choose the sound file that you want.**

    Flash lists all the sounds that you have imported into the Library. When you choose the sound file, you see the sound wave indicator on the sound's layer in the frame where you inserted the sound, as shown in Figure 8-3.

Figure 8-3:
When you add a sound to a button, the sound wave appears in the Timeline.

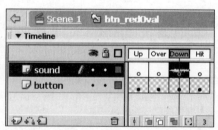

11. **From the Sync drop-down list of the Property inspector, choose Event.**

    The Event setting synchronizes the sound to the occurrence of an event: in this case, the clicking of the button. Event is the default setting.

12. **Click the scene name in the upper-left area of the layer list or the Back arrow to the left of the scene name.**

    Flash returns you to the regular Timeline and leaves symbol-editing mode.

13. **Drag the button symbol that you just created from the Library to wherever you want the button on the Stage.**

    You're done! Now test the button as we explain in the earlier section, "Putting Buttons to the Test."

Be sure to look in Chapter 11 for more information on adding sounds to buttons and movies.

If you've already added the sound to another movie, choose File⇨Import⇨ Open External Library and choose the other movie. Click the desired keyframe and drag the sound from the Library to anywhere on the Stage. Flash places the sound in the selected keyframe.

Adding a movie clip to a button

If you think that simple buttons are b-o-r-i-n-g, you can animate them. To animate a button, you must create a movie clip symbol and then insert the movie clip into one of the frames. Generally, button animation is localized in the area of the button. If you want to make an elaborate button, you can animate all three frames — Up, Over, and Down.

To add a movie clip to a button, you must first create the movie clip. Chapter 7 explains how to create a movie clip symbol, and Chapter 9 explains how to create the animation to put in the movie clip.

For the following steps, you can use the movie clip that we provide in the Ch08 folder of the CD-ROM. Open flower power.fla. It's a blank movie whose Library contains the symbols necessary to create a button with a movie clip.

If you've never created a button, review the steps in the section "Making a basic button," earlier in this chapter. Then, to create a button with a movie clip, follow these steps:

1. **If you're using the movie file included on the CD-ROM, open** flower power.fla **from the Ch08 folder; otherwise, open any new movie file.**

2. **Choose Insert⇨New Symbol to open the Create New Symbol dialog box.**

3. **In the Name text box, type a name for the button.**

4. **In the Behavior section, choose Button and click OK.**

5. Create the graphic for the Up state.

If you're using the movie from the CD-ROM, choose Window➪Library and drag to the Stage the graphic symbol named *Flower*. Click anywhere on the Stage to make it active, and press the arrow buttons on the keyboard (left, right, up, and down, as necessary) to center the flower symbol's registration point (shown by a little plus sign) exactly over the registration point (also a plus sign) on the Stage (see Figure 8-4). You can also cut and paste the symbol to center it. The flower graphic symbol is static, not animated.

6. Right-click (Windows) or Control+click (Mac) the Over frame and choose Insert Keyframe from the pop-up menu.

Flash inserts a keyframe.

7. Create the graphic for the Over state.

For this example, delete the graphic on the Stage (it's still there from the Up frame) and drag the movie clip called *Flower Rotating* to the center of the Stage. Click the Stage and use the arrow keys to perfectly center the flower. The Flower Rotating movie clip animates the flower by rotating it.

8. Right-click (Windows) or Control+click (Mac) the Down frame and choose Insert Keyframe from the pop-up menu.

9. Create the graphic for the Down state.

In this example, delete the graphic on the Stage and drag the Flower Light graphic symbol to the exact center of the Stage.

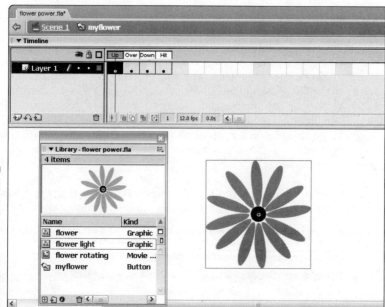

Figure 8-4:
You can use the Flower Power library to create an animated button.

10. **Right-click (Windows) or Control+click (Mac) the Hit frame and choose Insert Keyframe from the pop-up menu.**

11. **Use the Rectangle tool and drag a square to cover the entire area of the symbol, leaving the symbol on top; use the Selection tool to select and delete the symbol, leaving only the square.**

    If you don't perform this step, viewers must place the mouse cursor exactly over one of the petals to see the animation. By defining the Hit frame as a square, placing the cursor anywhere within that square activates the button. Your screen should look like Figure 8-4, shown with the Up frame active.

12. **Click the scene name (Scene 1) above the layer list to return to the regular Timeline.**

13. **Drag the button symbol that you just created from the Library to wherever you want the button placed on the Stage.**

    Congratulations! You have just created a button with a movie clip.

To test the button that you just created, choose Control⇨Test Movie. Place the cursor over the button, click the button, and watch the animation. If you used the Flower Power library from the CD-ROM, first save the file on your computer by choosing File⇨Save As and choosing a location on your hard drive. When you test this movie, the flower rotates when you pass the cursor over it and also lightens. When you click the flower, it seems to freeze. When you're done, click the Close box of the window.

If you want to see the final result of the preceding steps, check out `flower power final.fla` in the Ch08 folder on the CD-ROM.

Adding an action to a button

A button doesn't do anything except look pretty until you give it the proper instructions. For example, a button can link you to another Web page or start a movie. ActionScript is covered in Chapter 10, but in this section, we explain the basic principle of adding an action to a button — in this case, an action that links the user to another Web page by using the Behaviors panel, which is new in Flash MX 2004.

To add an action to a button, follow these steps:

1. **If you haven't already done so, drag an instance of the button onto the Stage. If the button isn't already selected, select it.**

2. **Choose Window⇨Development Panels⇨Behaviors to open the Behaviors panel.**

3. **Click the plus sign and choose whichever category and subcategory contains the action that you want. In our example, choose Web, then choose Go to Web Page.**

4. **Depending on the behavior that you chose, complete the information in the dialog box. In our example, complete the URL, as shown in Figure 8-5.**

   When typing the Uniform Resource Locator (URL), follow the same rules that you would to create any hyperlink on your Web site. For example, usually you can use local URLs (referring just to the page, for example) for other pages on the same Web site, but you need absolute URLs (that is, complete URLs, starting with http://) for hyperlinks to other sites.

Figure 8-5: The Go to URL dialog box.

5. **If you want, you can also change the Open In drop-down option, which determines how the URL opens.**

   For example, _blank opens a new browser window, and _self displays the URL in the same window.

6. **Click OK.**

   Figure 8-6 shows the Behaviors panel with the Go to Web Page action. Note that the top line of the ActionScript says that the event is On Release, which means that the button works when the mouse button is released.

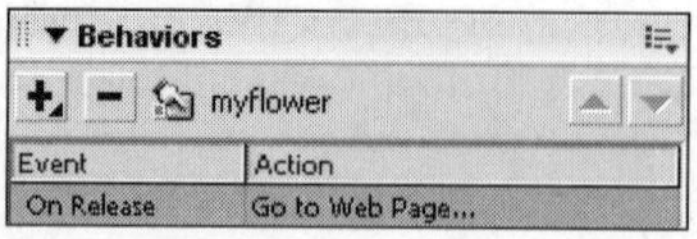

Figure 8-6: The Behaviors panel.

7. **If you want, choose another event by clicking the event and choosing from the drop-down list.**

   See Chapter 10 for a list of button events and how they work.

To view the ActionScript that you created, select the button and open the Actions panel (Window⇨Actions).

You can add your button to an existing Web page. In such a case, the button may be the only Flash element on the page. You can also include buttons as part of an environment completely created in Flash. Either way, buttons are a valuable piece of the Flash arsenal.

For a gorgeous example of a button, as shown in Figure 8-7, look for nav_button.fla in the Ch08 folder of the CD-ROM. Open the .fla file and choose Control⇨Test Movie to see how the button works. (Clicking the button results in your computer trying to go to the URL of the button's action.) Then close the window. Choose Control⇨Enable Buttons to turn off the button. Right-click the button (not the entire symbol) and choose Actions. Now you can see the Get URL action attached to this button. (*The nav_button.fla file is courtesy of Jeremy Wachtel, Vice President of Project Management at Macquarium Intelligent Communications —* http://www. macquarium.com.)

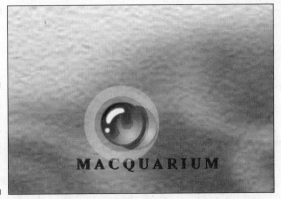

Figure 8-7: This Web site sports beautiful bubble buttons.

Creating a button that acts on text input

Here's a more advanced example of a button that uses an action to make a graphic respond to user input. As you can see in Figure 8-8, the example has a text box, a graphic, and a button. The text box is defined as input text, which means that the user can type text in it. (For more information on text, see Chapter 5.) When the user types a number in the text box and clicks the button, the graphic's width changes to the number of pixels specified in the text box. In this way, the user can interactively change the movie. You could use any graphic, and the button could change properties other than width.

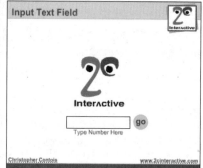

Figure 8-8: This movie's button changes the width of the graphic (in pixels) as specified by the number you type in the text box.

Before trying to re-create this example, look in the Ch08 folder of the CD-ROM for `inputTxtField.fla` to see how it works. Open the movie and press Ctrl+Enter (Windows) or ⌘+Return (Mac) to test the movie. Enter a number in the text box and click the button. (You can also press Enter [Windows] or Return [Mac].) Then enter a different number and try again. Have fun with it! *(Thanks to Christopher Contois, www.2cinteractive.com, for this movie. Christopher teaches classes in Flash.)*

Follow these steps to create this example:

1. **Create a symbol with a movie clip behavior.**

   This symbol will be the graphic that changes in width. For information on creating movie clips, see Chapter 7.

2. **Open the Library (choose Window⇨Library) and drag an instance of the symbol onto the Stage.**

3. **Open the Property inspector (choose Window⇨Properties). In the Instance Name text box, type a name for the instance. Later, you need to refer to this name.**

   For example, you could name the instance `ball`.

4. **Click the Text tool. In the Property inspector, choose Input Text from the Text Type drop-down list. Drag out a text box on the Stage.**

5. **If necessary, click the Expand arrow in the lower-right corner of the Property inspector to expand it to full size. In the Var text box, type a variable name for the input text box that you created on the Stage. In the sample movie, the variable name is `size`.**

6. **To the left of the Var text box is the Show Border around Text button. Click this button so that the border of the text box is visible when you publish the movie.**

7. **Click the Character button on the Property inspector to open the Character Options dialog box and choose Specify Ranges. Then choose Numerals [0–9] and click OK.**

8. **Create a button as we describe earlier in this chapter.**

   If you want, put some text on the button to help guide users to click the button. In the example, the word *Go* appears on the button.

9. **Drag an instance of the button onto the Stage.**

10. **With the button selected, open the Action panel (choose Window⇨Actions).**

11. **In the Actions panel, choose Global Functions⇨Movie Clip Control and then double-click** on.

    On is an event that defines when something happens. (For more information on events, see Chapter 10.)

    You see a list of options.

12. **Double-click Release from the list so that the button will function when the user releases the mouse button.**

13. **Click to the right of the left bracket at the end of the first line.**

14. **In the Actions panel, choose Built-in Classes⇨Movie⇨Movie Clip⇨Properties and double-click the property that you want. In our example, we used the** _width **property.**

    The Actions panel should look like this:

    ```
    on (release) {instanceName._width
        }
    ```

15. **To insert the instance name, double-click** instanceName. **Then click the Insert a Target Path button to open the Insert Target Path dialog box. Choose the instance name that you specified in Step 3 and click OK.**

    The target is the instance whose property you want to set.

    In our example, we want to change the width of the movie clip.

16. **To set the width equal to the value in the input text box, click at the end of the first line of code. Type an equal sign (=) and the variable that you created in Step 5. In our example, you would type the following:**

    ```
    =size
    ```

    This specifies where the instance ball1 gets the value for the property that you're setting. In this case, the value comes from the input text box. Your ActionScript should look like this:

    ```
    on (release) {ball1._width = size;}
    ```

17. **Collapse or close the Actions panel. Add some text that explains to users what to do and make the rest of the Stage look pretty, if you want.**

18. **Test the movie! Press Ctrl+Enter (Windows) or ⌘+Return (Mac). Try different numbers and click the button. Make the symbol skinny or fat!**

Testing your button's Get URL action

To properly test a button with a Get URL action, you need to publish your movie, upload it to your Web page, go online, and try it out. You can test the button on your hard drive first, however, so that you can be fairly sure that it will work when you put it on your Web page.

Suppose that you want your button to link to another Web page on your Web site. Perhaps that page's local URL is tips.html. Assume that tips.html is in the same folder as the Web page containing your Flash button so that you can use this simple local URL.

To test your button's Get URL action, follow these steps:

1. **After creating the button and its Get URL action with a URL of** tips.html **(or whatever's appropriate in your situation), choose File⇨Save to save the movie file.**

2. **Choose File⇨Publish.**

   Flash publishes the file, creating a HyperText Markup Language (HTML) and an .swf file in the same folder as your .fla file. (These are default settings. See Chapter 13 for more information on publishing movies.)

3. **To test the button, you need a file on your hard drive with the same URL that you used in your button. Create a file named** tips.html **(or whatever URL you used) on your hard drive in the same folder as**

your movie. You can use either of two methods:

✔ Make a copy of the existing tips.html (if you have it on your hard drive) and move it to the folder containing your movie.

✔ Create a new HTML document and save it as tips.html in the same folder as your movie. This document can be a dummy document — you can put any text you want in it. For example, you can type **This is a test HTML document**. If you create this document in a word processor, be sure to save it as an HTML document. Otherwise, use the software that you normally use to create HTML documents.

4. **Working offline, open your browser, choose File⇨Open, and open the HTML file for your Flash movie. (It has the same name as your movie.)**

5. **Click your button.**

   You should see tips.html displayed. If you don't, go back and check your action settings.

You can also test your button without publishing it by choosing Control⇨Test Movie and clicking a button with a Get URL action. If you have used an absolute (complete) URL, you should have no problem. However, a relative (local) URL may not be available.

Part IV
Total
Flash-o-Rama

The 5th Wave   By Rich Tennant

©RICHTENNANT

Jeez–that's impressive! Let's see that airbrush effect again.

In this part . . .

Moving imagery is the heart and soul of Flash, and in this part you make your Flash creations come to life through the power of animation and video. You find out about moving objects, changing their shape (or *morphing* them), letting Flash create animation for you, and easy ways to integrate video into your Flash movies.

After you create your movie, you can make it interactive so that the Web experience is more meaningful and engaging. Flash ActionScript offers infinite potential, so let your imagination soar. We show you how to combine your animation with your symbols and then add actions to script your entire movie.

The world is not silent, and your Flash movies don't have to be either. Find out how to add sounds and music to your movies — from the simplest sound of a button click to the majestic tones of a full-fledged symphony.

Chapter 9

Getting Animated

. . . .

. . . .

*W*hy do you create graphics in Flash? To animate them, of course. In this chapter, we explain animation — the heart and soul of Flash — and making your graphics move. Hold on to your hats!

We start by explaining the basics of animation, including how to prepare for animation and how to work with the Timeline. Then we go into the specific techniques — Timeline effects, frame-by-frame animation, and tweening — that you can use to create great, animated effects in Flash. We cover both motion and shape tweening and then give you the details of editing your animation. So let's get moving!

Who Framed the Animation?

The secret of animation in Flash, as in the movies, is that ultimately, nothing ever really moves. A Flash movie creates the illusion of movement by quickly displaying the sequence of still images. Each still image is slightly different. Your brain fills in the gaps to give you the impression of movement.

One of the great things about Flash is that you can easily create complicated, spectacular extravaganzas of animation. Flash stores lots of information in super-compact vector format. Because the files are so small, they download quickly. So Flash = spectacular animation + fast download. That's good for your Web site viewers.

Just as in a movie, each still image is contained in a frame. Each *frame* represents a unit of time. You create the animation by placing images in the frames. A frame may contain one object or none or many, depending on how crowded of a scene you want to create.

Time is your ally in Flash because you have complete control over it. You can look at each individual image in time and tweak it to your heart's content. Then you can step on the gas, play everything back at high speed, and watch everything appear to move.

In Flash, you create animation in three ways:

- **Frame by frame:** You move or modify objects one frame at a time. This frame-by-frame animation is time consuming but is often the only way to create complex animated effects. This method can certainly satisfy your appetite for total control.

- **Tweening:** You create starting frames and ending frames and let Flash figure out where everything goes in the in-between frames, which is why it's called *tweening*. Tweening is much more fun and easier than frame-by-frame animation. If you can create the animation that you want by tweening, it's definitely the way to go. Flash offers two types of tweening: *motion* tweening and *shape* tweening, both of which we describe later in this chapter.

- **Timeline effects:** You choose from a list of prebuilt animations, adjust a few settings, and then instantly apply them to your text, graphics, buttons, or movie clips. Flash automatically creates the tweens for you. This is a cool, new feature in Flash MX 2004.

In tweening, the starting and ending frames are called *keyframes* because they are the key moments in time that the software uses to calculate the in-between frames. Tweening not only means less work for you but also creates smaller files (which download faster) because you're describing your animations more concisely. In frame-by-frame animation, every frame is a keyframe because every frame defines a change in the action.

Preparing to Animate

You probably want to get started animating already, but you need to set the stage first so that your animation works properly. Here are the steps that you need to take before you can begin creating your animation:

1. **Choose Insert⇨Timeline⇨Layer to create a new layer for your animation and put your starting graphic or graphics on that layer.**

You should always animate on a layer that has no other objects on it. Otherwise, your animated objects may erase, connect to, or segment other objects . . . with messy results. Refer to Chapter 6 for more information on layers.

2. **If you plan to use motion tweening, turn your graphic into a symbol or group; if you plan to use shape tweening, make sure that your graphic is a shape; and if you plan to do frame-by-frame animation, your graphic can be anything that you want.**

   See the section "The Animation Tween," a little later in this chapter, to find out more about motion tweening and shape tweening. Your graphic absolutely must be a symbol, a group, or text in order for your motion tweening to work properly. (Refer to Chapter 7 for more about symbols and Chapter 4 for the lowdown on grouping objects.) For shape tweening, the rule is the opposite of motion tweening. If your graphic is a symbol or a group or both, you can't shape tween it, so just draw a shape by using the drawing tools.

3. **Set a frame rate. (See the later section "Turtle or hare?" for more information.)**

When you animate, you often need to play back your animation during the process. The simplest way is to press Enter (Windows) or Return (Mac), which plays the movie. Sometimes, however, you may want more control — perhaps to play part of your movie. In this case, the Controller is invaluable. The Controller, as shown in Figure 9-1, is a simple toolbar that looks like the controls on a tape recorder. Use it to play, rewind, fast-forward, and stop your animation.

Figure 9-1:
The
Controller.

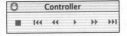

Master of the Timeline

The *Timeline* is the map of your animation sequence. If the Timeline isn't visible, choose Window⇨Timeline. Each layer has its own Timeline row. The Timeline has its own coding to help you understand the structure of your animation, as shown in Figure 9-2.

The Timeline can be undocked from the main Flash window and resized. Just grab the Timeline in the gray area below the title bar and to the left of the Eye icon, and drag it to where you want it. Then you can resize it as an independent window by dragging the lower-right corner (Windows) or by dragging the Size box in the lower-right corner (Macintosh).

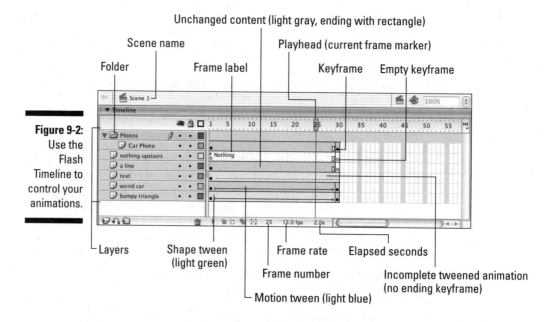

Figure 9-2:
Use the
Flash
Timeline to
control your
animations.

Half the power of the Timeline is that it divides motion into *frames* — bits of time that you can isolate and work with — one at a time. The other half of the Timeline's power is that you can organize different components of your animation into different layers.

Always animate one layer at a time.

Click any frame to make it active. Remember to click in the row of the layer containing the graphics that you want to animate. By clicking any frame, you can view your animation frozen in a moment of time.

As you read through the examples and steps in this chapter, you quickly get the hang of working with the Timeline.

Hide the layers that you're not interested in (click beneath the Eye icon) to help you visualize the animation. But don't forget to check the animation with all the layers displayed to see how everything looks together. You should also lock layers when you're finished with them to avoid unwanted changes. Refer to Chapter 6 for further instructions on hiding and locking layers.

Turtle or hare?

All you need to do to make animation work is to view your sequence of still images over time at high speed. Unless you have a remarkable attention span, one image per second is way too slow. Silent movies were typically

16 or 18 frames per second (fps). With the arrival of talkies, the speed got bumped up to 24 fps for better quality sound. On your television, the speed is roughly 30 images per second.

The smoothness of the playback of your animation depends not only on the frame rate that you specify but also on the complexity of the animation and the speed of the computer that's playing it. Generally, 12 fps is a good choice for Web animation. Luckily, that's the default rate in Flash.

To change the frame rate for your animation, follow these steps:

1. **Double-click the Frame Rate box (which displays a number and the letters fps) at the bottom of the Timeline to open the Document Properties dialog box.**

   Alternatively, you can choose Modify⇨Document.

2. **In the Frame Rate text box, type a new number (in frames per second).**

   You can set only one frame rate for all the animation in your current Flash file, and you should set the frame rate before you start animating.

3. **Click OK to set the new speed and close the dialog box.**

A Flash movie's frame rate represents the maximum speed at which the movie runs. Flash animation has no guaranteed minimum speed. If your animation is lagging or bogging down, increasing the frame rate doesn't help at all; in fact, it may make things worse.

Animating with Keyframes

Keyframes are the frames that are key to your animation. In frame-by-frame animation, every frame is a keyframe. In tweened animation, only the first and last frames of a tween are keyframes. By creating keyframes, you specify the duration and therefore the speed of an animated sequence.

To create a keyframe, select a frame on the Timeline and choose Insert⇨Timeline⇨Keyframe. For faster service, right-click (Windows) or Control+click (Mac) a frame on the Timeline and choose Insert Keyframe from the shortcut menu that appears. You can also press F6.

You can change the display of the appearance of frames on the Timeline by clicking the Frame View button in the upper-right corner of the Timeline. This action brings up the Frame View pop-up menu. With this menu, you can

✔ Set the width of frame cells to Tiny, Small, Normal, Medium, or Large.

✔ Decrease the height of frame cells by choosing Short.

✔ Turn on or off the tinting of frame sequences.

✔ Choose to display a thumbnail of the contents of each frame. If you choose Preview, the thumbnail is scaled to fit the Timeline frame; if you choose Preview in Context, the thumbnail also includes any empty space in the frame.

Creating Animations Instantly with Timeline Effects

In Flash MX 2004, you can now instantly create complex animations simply by choosing from a list of Timeline effects and applying one to your art. With Timeline effects, you can use prebuilt animations to make your art spin, shrink, explode, expand, fade in or out, and do many other tricks, with just a few clicks of your mouse.

To add animation by using Timeline effects, do the following steps:

1. **Select an object that you want to animate.**

   For the Timeline effect to work, the object must be a shape, text, a bitmap image, a graphic symbol, a button symbol, or a group.

2. **Choose Insert⇨Timeline Effects⇨Assistants, Insert⇨Timeline Effects⇨Effects, or Insert⇨Timeline Effects⇨Transform/Transition.**

   A list of effects appears. The list contains various effects for different kinds of objects. Any effects that don't work with your type of object appear grayed-out on the menu.

3. **Select an effect from the list.**

   A dialog box opens for the effect that you select.

4. **In the Effects Settings dialog box, modify any of the default settings if you want to change them, and then click OK.**

   The dialog box disappears. Flash automatically renames layer containing your object. The layer has the same name as the effect but with a number appended corresponding to the number of Timeline effects that you've created so far.

   Flash also automatically puts your object inside a new symbol, which is in turn inside a new graphic symbol containing all the new tweens and transformations needed for the effect.

5. **Choose Control⇨Test Movie to view your animation.**

   Your movie is exported to a Flash Player ("swf") window.

6. **To further adjust your Timeline effect, close the Flash Player ("swf") window and click the Edit button in the Property inspector.**

   The dialog box for your Timeline effect reappears.

7. **Repeat Steps 4 through 6 as desired.**

To delete a Timeline effect, follow these steps:

1. **On the Stage, right-click (Windows) or Control+click (Macintosh) the object with the Timeline effect that you want to remove.**

   A contextual menu appears.

2. **Choose Timeline Effects⇨Remove Effect from the contextual menu.**

   The Timeline effect is removed.

Frame after frame after frame

If your animation isn't a simple motion in an easily definable direction or a change of shape or color — and isn't one of the prebuilt Timeline effects — you probably need to use frame-by-frame animation.

If you must, you must. Some complex animations just have to be created frame by frame. The basic procedure is simple.

To create an animation by using the frame-by-frame technique, follow these steps:

1. **Select a frame in the row of the layer that you want to use.**

   The animation starts in that frame.

2. **Right-click (Windows) or Control+click (Mac) the frame and choose Insert Keyframe from the menu that appears.**

   The first frame on a movie's Timeline is automatically a keyframe, so you don't have to create it.

3. **Create the graphic for the first frame.**

   You can import a graphic, paste a graphic from the Clipboard, or use the Flash drawing tools. (Refer to Chapter 3 for help with creating or importing a graphic.)

4. **Right-click (Windows) or Control+click (Mac) the next frame and choose Insert Keyframe again.**

   The next frame on the Timeline now has the same graphic as the preceding one.

5. **Modify the graphic to create the second frame of the animation.**

6. **Repeat Steps 4 and 5 until you've created all the frames that you need for your animation.**

7. **While you work, you can continually check your cool animation by pressing Enter (Windows) or Return (Macintosh) to play it back.**

Figure 9-3 shows frames of an animation as the word *New!* is created from a few specks on the page.

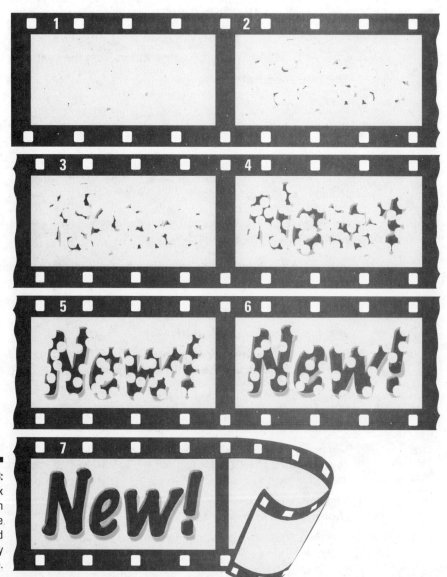

Figure 9-3: A complex animation must be created frame by frame.

Stillness in the night

Regular frames cannot contain changes. Therefore, if you insert a graphic in the first keyframe, the graphic remains throughout the Timeline until it reaches another keyframe with a new graphic.

For several reasons, you may need to copy objects over a number of frames. Sometimes, you want a still image to sit unmoving for a while on a layer of your animation — as a background image, for example — while your animation moves in front. A background gives context to your animated objects. Even animated objects often need to remain on the Stage after they've finished moving about.

To make this happen, add a new layer for your background or other object. With that layer active, create or paste your object (or objects) at the starting frame you choose. Then click your chosen ending frame and choose Insert⇨Timeline⇨Frame. Flash duplicates your image throughout all intermediate frames.

As a shortcut, after you have your object or objects in the starting frame, Alt+drag (Windows) or Option+drag (Mac) the frame along the Timeline until you reach the last frame that you want to contain the object. Flash copies the contents of the first keyframe through all the frames.

If you copy the objects to a keyframe, they remain on the Stage until the next keyframe.

The Animation Tween

If your animation follows some simple guidelines, you can save yourself lots of work (and control your file size, too) by asking Flash (say, "Please") to interpolate the in-between frames for you automatically. You just create the first and last keyframes, and Flash figures out what should go in-between. In animation technobabble, that's called *tweening* — a quick, fun way to create great animations.

The Flash tweening capabilities are impressive. Here's what you can do with tweening:

✔ **Motion tweening:** This is probably the most common type of tweening. Simple motion tweening moves your objects in a straight line from here to there. Flash can, however, easily handle animation along any path that you create, even one with lots of curves.

✔ **Shape tweening:** This type of tweening gradually changes any shape to another shape. You create the first and last shapes. Your kids call it *morphing.* You can add *shape hints* to tell Flash exactly how you want your shape to morph.

✔ **Change an object's size (both motion and shape tweening):** For example, if you make an object smaller as you move it, the object often appears to be moving away from the viewer.

✔ **Rotate an object (both motion and shape tweening):** You specify the amount of the rotation. Flash combines the motion or shape tweening with the rotation so that you get both effects at one time.

✔ **Change color and/or transparency (both motion and shape tweening):** Flash creates a gradual change in color based on your starting and ending colors.

Animating your graphic's transparency is a particularly cool effect because it lets you fade objects in and out, making them magically appear and disappear at just the right moment.

Of course, you can create several animations, one after another, to mix and match the effects. You can also combine frame-by-frame animation with tweened animation. Let your imagination soar!

From here to there — motion tweening

In motion tweening, you move an object from one place to another. The movement can be a straight line or any path that you can draw with the Pencil tool. Figure 9-4 shows a few frames from a motion tween that uses a looped path. While the animation progresses, the skateboarder image also scales down to 50 percent of its original size so that it appears to be moving away from you. In this example, the path is made visible so that you can see how the animation works. You usually hide the layer containing the path.

Moving symbols, groups, and type

You can motion tween instances of symbols, objects that you've made into a group, or type (text). You can not only move them but also change their size, rotation, and skew. And, in the case of instances, you can also motion tween their color. (To change the color of groups or text during motion tween, you have to convert them into symbols first.) See Chapter 7 to discover all about symbols and instances.

To *skew* an object means to slant it along one or both axes.

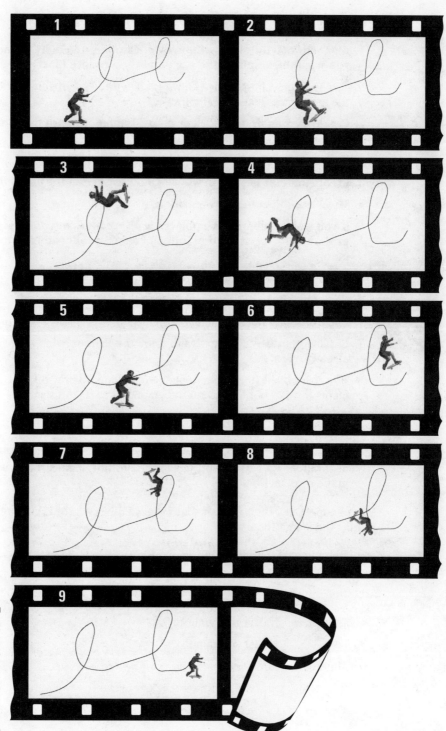

Figure 9-4:
You can draw any path and animate an object along the path.

To create a simple motion tween animation, follow these steps:

1. **Right-click (Windows) or Control+click (Mac) an empty frame where you want the animation to start and then choose Insert⇨Keyframe.**

   The Timeline's first frame is always a keyframe, so if you're starting from the first frame, just click the frame.

2. **Create a group or text block or drag a symbol instance from the Library.**

   Refer to Chapter 7 for the details on creating symbols and instances. Refer to Chapter 2 for the lowdown on using the Library.

3. **Create another keyframe where you want to end the animation.**

4. **Move the object to a new position.**

5. **If you want to change the object's size, rotation, or color (as we explain in the sections that follow), make the adjustments at this point.**

   See the next two sections of this chapter for details.

6. **Click anywhere in the tween before the last keyframe.**

   The frame just before the last keyframe is a good place to click.

7. **Choose Window⇨Properties to open the Property inspector if it's not already open.**

   Windows only: If necessary, click the collapse arrow on the Property inspector title bar to expand the inspector to its full size.

8. **From the Tween drop-down list in the Property inspector, choose Motion.**

   Flash creates the motion tween. If you want to change the object's size or rotation, specify the settings in the Property inspector, as we explain in the next section.

You're done! Click the first frame and press Enter (Windows) or Return (Mac) to play the animation.

Here's a silly phrase to help you remember the procedure for creating a motion tween:

Funny	First keyframe
Objects	Object — place it
Love	Last keyframe
Moving	Move object
In	In the middle — click between the keyframes
Tweens	Tween — choose Motion from the Tween drop-down list

Scaling and rotating an animated object

Okay, so you're creative and ambitious and want to do more. Changing other properties of your graphic while you're moving it is easy. In Step 5 of the procedure just listed, you can scale and rotate (including skewing) your object.

Use the Free Transform tool in the Tools panel or any other method of changing size or rotation. (Refer to Chapter 4 for instructions on scaling and rotating objects.)

In Step 7 of the motion tweening procedure just listed, complete the rest of the settings in the Property inspector, as shown in Figure 9-5 (and described in the following text).

Figure 9-5:
The
Property
inspector.

After you specify motion tweening, settings in the Property inspector appear that let you specify how your motion tweening will work:

- ✔ **To put into effect any scaling changes you made, select the Scale check box.** Enabling Scale has no effect if you don't change the object's size when you create the motion tween. Clearing Scale disables the scaling.

- ✔ **To rotate your graphic, choose one of the Rotate options from the drop-down list.** The Auto option automatically rotates the graphic once in the direction that uses the least movement. Or, you can choose to rotate it clockwise (CW) or counterclockwise (CCW) and then type the number of times that you want to rotate your graphic. These options rotate your object even if you didn't rotate it in Step 5 of the motion tweening procedure. If you did rotate the object, however, Flash adds the two rotations to end up with the rotation angle that you specified.

- ✔ **To control the acceleration or deceleration of the movement, use the Easing slider.** By default, the slider is in the middle, which creates a constant rate of movement throughout all the frames. Move the slider down to start slowly and get faster at the end. Move the slider up to slow down at the end. You can create a sense of anticipation or excitement by using this technique.

- ✔ **To ensure that your graphic symbol animation loops properly, select the Sync check box.** If your animation is in a graphic symbol and the number of frames it takes up isn't an even multiple of the frames that the symbol occupies on the main Timeline, Flash synchronizes the two timelines so that the graphic symbol loops properly in the main Timeline.

The Snap and Orient to Path settings are covered later in this chapter in the section, "Tweening along a path." The Sound, Effect, and Sync settings are covered in Chapter 11.

Look for `weldersmall.fla` in the Ch09folder of the CD-ROM for a nice example of a motion tween that includes rotation. This animation was part of the `www.weldersmall.com` Web site. *(Thanks to George Andres, of Acro Media Inc., at `www.acromediainc.com`, for this Flash file.)*

Another cool example of motion tweens is `thevoid.fla`, part of the `www.thevoid.co.uk` Web site. Look in the Ch09 folder of the CD-ROM. *(Thanks to Luke Turner, creative director of thevoid new media, for this Flash movie.)*

Tweening colors and transparency

To change an object's color, click the frame on the Timeline where you want to change its color. Then click the object. Choose Window⇨Properties to open the Property inspector if it's not already open. If necessary (in Windows only, not Macintosh) click the collapse arrow on the Property inspector's title bar to expand the inspector to its full size. If your object is an instance, choose one of the options (such as Tint or Alpha) from the Color drop-down list and make the desired adjustments. (Chapter 7 explains how to modify instances of symbols and provides much more detail about using the options on the Color drop-down list.) If your object is a shape rather than an instance, you can simply change its color and opacity in the Color Mixer panel. (See Chapter 3 for more on the Color Mixer.)

You can mix and match motion animation with scaling, rotation, color, and transparency changes to create exciting effects. If an object spins and gets smaller while it moves, it can seem to be rolling away from the viewer. Animating semitransparent objects in front of each other creates interesting mixtures of color and gives a semblance of texture and depth in the 2-D world of the Web. Decreasing alpha (opacity) during a tween makes the object appear to fade as it becomes more transparent. Try out some possibilities and come up with ideas of your own.

Color fades are faster than alpha fades. If you need an object to fade in or out, your movie loads faster if you tween to or from the background color rather than tween to or from transparency.

Tweening along a path

You can create animation that doesn't move in a straight line by motion tweening along a path that you draw. Suppose that you want to get the skateboarder shown in Figure 9-4 to do some tricks. The following steps show you how to do that.

If you want to follow along with these steps, you can import the skateboarder from the CD-ROM. Choose File⇨Import⇨Import and look in the Ch09 folder for skateboarder.bmp. (We made him in Poser — a cool program for generating 3-D people, in case you're interested. You can find out more about Poser at www.curiouslabs.com.)

To tween along a path, follow these steps. (The first steps are the same as the ones provided earlier in this chapter for motion tweens.)

1. **Create the first keyframe (if necessary).**

2. **Place your instance, text block, or group on the Stage.**

   If you're using the skateboarder, drag it from the Library to the left side of the Stage.

3. **Create the ending keyframe.**

   Don't move the object as you usually would when creating a motion tween.

4. **Click anywhere between the two keyframes.**

5. **Choose Window⇨Properties to open the Property inspector if it's not already open.**

   If necessary, click the collapse arrow in the Property inspector's title bar (Windows) or bottom-right corner (Macintosh) to expand the inspector to its full size.

6. **From the Tween drop-down list, choose Motion.**

   You now have a motion tween with no motion.

7. **In the Property inspector, select the Snap check box to snap the registration point of the object to the motion path.**

8. **Select the Orient to Path check box if you want to rotate the object with the angle of the motion path.**

9. **Right-click (Windows) or Control+click (Mac) the object's layer and choose Add Motion Guide.**

   A new layer appears on the Timeline. It's labeled Guide and has a motion guide icon. (If you want, you can create this layer before you start the process of creating the animation.)

10. **Draw your path, making a few curves or loop-the-loops, if you want.**

    You can use any of the drawing tools: Pen, Pencil, Line, Circle, Rectangle, or Brush. You can also use the Straighten or Smooth modifiers if you're using the Pencil tool. (The path shown in Figure 9-4 was created by using the Pencil tool with the Smooth modifier.)

Lock the object's layer before drawing the guide path so that you don't move the object by accident. Refer to Chapter 6 for further instructions on hiding and locking layers.

11. Click the first frame of the animation and drag the object by its registration point (shown by a small plus sign) to the beginning of your path; let go when the registration point snaps to the beginning of the path.

12. Click the last keyframe and drag the object by its registration point to the end of the path; let go when the registration point snaps to the end of the path.

13. Press Enter (Windows) or Return (Macintosh) to play the animation — you should see a few moments of death-defying skateboarding (or whatever animation you've created).

You can find the completed animation, `skateboarder.fla`, in the Ch09 folder of the CD-ROM.

Not quite ready for prime time — yet

The steps listed in the preceding section for tweening along a path provide only the basic process. You often need to make several refinements to motion animation along a path.

Not satisfied with your motion path? No problem. Here's a really great feature that lets you easily modify your path. Select the motion guide layer. Choose the Selection tool and reshape the line by dragging from any point on the line. (Just be sure not to break the line apart!) Press Enter (Windows) or Return (Macintosh) again, and the skateboarder follows the revised path.

Want to get rid of that unsightly motion guide? That's easy, too. Click the eye column of the motion guide layer to hide it. Press Enter (Windows) or Return (Macintosh) to play back the animation. (Even if you don't hide the motion guide layer in this way, the motion guide is not visible when the movie is published.)

Symbols, groups, text, and bitmap images have a registration point that's usually at the center of the graphic. When you tween along a path, you may want another point to follow the path. In the section on groups in Chapter 4, you find out how to change the registration point to get the results that you want.

What if you've already got a motion guide and you want to link it to an object on a different layer? Perhaps you draw an oval and then decide that you want an electron revolving along the oval, so you make its layer a motion guide layer. You have several choices:

✔ Create a new layer under the motion guide layer. The new layer appears indented under the motion guide layer, showing that it's linked to the motion guide, as shown in Figure 9-6. Then, any objects that you put on the new layer snap automatically to the motion guide. After putting your objects on the new layer, all you need to do is click the starting keyframe, drag your object to snap to the beginning of the path, click the ending keyframe, and snap to the end of the path.

Figure 9-6:
A guide
layer.

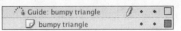

✔ If you already have a layer that you want to attach to your path, drag the layer with your graphics so that it's under the motion guide layer. When the new layer appears indented under the motion guide layer, you know that it's linked.

✔ A third option to link a graphics layer to a path is to select your graphics layer and then choose Modify⇨Timeline⇨Layer Properties. The layer must be listed somewhere under the guide layer. In the Layer Properties dialog box, select Guided and click OK.

For a nice example of a motion tween along a path, open flashsite_big. fla from the Ch09 folder of the CD-ROM. The motion tween is hidden in a movie clip, so you have to find it. Choose Window⇨Library and select the "intro movie" movie clip. (It has the movie clip symbol.) On the Stage, use the Selection tool to create a selection box around the little plus sign and circle. Choose Edit⇨Edit Selected. You should now be in the intro movie clip. Press Enter (Windows) or Return (Macintosh) to watch the "electrons" revolve around their orbits. *(The Flash movie is courtesy of Daniel Zajic.)*

Tweening shapes

In shape tweening, you change an object's shape at one or more points in the animation, and the computer creates the in-between shapes for you. You can get some great animation effects by using shape tweening. This process is often called *morphing*. You can see an example shown in Figure 9-7.

You can combine shape tweening with motion tweening as well as changes in size, color, and transparency. As with motion tweening, you should work with one shape per layer to avoid problems.

You can shape tween objects that you have created by using the Flash drawing tools.

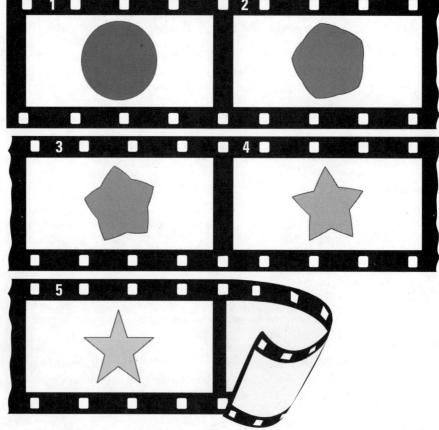

Figure 9-7:
You can
twist and
deform your
objects by
using shape
tweening,
and a circle
becomes
a star!

You can't shape tween a symbol instance, text (type), or group unless you break them apart into shapes by selecting them and choosing Modify⇨Break Apart. And you have to break apart text blocks twice — once to break the text block into individual letters and once to break the letters into shapes. You can also try to shape tween a bitmap image after breaking it apart, but the results may be unpredictable.

If you break apart a symbol instance, text block, bitmap image, or group by using Modify⇨Break Apart, you may have a number of shapes to animate. Be sure to put each animated object on a separate layer. You can do this easily by selecting the objects and choosing Modify⇨Timeline⇨Distribute to Layers, which we explain in Chapter 6.

To create a simple shape tween, follow these steps:

1. **Right-click (Windows) or Control+click (Mac) an empty frame where you want the animation to start and then choose Insert⇨Timeline⇨ Keyframe.**

2. **Use the drawing tools to create the beginning shape.**

   You can create complex objects by merging objects of the same color or creating cutouts with objects of differing colors. (Refer to Chapter 3 for details.)

3. **Create a new keyframe after the first keyframe wherever you want it on the Timeline by using the same technique that you used in Step 1.**

4. **Create the ending shape.**

   You can erase the old shape and draw a new one; or use the first shape, still on the Stage, and modify it. You can also move the shape and change its color/transparency. You can quickly change the color by using the Color modifiers in the toolbox. Use the Color Mixer panel to change opacity (alpha). Refer to Chapter 3 for more information on colors and transparency.

5. **Click anywhere in the tween before the last keyframe.**

   The frame just before the last keyframe is a good place to click.

6. **Choose Window⇨Properties to open the Property inspector if it's not already open.**

   If necessary, click the collapse arrow on the Property inspector's title bar (Windows) or bottom-right corner (Mac) to expand the inspector to its full size.

7. **Choose Shape from the Tween drop-down list.**

8. **Choose whether you want an Angular Blend or Distributive Blend type.**

   Choose the Angular Blend type for blending shapes with sharp corners and straight lines. It preserves corners and straight lines in the in-between shapes of your animation. If your shapes don't have sharp corners, use the Distributive Blend type (the default) for smoother in-between shapes.

9. **You're finished! Click the first frame and press Enter (Windows) or Return (Macintosh) to play the animation.**

Look in the Ch09 folder of the CD-ROM for a great example of shape tweening. The file is named `opening movie.fla`. Here, Jennie Sweo takes two circles and changes them into words using shape tweening. Amazingly, Flash handles this process automatically. To shape tween one circle into a word, start with a circle. When you get to Step 4 of the shape tweening process, delete the circle and create the text wherever you want. Choose any size, color, and font and then break apart the text (choose Modify⇨Break Apart). This command breaks the text into letters. Then break apart the text again (choose Modify⇨Break Apart) to break the letters into shapes. Finish the shape tween and you're done! To create the effect that Jennie created, create a second, similar shape tween on another layer. To view the effect, choose Control⇨ Test Movie. *(The Flash movie is courtesy of Jennie Sweo. You can see this movie on the Web at* `http://sweo.tripod.com`.*)*

Get the hint — using shape hints

Now you've got your shape animation, but does its transformation from one shape to another look strange? Flash tries to figure out the simplest and most probable way to change one of your shapes into another, but this solution may not turn out the way that you expect or want.

Never fear. You can use the Flash shape hints feature to fix this problem. A *shape hint* is a marker that you attach to a point on a shape at the beginning and end of a shape change. The shape hints signal to Flash exactly how you want this point and the area around it to move from start to end of the shape tweening process.

You can use up to 26 shape hints per layer. Shape hints are displayed on the Stage as small, colored circles with a letter (a–z) inside. On the starting keyframe, the shape hint is yellow; and on the ending keyframe, it's green. When you first insert a shape hint — before you move it onto your shape — it's red. Figure 9-8 shows an example of beginning and ending shapes with shape hints.

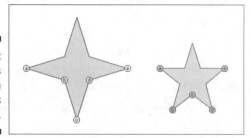

Figure 9-8:
Shape hints guide Flash as it tweens your shape.

You can find the beginning and ending shapes on this book's CD-ROM in the Library folder, in `Flash MX for Dummies Library.fla`. (Appendix D explains how to use this Flash movie as a permanent library.) Also look for the Flash movie file `4 to 5 point star with shape hints.fla` in the Ch09 folder.

To use shape hints, follow these steps:

1. **Create a shape animation by using shape tweening. (Refer to the preceding set of steps if you need help with this task.)**

2. **Click the keyframe where you want to add your first shape hint.**

3. **With the object selected, choose Modify⇨Shape⇨Add Shape Hint or press Ctrl+Shift+H (Windows) or ⌘+Shift+H (Mac).**

   Your beginning shape hint appears as the letter *a* in a small, red circle somewhere on the Stage.

4. **Click the small, red circle and drag it to the part of your graphic that you want to mark.**

5. **Click the keyframe at the end of the shape animation.**

   The ending shape hint appears somewhere on the Stage, again as the letter *a* in a small, red circle.

6. **Click the small, red circle and drag it to the point on your shape to which you want your beginning point to move.**

   The ending shape hint turns green. If you go back to the first frame of the animation, the beginning shape hint turns yellow.

7. **Press Enter (Windows) or Return (Macintosh) to play your movie.**

You can drag shape hints off the Stage to remove them. Or choose Modify↪ Shape↪Remove All Shape Hints to nuke them all — but the layer and keyframe with shape hints must be selected. Choose View↪Show Shape Hints to see all the shape hints in your current layer and keyframe. Choose it again to hide them. (Again, the layer and keyframe with shape hints must be selected.)

Adjusting shape hints

To tweak your animation, click the keyframe at the start or end of your shape animation and move your shape hint. Then play your animation again to see the new result. The more complicated your shape animation, the more shape hints you need to use. For more complicated shape animations, you can also use more keyframes. Do this by creating intermediate shapes and tweening them (using plenty of shape hints, of course). In other words, you can create two shape tweens, one immediately following the other.

If you aren't getting the results that you want, make sure that you have placed your shape hints logically. If you have a curve with shape hints a, b, and c — in that order — don't have them tween to a curve with the shape hints in c, b, a order unless you want some unusual effects. Flash does a better job with shape hints when you arrange them in counterclockwise order, starting from the upper-left corner of your object.

Editing Animation

Of course, nothing is perfect the first time, and Flash is quite forgiving. You can edit keyframes in assorted ways.

You can't edit tweened frames directly — you can view them, but you can edit only the keyframes, not the tweened frames. You can overcome this restriction and edit your tweened frames by inserting a new keyframe between your beginning and ending keyframe and then editing the new keyframe. You do this by choosing Insert↪Timeline↪Keyframe. Don't choose Insert↪Timeline↪Blank Keyframe unless you want to nuke your existing tween animation. Of course, you can always edit tweened frames by simply changing the starting or ending keyframe that defines them. When you edit a keyframe of a tweened animation, Flash automatically recalculates the entire tween.

The following sections explain some useful techniques for editing and managing your animations.

Adding labels and comments

Animation can get confusing after a while. You may find it helpful to add comments to the Timeline to explain what each part of the Timeline is doing. Also, when you start adding interactivity to your movies, you can add labels to frames and then refer to them in your ActionScript. (You can find out more about ActionScript in Chapter 10.)

To add a label or a comment to a frame, follow these steps:

1. **Select a frame.**

   See the next section for information on selecting a frame.

2. **Choose Window⇨Properties to open the Property inspector if it's not already open.**

   Windows only: If necessary, click the collapse arrow on the Property inspector's title bar to expand the inspector to its full size.

3. **In the Frame Label text box, type the text for the label or comment and press Enter (Windows) or Return (Macintosh).**

   To make the text function as a comment, type two slashes (//) at the beginning of the comment. (If you get long-winded and go to a new line, type the two slashes at the beginning of the new line as well.)

Selecting frames

Flash offers two styles of making selections on the Timeline.

The default method is frame-based selection. In this method, if you click a frame or a keyframe, it's selected. To select a range of frames, you can click and drag over the frames that you want to select, or you can click the first frame, press Shift, and then click the last frame in the range.

The other style of selection is span-based selection. In this method, if you click a frame, it selects the entire sequence containing that frame, from one keyframe to the next. Clicking and dragging moves the entire sequence (between the keyframes) along the Timeline in either direction. To select an individual frame, you need to press Ctrl (Windows) or ⌘ (Mac).

You can change the style of selection by choosing Edit⇨Preferences (Windows) or Flash⇨Preferences (Mac), clicking the General tab in the Preferences window, and then selecting the Span Based Selection check box in the Timeline Options section.

In span-based selection, when you click the first or last keyframe of a tween and drag, you change the length of the tween rather than just select frames.

Copying and pasting

You can copy frames that contain contents you want elsewhere. Then you can paste the frame in another location.

To copy and paste frames, follow these steps:

1. **Select one or more frames.**

2. **Choose Edit⇨Timeline⇨Copy Frames to copy the frames to the Clipboard.**

3. **Select the first frame of your destination or select a sequence of frames that you want to replace.**

4. **Choose Edit⇨Timeline⇨Paste Frames to paste the frames into their new location.**

You can also copy frames by pressing and holding Alt (Windows) or Option (Mac) while you drag the keyframe or range of frames to a new location. You see a small plus sign while you drag.

Moving frames

You can move frames and their contents. Select the layer and place the cursor over a frame or range of frames. Then drag them to their new home, as shown in Figure 9-9.

Figure 9-9:
Move frames by select-ing and dragging them.

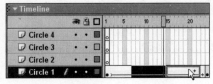

Adding frames

You can stretch out your animation by right-clicking (Windows) or Control+ clicking (Mac) and choosing Insert Frame. (Or you can select a frame and then press F5 to insert a frame.) Because you now have more frames between your first and last keyframes, the animation takes longer to complete and therefore appears to be slower. Use this technique to slow down the rate of animation.

Deleting frames

Delete frames by selecting one or more frames. Then right-click (Windows) or Control+click (Mac) on one of the frames and choose Remove Frames from the shortcut menu that appears. If you delete frames within a tweened animation, the animation is completed more quickly and appears to be faster.

Turning keyframes back into regular frames

If you don't like a keyframe, you can change it back to a regular frame by right-clicking (Windows) or Control+clicking (Mac) the offending keyframe and choosing Clear Keyframe. Changing a keyframe into a regular frame removes the change that occurred at that keyframe. You can use this technique to merge two consecutive tweens into one tween — change the keyframe in the middle to a frame.

Reversing your animation

You can make your animation play backward by selecting the relevant frames in one or more layers and choosing Modify➪Timeline➪Reverse Frames. Your selection must start and end with keyframes.

Faster or slower?

After you set up your animation, play your movie to check the speed. If one part of your tweened animation is too fast or too slow, you can slide keyframes around on the Timeline to shorten or lengthen the time between keyframes. You can do this simply by clicking a keyframe and dragging it to another point on the Timeline. This technique gives you lots of control over the timing of your animation.

If you have difficulty dragging an ending keyframe, create a new keyframe somewhere to the keyframe's right and then drag the obstinate keyframe.

Figure 9-10 shows two possible versions of the Timeline for the shape tween shown in Figure 9-8. To create the version on the bottom, we dragged the last keyframe to the right, thereby lengthening the tween. Because the same change in shape now occurs over a longer period, the tween appears slower.

Figure 9-10: You can change the length of a tween.

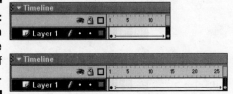

The effect is even more noticeable with a motion tween. For example, if a symbol moves from the left of the Stage to the right and you shorten the tween, the symbol appears to move across the Stage more quickly because it must get from the left to the right in fewer frames.

Changing the animation settings

You can always go back and change some of the settings in the Property inspector. For example, you can add easing or change the blend type of a shape tween in the Property inspector. These settings are explained earlier in this chapter.

Onion skinning

To help you visualize the flow of your animation, you can turn on the onion-skinning feature. Onion skinning lets you see a "ghost image" of some or all of the frames in your animation. (Normally, you see only the current frame on the Stage.) Figure 9-11 shows an example of both regular and outlined onion skinning. Onion skinning displays frames as transparent layers, like the transparent layers of an onion skin.

 To display onion skinning, click the Onion Skin button at the bottom of the Timeline.

 To display onion skinning with outlines, click the Onion Skin Outlines button.

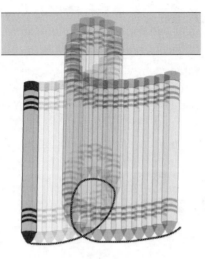
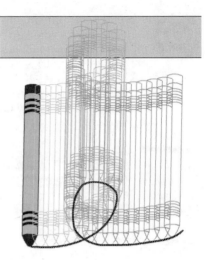

Figure 9-11:
Onion skinning helps you to see where your animation is going.

When you display onion skinning, Flash places markers at the top of the Timeline around the frames that are displayed as onion skins. (See Figure 9-12.) Usually, these markers advance automatically when the current frame pointer advances. You can manually adjust the beginning and ending of the onion-skinning effect by clicking and dragging either the left or right marker to a new location on the Timeline.

Onion skin markers

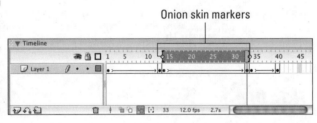

Figure 9-12:
When you display onion skinning, markers are placed on the Timeline.

 To edit any of the frames on the Timeline no matter where your current frame pointer is, click the Edit Multiple Frames button. If you also have onion skinning turned on, you can then edit any frame while viewing all the other onion-skinned frames.

 Click Modify Onion Markers to display a menu to help you adjust the way that your onion markers work:

✓ **Always Show Onion Markers:** Shows onion markers even when you've turned off onion skinning

✔ **Anchor Onions:** Locks the onion markers in their current position and prevents them from moving along with the current frame pointer, as they normally do

✔ **Onion 2:** Applies onion skinning to the two frames before and the two frames after the playhead (the current frame pointer)

✔ **Onion 5:** Applies onion skinning to the five frames before and the five frames after the playhead

✔ **Onion All:** Applies onion skinning to all the frames on your Timeline

Hidden or locked layers never show as onion-skinned. Hide or lock layers to isolate them from the layers that you really want to change and to keep your onion skinning from getting out of control. Chapter 6 explains how to hide and lock layers.

Moving everything around the Stage at once

If you move a complete animation on the Stage without moving the graphics in all frames and all layers at one time, you may quickly go nuts when you discover that every little thing must be realigned. Instead, retain your sanity and move everything at one time.

To move a complete animation, follow these steps:

1. **Unlock all layers that contain the animation you want to move, and then lock or hide any layers that you don't want to move.**

2. **Click the Edit Multiple Frames button at the bottom of the Timeline.**

3. **Drag the onion skin markers to the beginning and ending frames of your animation.**

   Alternatively, if you want to select all frames, click the Modify Onion Markers button at the bottom of the Timeline and choose Onion All.

4. **Choose Edit⇨Select All.**

5. **Drag your animation to its new place on the Stage.**

Making the Scene

Animations can get complicated fast, and one way to manage that complexity is by organizing them in layers and layer folders. (Refer to Chapter 6 for the lowdown on layers and layer folders.) Another great way to manage the complexity of your animations is to break them into chunks of time — into scenes. You can then use scenes as the modular building blocks of your movies, which you can then rearrange in any way that you want.

When is a good time to break up your movie into scenes? If your movie is simple, one scene may be all that you need. But if the movie gets more complex, you may want to break it up into a loading message, an introduction, the main act, the ending, and the credits.

Or, if your Timeline is starting to get longer than one screen will hold at a time, you may want to find logical places to separate segments of your animation into scenes. If your cast of graphics characters changes at a particular time, that may be a good place to break into a new scene. And if a section of your movie can conceivably be reused elsewhere in other movies, you may have an excellent reason to break it out into its own scene.

Breaking your movie into scenes

When you create a new Flash movie file (by running Flash for the first time or by choosing File⇨New and selecting a Flash Document under the General tab), by default the file contains one empty scene, cleverly titled *Scene 1*. Any animations that you create then become part of Scene 1.

If you want to add a scene, choose Insert⇨Scene. The Stage clears, and the Timeline is labeled *Scene 2*.

Manipulating that scene

To keep track of your scenes, open the Scene panel by choosing Window⇨ Design Panels⇨Scene, as shown in Figure 9-13. The Scene panel lists all the scenes in your movie. When you choose Control⇨Test Movie, the scenes play in order from the top of the list down.

Figure 9-13:
The Scene panel lets you make a big scene.

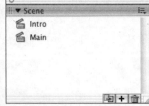

Here's how to use the Scene panel to control your scenes:

- ✔ **To change the order in which scenes play,** drag a scene's name on the Scene panel to a new place in the list.

- ✔ **To rename a scene,** double-click the scene's name in the Scene panel, type the new name, and then press Enter (Windows) or Return (Mac).

 To delete a scene, select that scene and click the Delete Scene button at the bottom of the Scene panel.

 To duplicate a scene, click the Duplicate Scene button at the bottom of the Scene panel.

To view a particular scene, click its name on the Scene panel. Or, choose View⇨Go To and the name of the scene that you want on the submenu.

 Look in the Ch09 folder of the CD-ROM for `picturetour.fla`, which is a nice example of a Flash movie divided into scenes. This movie is part of The Raj's Web site, at `www.theraj.com`. *(Thanks to Lindsay Oliver, of The Raj, and Jesse Spaulding, the movie's creator, for this Flash movie.)*

Chapter 10

Getting Interactive

● ●

In This Chapter

▶ Getting familiar with actions

▶ Using behaviors to instantly create interactivity

▶ Adding actions to frames

▶ Using actions with buttons

▶ Adding actions to movie clips

▶ Working with actions

▶ Using methods to control objects

▶ Investigating advanced ActionScript features

● ●

*T*he real fun with Flash begins when you start to make your art and animations interactive. *Interactivity* means that a computer user's input triggers immediate changes on the computer screen, which the user can then respond to further, as if a conversation is taking place between the user and the computer. Examples include clicking a button to go to another Web page and choosing to stop the music.

Flash uses actions to specify how the interactivity works. *Actions* are simply short instructions that tell Flash what to do next. By combining actions, you can create very complex sets of instructions to give your Flash movies sophisticated capabilities. You can use actions to control your animation without interactivity, if you want. Flash actions offer a great deal of flexibility, and only your imagination limits what you can do.

Understanding Actions

Flash lets you put actions in only four places:

- ✔ A frame on the Timeline.
- ✔ A button.

✔ A movie clip.

✔ A separate ActionScript file that is loaded by your Flash movie. (See the section, "External scripting," later in this chapter.)

You cannot assign actions to graphics.

When you create an action, you first specify what has to occur for the action to be executed. This is the *when* part of the process. For example, if you add an action to a button instance, you can specify that the action will happen *when* the user releases the mouse button after clicking it.

Next you specify the action itself — *what* will happen. The action must come from the list of actions in Flash. Many actions have parameters that you must add. For example, to get a button to bring your viewer to another Web page, you use the `getURL` action and add the exact Uniform Resource Locator (URL; Web page address) as a parameter.

Using Behaviors

In Flash MX 2004, you can now easily add ActionScript to your movies by inserting behaviors with a click of the mouse. *Behaviors* are prewritten collections of ActionScript code that you add from the Behaviors panel. You can add them to frames, buttons, and movie clips in your Flash movies.

To add a behavior, follow these steps:

1. **Click a frame if you want to add an action to a frame. Create a symbol and place an instance of the symbol on the Stage if you want to add an action to a symbol.**

   For example, to create a button that links to a Web site, select the button instance. Refer to Chapter 8 if you need help with creating buttons.

2. **With the frame or instance selected, choose Window➪Development Panels➪Behaviors to open the Behaviors panel, as shown in Figure 10-1.**

   If necessary, click the collapse arrow on the Behaviors panel's title bar to expand the panel. (You can also call the collapse arrow the *expand arrow* because clicking the arrow collapses the panel when the panel is expanded and expands the panel when the panel is collapsed.)

3. **Click the plus button on the upper left of the Behaviors panel and choose a category; then choose one of the behaviors listed in that category. In our example, choose Web➪Go To Web Page from the pop-up menu.**

   The categories and the behaviors that they contain are listed after these steps. The behaviors that are available depend on the type of object that you choose. In our example, the Go To URL dialog box appears. Other behaviors prompt you for the appropriate information.

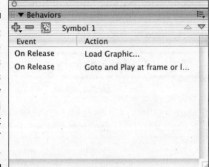

Figure 10-1:
The
Behaviors
panel lets
you instantly
add
ActionScript
to your
movie.

4. **Enter the required information in the dialog box that appears. In our example, type a URL in the URL text box, such as** `http://www.infinityeverywhere.net.`

5. **Click OK.**

   You see the behavior listed in the Behaviors panel. If you chose a button or a movie clip, an event may be listed as well. An *event* describes under what circumstances the behavior occurs, such as releasing the mouse button or pressing a key on the keyboard. In our example, you would see the `On Release` event.

6. **If you chose a button or a movie clip and want to change the event, click the event to display a drop-down list. Choose a new event from the drop-down list.**

   See Table 10-2 for events available for buttons and Table 10-3 for events for movie clips (both later in this chapter).

7. **To see your brand new ActionScript code, choose Window↪ Development Panels↪Actions to open the Actions panel if it's not already open (see Figure 10-2).**

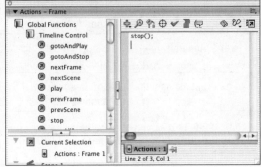

Figure 10-2:
The Actions
window is
your key to
adding
actions to
your frames.

Flash's behaviors allow you to add interactivity for controlling graphics, movie clips, sound, video and more. Table 10-1 lists the available behaviors.

Table 10-1	ActionScript Behaviors	
Category	*Behavior*	*Description*
Data	Trigger Data Source	Loads and manipulates information from data sources.
Embedded Video	Fast Forward	Fast forwards embedded video by the number of frames that you specify. For more information, see Chapter 11.
Embedded Video	Hide	Hides the video.
Embedded Video	Pause	Pauses the video.
Embedded Video	Play	Plays the video.
Embedded Video	Rewind	Rewinds the video by the number of frames that you specify.
Embedded Video	Show	Displays the video.
Embedded Video	Stop	Stops playing the video.
Movie Clip	Bring Forward	Brings the movie clip one level higher in the stacking order.
Movie Clip	Bring to Front	Brings the movie clip to the top of the stack, so it's on top of all other movie clips.
Movie Clip	Duplicate Movie Clip	Duplicates a movie clip. You can offset the new movie clip by a specified x and y distance.
Movie Clip	Go to and play at frame or label	Plays a movie clip. You can specify the frame.
Movie Clip	Go to and stop at frame or label	Stops a movie clip. You can specify the frame.
Movie Clip	Load external movie clip	Loads an external SWF file into a movie clip.
Movie Clip	Load Graphic	Loads a JPEG graphic file that is external to the movie (FLA) file.

Category	Behavior	Description
Movie Clip	Send Backward	Sends the movie clip one level lower in the stacking order.
Movie Clip	Send to Back	Sends the target movie clip to the bottom-of the stack.
Movie Clip	Start Dragging Movie Clip	Starts dragging a movie clip. For more information about dragging movie clips, see Chapter 14.
Movie Clip	Stop Dragging Movie Clip	Stops the current drag.
Movie Clip	Unload Movie clip	Removes a movie loaded with the Load Movie behavior or action.
Projector	Toggle Full Screen Mode	Toggles full screen mode on and off when you play a movie with a projector (a self-playing movie). For more information on projectors, see Chapter 13.
Sound	Load Sound from Library	Loads a sound from a runtime shared library. For more information, see Chapter 12.
Sound	Load Streaming MP3 File	Loads an MP3 sound file.
Sound	Play Sound	Plays a sound.
Sound	Stop All Sounds	Stops all sounds.
Sound	Stop Sound	Stops a specific sound.
Web	Go to Web page	Opens a specified Web page.

Adding Actions to Frames

You add an action to a frame to control what happens when the movie reaches that frame. *Frame actions* are often used to play a movie clip or to loop a movie so that a certain section of the animation is repeated. Another use for frame actions is to stop a movie or to automatically link to another URL (such as a Web page address). You can also use frame actions for more complex programming of Flash.

To add a basic action to a frame, follow these steps:

1. **Create a new layer for your actions (if you haven't already done so).**

   Chapter 6 explains how to add a new layer.

2. **Click a keyframe.**

   If the frame that you want to use is not a keyframe, right-click it (Windows) or Control+click it (Mac) and choose Insert Keyframe.

3. **Choose Window⇨Development Panels⇨Actions to open the Actions panel if it's not already open (refer to Figure 10-2).**

   If necessary, click the collapse arrow on the Actions panel title bar to expand the panel.

4. **Click a category and subcategory in the left pane of the Actions panel and either double-click an action or drag the action to the right side.**

   You can also click the plus sign, choose a category, and then choose an action from the submenu.

   If the action requires parameters, either a pop-up menu of suggested parameters appears or a hint appears in a yellow box over the cursor in your ActionScript code. If there is more than one hint, you can browse through them by clicking the forward and backward arrowheads in the yellow hint box.

5. **If the action requires parameters, type the required information at the cursor.**

   We list the details of specific actions and their parameters later in this chapter. You can continue to add actions by repeating Steps 4 and 5.

6. **If you want to get the Actions panel out of the way, right-click (Windows) or Control+click (Mac) the panel's title bar and choose Close Panel. Or use the handy keyboard shortcut and press F9.**

A simple example of using a frame action is to place a Stop action at the beginning of the movie, as illustrated in Figure 10-2. You may provide a button that starts the movie so that viewers can choose whether they want to see it. (They may want to get down to business right away and purchase something. Who are you to make them wait?) In this example, the movie loads, but the first thing that it encounters is a command to stop. Nothing happens until someone clicks a button to start the movie. Of course, the Web page should contain other buttons and information that viewers can use to navigate through your Web site.

To add the Stop action to your movie, follow these steps:

1. **Create your animation.**

2. **Choose Control⇨Test Movie and watch your animation run.**

3. **Create a layer for your action and name it** Actions.

    Chapter 6 explains how to create and name layers.

4. **Click the keyframe where you want to add the action.**

5. **Choose Window⇨Actions to open the Actions panel if it's not already open.**

    If necessary, click the collapse arrow on the Actions panel's title bar to expand the panel.

6. **Click Global Functions, click Timeline Control, and then double-click Stop from the list of actions.**

7. **To close the Actions panel, right-click (Windows) or Control+click (Mac) the Actions panel title bar and choose Close Panel.**

8. **Choose Control⇨Test Movie again.**

    This time, the movie doesn't run because of the Stop action.

You can add many actions to frames. Later in this chapter, we list the major actions and how to use them.

To test a frame action without leaving the main Timeline, choose Control⇨Enable Simple Frame Actions. Then run your animation.

For a lovely example of a frame action, open bounce.fla from the Ch10 folder of the CD-ROM (see Figure 10-3). To see how the movie works, save the movie to your hard drive and choose Control⇨Test Movie. Then close the window. Click the last frame of Layer 1, the one with the *a* in it. Choose Window⇨Actions to open the Actions panel if it's not already open. You see gotoandplay(1) on the Actions panel. This action simply tells Flash to go to Frame 1 and play; in other words, it loops the movie over and over again, creating the bouncing effect. (*The* bounce.fla *file is courtesy of Jeremy Wachtel, Vice President of Project Management at Macquarium Intelligent Communications.*)

Figure 10-3:
The bouncing marble from Macquarium.

Adding Actions to Buttons

A common way to add interactivity is to create a button. The viewer clicks the button and something happens (or stops happening). Usually, you add text near or on the button so that your viewers know what the button is for.

If you already work on a Web site, you're familiar with the concept of hyperlinks. If you know HyperText Markup Language (HTML) — the language behind Web pages — you know that you can create hyperlinks by using the <HREF> tag. This tag links text or an image to another URL. When people click the text or the image, they are teleported to that URL. You can create Flash buttons that accomplish the same purpose but with much greater flair.

Buttons can do more! They can start or stop animation, jump to different parts of a movie, and stop sounds, among other things.

The process of adding an action to a button is simple (see Figure 10-4). The difficult part is deciding which actions to use. Later in this chapter, we review all the possible actions and how to use them. (Refer to the end of Chapter 8 for an example of a button that links to a different Web page. You can also add an action to a button using behaviors, as we explain earlier in this chapter.)

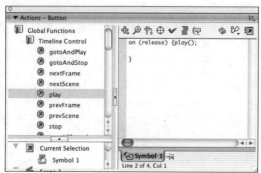

Figure 10-4:
In this example, a Play action has been added to the button.

To create a button with actions, follow these steps:

1. **Create the button and place an instance of the button on the Stage.**

   Refer to Chapter 8 if you need help with creating buttons.

2. **With the instance selected, choose Window⇨Development Panels⇨Actions to open the Actions panel.**

   If necessary, click the collapse arrow on the Actions panel's title bar to expand the panel.

3. **You probably want to make something happen when your audience clicks the button, so click the Global Functions category and the Movie Clip Control subcategory in the left pane of the Actions panel and double-click the on action from the list.**

   In the Script pane on the right of the Actions panel, the on statement appears along with a pop-up menu of suggested parameters.

   You use the on action to respond to the mouse button, the motion of the mouse, and keypresses.

4. **You probably want to make the button do something when the user clicks and releases the button, so choose the release parameter from the list of parameters in the pop-up menu.**

   The release parameter appears in the on statement in the Script pane on the right of the Actions panel.

5. **Click to reposition your cursor at the end of the current line.**

6. **To specify what happens when the button is released, click a category and subcategory in the left pane of the Actions panel and double-click an action from the list. For example, to rewind the movie to the first frame and play it again, choose Global Functions⇨Timeline Control⇨gotoAndPlay.**

   If the action requires parameters, a code hint or a pop-up menu of suggested parameters appears. In our example, the code hint says gotoAndPlay(frame) to tell you to enter the frame number between the parentheses.

7. **If the action requires parameters, choose a parameter from the list (if a list of parameters appears in a pop-up menu) or type in the parameter suggested by the code hint (if a code hint appears). In our example, type 1 between the parentheses.**

   The example code now looks like this in the Actions panel:

   ```
   on (release) {gotoAndPlay(1);

   }
   ```

   Some of the most common actions and their parameters are listed later in this chapter, in the "Using Actions" section. You can continue to add actions by repeating Steps 5, 6 and 7.

8. **If you decide that you want to change the on (release) statement, double-click the word release to select it and then click the Show Code Hint button near the top of the Actions panel.**

   The pop-up menu of suggested parameters appears again.

   See the upcoming Table 10-2 for more information on the statements that you can use to define when a button action goes into effect.

9. **Choose a new parameter from the list of parameters in the pop-up menu.**

10. **Click the collapse arrow on the Actions panel title bar to collapse the panel.**

Table 10-2	Button Action Statements
Statement	*When the Action Occurs*
Press	When the user clicks the button
Release	When the user releases the mouse button
Release Outside	When the user moves the mouse outside the hit area and releases the mouse button
Key Press	When a key that you specify is pressed (for example, *keyPress "<Left>"* specifies the left arrow key)
Roll Over	When the mouse cursor moves over the hit area of the button without clicking
Roll Out	When the mouse cursor moves out of the hit area of the button without clicking
Drag Over	When the mouse cursor moves over the hit area of the button with the mouse button held down
Drag Out	When the mouse cursor moves out of the hit area of the button with the mouse button held down

The hit area of a button is the button's *active area* — the area which responds to mouse clicks and other user interactions. Refer to Chapter 8 to read all about buttons.

Adding an Action to a Movie Clip

You add an action to a movie clip in the same way you add one to a button; both are objects to which you can add an action. Actions in movie clips work within the Timeline of the movie clip, not on the main Timeline of the entire movie. Therefore, you can create movie clips that are interactive within themselves.

You can use actions in movie clips to do all kinds of things. You can use ActionScript within one movie clip to control a second movie clip — the ActionScript could set the second movie's properties, for instance, and change its size, visibility, and so on. You can use ActionScript to start or stop a movie clip from playing and to replace one movie clip with another. You can use the `onClipEvent()` action to wait for an event while the movie clip is playing. If the event is a mouse movement for instance, you can use a little more ActionScript to do something in response to the position of the mouse while it moves.

You can also add actions to movie clips by using behaviors, as we explain earlier in this chapter.

To add an action to a movie clip, follow these steps:

1. **Create the movie clip and place an instance of the movie clip on the Stage.**

   Chapter 8 explains how to create movie clips if you need a refresher.

2. **With the instance selected, choose Window⇨Development Panels⇨Actions to open the Actions panel.**

   If necessary, click the collapse arrow on the Actions panel title bar to expand it.

   You can attach many kinds of actions to movie clips. A typical example might be that you want something to happen when the movie clip loads.

3. **Find the action that you want in the left pane of the Actions panel and double-click it. For example, say that you want to define when an action will happen in a movie clip. In that case, click the Global Functions category and the Movie Clip Control subcategory in the left pane of the Actions panel and double-click the `onClipEvent` action from the list.**

   In the Script pane on the right of the Actions panel, the action appears (in our example, the `onClipEvent` statement) along with a pop-up menu of suggested parameters or methods.

4. **Choose a parameter (for instance, `load`) from the list of parameters in the pop-up menu.**

   The parameter appears in the `onClipEvent` statement in the Script pane on the right of the Actions panel.

5. **Click to reposition your cursor at the end of the current line.**

6. **Click a category and subcategory in the left pane of the Actions panel and double-click an action from the list.**

   Say that you want your movie to suddenly go silent as soon as the movie clip loads (that is, at the moment when the movie clip first appears in the Timeline). In that case, click the Global Functions category and the Timeline Control subcategory in the left pane of the Actions panel and double-click the `stopAllSounds` action from the list.

TIP

If the action requires parameters, a code hint or a pop-up menu of suggested parameters appears.

7. **If the action requires parameters, choose a parameter from the list (if a list of parameters appears in a pop-up menu) or type in the parameter suggested by the code hint (if a code hint appears). In our example,** stopAllSounds **doesn't require any parameters, so you can skip this step.**

The example code now looks like this in the Actions panel:

```
onClipEvent (load) {stopAllSounds();
```

Some of the most common actions and their parameters are listed later in this chapter, in the "Using Actions" section. You can continue to add actions by repeating Steps 5, 6, and 7.

8. **If you decide you want to change the** onClipEvent (Load) **statement, double-click the word** load **to select it, and then click the Show Code Hint button near the top of the Actions panel.**

The pop-up menu of suggested parameters appears again.

See Table 10-3 for a list of the events available for onClipEvent.

9. **Choose a new parameter from the list of parameters in the pop-up menu.**

10. **Click the collapse arrow on the Actions panel title bar to collapse the panel.**

Table 10-3	Movie Clip Action Statements
Statement	*When the Action Occurs*
Load	As soon as the movie clip loads into memory (that is, when the movie clip first appears on the Timeline)
EnterFrame	When the movie clip enters each frame
Unload	In the first frame after the movie clip is removed from the Timeline
Mouse Down	When the (left) mouse button is clicked
Mouse Up	When the (left) mouse button is released
Mouse Move	When the mouse is moved (anywhere on the screen)
Key Down	When any key is pressed
Key Up	When any key is released
Data	When data is received from either a loadVariables or loadMovie action

Using Actions

Before you can create actions, you need to know which actions are available. In this chapter, we explain only the basic actions. For more information about advanced actions and programming in ActionScript, choose Help⇨ActionScript Dictionary. Then refer to the preceding sections for instructions on inserting actions into frames, movie clips, and buttons.

The following sections describe the most common actions.

Timeline Control actions

First, we look at the actions that you find in the Timeline Control category of the Actions panel. (To see this list, choose Window⇨Development Panels⇨Actions to open the Actions panel and, if necessary, click the collapse arrow on the Actions panel title bar to expand the panel. Then click Global Functions and then Timeline Control in the left pane of the Actions panel.)

gotoAndPlay

gotoAndPlay tells your movie to go to a different frame and play from there. Use this action when you want to jump to a new area of the movie and play the animation there. This option is commonly used to loop a movie. On the last frame, you insert an action that goes to the first frame and plays the movie over again. gotoAndPlay is also used in *preloaders,* which are short scenes that encourage the viewer to wait while a bigger movie is loading. (See Chapter 12 for more information on preloaders.)

To define the frame, insert the action, and then type in the frame number, the frame label, or an expression that calculates the frame number.

Using a label is preferable if you may move frames to a different location on the Timeline, thereby changing their number. If you move a frame with a label, the label follows the frame. (Create a label by typing it in the Frame Label text box of the Property inspector.)

If you've written some ActionScript to calculate a frame number, you can use the ActionScript expression to specify the frame.

gotoAndStop

gotoAndStop tells your movie to go to a different frame and stop playing. You may want to choose this option if you want to wait for the user to press a button at that frame's location.

You define the frame the same way you do with the gotoAndPlay action — insert the action, and then type in the frame number, the frame label, or an expression that calculates the frame number.

Play

The Play action tells a movie to start playing.

Stop

Stop stops a movie from playing. (Did you guess?) One important use is at the end of a movie clip because otherwise, movie clips automatically loop. You can also put a Stop action on a button so that users can stop an introduction and get to the rest of your site. For a tidy ending to a movie, Flash users often place a Stop action at the end.

Look for Jay M. Johnson YE2k.fla in the Ch10 folder of the CD-ROM. In Frame 470, you see a Stop action. Because the music continues after that frame, the Stop action neatly stops everything at the point where the movie displays some buttons for you to press. Choose Control⇨Test Movie to see how it works. *(Thanks to Jay M. Johnson for this Flash movie.)*

stopAllSounds

The stopAllSounds action simply stops all sounds from playing.

Browser/Network actions

Next, we look at some actions that you find in the Browse/Network category of the Actions panel. (To see this list, choose Window⇨Actions to open the Actions panel and, if necessary, click the collapse arrow on the Actions panel's title bar to expand the panel. Click Global Functions and then Browser/Network in the left pane of the Actions panel.)

fscommand

You can use the fscommand to control the Flash Player or other applications, like browsers. For example, the fscommand lets you execute JavaScript that you have written on the Web page. To use this action, double-click fscommand in the list in the Actions panel. Then type the name of the JavaScript command that you've created and add any arguments that your command requires or takes.

You need to add some code to the HTML page. For more information, see the fscommand in the ActionScript Dictionary (choose Help⇨ActionScript Dictionary).

getURL

The getURL action is the Flash equivalent to a hyperlink in HTML, which is the language used to code Web pages. getURL is often used on buttons, so when you click the button, you jump to another Web page. You need to supply the URL so that Flash knows where to send your viewers.

To use this action, double-click getURL in the list in the Actions panel; then, type in the URL (such as http://www.infinityeverywhere.net), then a comma, and then the kind of window that you desire: _self, _blank, _parent, or _top.

- ✔ _self: Opens the new Web page in the current window. Viewers can return to the previous window by using the Back button of their browsers.

- ✔ _blank: Opens a new window. Viewers can close this window (by clicking the Close box) to return to the previous window that is still displayed.

- ✔ _parent: If you have a movie within a nested frame, puts the new Web page in the parent of the nested frame (that is, one level above the nested frame).

- ✔ _top: If your movie is in a frame within a window, blows away all the frames and replaces them with the new Web page.

loadMovie

The loadMovie command lets you load any Flash Player movie (a .swf file) or JPEG image file that Flash can find. It can be another Flash Player movie or JPEG image residing in the same folder or somewhere else on the Web. You can use loadMovie to let users choose what they want to see next. This type of transition is smoother than using getURL to load new Web pages.

To use this action, double-click loadMovie in the list in the Actions panel and then type in the URL. Optionally, you can also then type in a comma and the target. Here is what you need to know to set these parameters:

- ✔ **URL:** If the movie or image that you're loading is in the same folder as the current movie, you can just type its name. If it's in a subfolder, for example, just type the path to the file, such as movies/mymovie.swf. But if the movie or image is elsewhere on the Web, type the entire URL (for instance, http://www.mum.edu/arts/artwork/digital/digital.swf).

  While you're testing your movie, you must place the SWF or JPEG file in the same folder as the open movie and simply list the filename. Therefore, if you will use a different arrangement on the Web, be sure to change the reference to the file as necessary.

✔ **Target:** You can specify a target if you want to replace a particular movie clip. Type the name of a movie clip that you want to replace. Specifying the URL and the target lets you replace a movie clip (the target) with an external movie or image (the URL). Note that the new movie or image will be placed in the same location as the original movie clip, with the same rotation and scale.

unloadMovie

unloadMovie unloads Flash Player movies that you have loaded by using the loadMovie command. To use this action, double-click unloadMovie in the list in the Actions panel, and then type in the target as we explain in the preceding section. Using this command helps to make sure that transitions are smooth and also frees up your computer's memory sooner rather than later.

loadMovieNum

The loadMovieNum command lets you load a Flash Player movie (a .swf file) or JPEG image file into a level number that you specify. Use loadMovieNum if you want to maintain more than one open movie or image at a time. To use this action, double-click loadMovieNum in the list in the Actions panel, type in the URL, a comma, and then the level number that you desire.

✔ **To replace the main (original) open movie or image (and any other loaded movies or images) with the new one:** Specify level 0. This is like switching movies or switching images in a slideshow.

✔ **To load a new movie or image without replacing the original (or any other loaded movie or image):** Specify a level number not used by any other movie or image. You can continue to load movies and images on different levels above the one in level 0. The frame rate, background color, and movie size are determined by the movie on the lowest level.

✔ **To replace a movie or image that is already loaded:** Use the level number of that movie or image.

unloadMovieNum

unloadMovieNum unloads Flash Player movies that you have loaded with the loadMovieNum command. To use this action, double-click unloadMovieNum in the list in the Actions panel, and then type in the level as we explain in the preceding section. This action gives you the same benefits as unloadMovie.

Making Objects Work For You

In ActionScript, information is organized into classes that share similar properties and capabilities. (The capabilities are called *methods.*) You can create multiple instances of a class in ActionScript to use in your scripts. These instances are called *objects.*

ActionScript comes with many objects already built-in and ready to use. Buttons, for example, are one kind of object in ActionScript, and sounds are another.

Objects like buttons, text, movie clips, and sounds have properties and methods built into them in ActionScript, and this makes it easy to use ActionScript to control them.

Method acting

You can make an object work for you by calling on one of its built-in methods. Doing this is easy: You specify the object by name, followed by the dot (.) operator, followed by the method and the parameters that you want to pass to it, like this:

```
snazzySound.setVolume(75);
```

In this example, snazzySound is a sound that you imported into Flash, setVolume is one of its methods, and 75 is the volume level at which you want to set it. (The setVolume method comes with a volume range from 0–100.)

As usual, Flash makes it easy for you to control objects with their built-in methods — you can just click on methods on the list of actions on the Actions panel, and Flash shows you the parameters you need to fill in. Let's look at some examples of how this process works with two examples: animated masks and dynamically loaded music.

Creating animated masks with movie clips

Flash has loads of useful methods built-in to its objects. One is the movie clip's setMask method, which you can use to create an animated mask. When a mask is animated, the mask reveals the background beneath while it moves. (For more on masks, refer to Chapter 6.)

To use the setMask method to make a movie clip into a mask, follow these steps:

1. **Create a movie clip and place an instance of it on the Stage.**

   This instance will be the background movie clip behind the mask. If you need to know how to create movie clips, refer to Chapter 8.

2. **With the instance selected, choose Window⇨Properties to open the Property inspector.**

   If necessary (Windows only), click the collapse arrow on the Property inspector title bar to expand the inspector.

3. **Enter an instance name for the movie clip (such as Background) in the text field near the upper-left corner of the Property inspector.**

4. **Create another movie clip and place an instance of it on a new layer on the Stage. Create some animation for this movie clip so that it moves over the background movie clip.**

   This instance will be the mask movie clip. Check out Chapter 6 for information on creating new layers. See Chapter 9 for information on creating animation.

5. **Enter an instance name (such as Mask) for the second movie clip in the Property inspector.**

6. **Click Frame 1 of the new layer on the Timeline.**

7. **With the frame selected, choose Window⇨Actions to open the Actions panel.**

   If necessary, click the collapse arrow on the Actions panel title bar to expand the panel.

8. **In the left pane of the Actions panel, choose Built-in Classes⇨Movie⇨MovieClip⇨Methods, and then double-click `setMask`.**

   The code `instanceName.setMask()`; appears in the Script pane of the Actions panel.

9. **Between the parentheses, type the mask movie clip's instance name, such as Mask — the one you named in Step 5.**

10. **Double-click `instanceName` in the Script pane of the Actions panel to select it. Type the instance name of the first movie clip (such as Background) — the one you named in Step 3.**

    If your mask movie clip's instance name is `Mask` and your other movie clip instance is named `Background`, the code should look like this:

    ```
    Background.setMask(Mask);
    ```

11. **Choose Control⇨Test Movie and enjoy the new animation.**

Dynamically loading music from the Web

You can use an ActionScript to load music into your movie live from the Web by using the ActionScript `loadsound` method.

To load an MP3 file on the Web into your movie while your movie is playing, follow these steps:

1. **Create a new layer (if you haven't already done so).**

   Chapter 6 explains how to add a new layer.

2. **Click a keyframe.**

   If the frame that you want to use is not a keyframe, right-click it (Windows) or Control+click it (Mac) and choose Insert Keyframe.

3. **Choose Window⇨Actions to open the Actions panel.**

   If necessary, click the collapse arrow on the Actions panel title bar to expand the panel.

4. **In the left pane of the Actions panel, choose Built-in Classes⇨ Media⇨Sound and then double-click** new Sound.

   new Sound() should appear in the Script pane of the Actions panel.

5. **Decide on an instance name, such as** mySound, **and type this name and an equal sign to the left of the existing code. Then type a semicolon at the end of the line and press Enter (Windows) or Return (Mac).**

   The text in the Script pane should be

   ```
   mySound = new Sound();
   ```

   This step creates an instance of a new sound object with the name mySound.

6. **In the left pane of the Actions panel, choose Built-in Classes⇨Media⇨ Sound⇨Methods, and then double-click** loadSound.

   The text in the Script panel should now be

   ```
   mySound = new Sound();
   instanceName.loadSound();
   ```

7. **Within the parentheses of the second line of code, type the URL (enclosed in quotation marks) of an MP3 file. Follow the URL with a comma and then the word** true.

   This step signifies that it's true you want to stream the sound. Now the Parameters text field contains

   ```
   "http://www.yoursite.com/fun-sound.mp3", true
   ```

   and your code in the Script pane of the Actions panel should look like this (except with your own URL):

   ```
   mySound = new Sound();
   instanceName.loadSound("http://www.yoursite.com/
        fun-sound.mp3", true);
   ```

8. **Double-click** `instanceName` **in the Script pane of the Actions panel to select it. Type in the instance name that you chose (in our example,** `mySound`**).**

   Now your code in the Script pane of the Actions panel should look like this (except with your own URL):

   ```
   mySound = new Sound();
   mySound.loadSound("http://www.yoursite.com/
           fun-sound.mp3", true);
   ```

9. **Choose Control⇨Test Movie and enjoy the music.**

Exploring Advanced ActionScript

Flash contains approximately one zillion more actions than the basic actions that we cover in this chapter. For more information, choose Help⇨ActionScript Dictionary. In this section, we briefly explain a few of the more advanced aspects of ActionScript programming to give you an idea of some of the possibilities.

Programming constructs

If you're familiar with programming, you will recognize several familiar commands, such as `For` and `While`, which let you process certain actions repeatedly while certain conditions that you specify are true. The `If` and `Else` statements create conditional expressions.

Start-and-stop drag

Flash lets you create objects that your audience can drag around the screen. Draggable objects are used for games, slider bars, and other fun purposes. See Chapter 14 for details on creating your own draggable objects.

Making comments

To help make your ActionScript clear when you look back at it a few months from now, you should add comments that explain the purpose of the ActionScript. To do this, you can type two slashes, //, and then your comments. Anything on the line after the two slashes is ignored when running the animation. If you need more than one line for comments, you can type the two slashes at the beginning of each comment line.

ActionScript 2.0

ActionScript is available in a major new version in Flash MX 2004 — ActionScript 2.0. The new version adds new commands to ActionScript that are mostly of interest to intermediate or advanced programmers who are building applications in Flash which implement new classes and subclasses of objects. Now more than ever you can use Flash to build extremely sophisticated applications that easily support rich media formats.

External scripting

You can keep your actions in separate text files that your Flash movie can load when needed. This makes it easier to reuse your beautiful ActionScript code in multiple movies. You can create your ActionScript files with any text editor that you like. When starting to learn Flash, though, it's probably easier to stick with putting your actions in frames, buttons, or movie clips.

In Flash MX 2004 Pro only, you can create a separate new ActionScript file within Flash. Choose File⇨New and then choose ActionScript File from the General tab of the New Document dialog box. You can type in your ActionScript code in this file and save it.

If you have Flash MX 2004 but not the Pro version, you can create separate ActionScript files by using Dreamweaver or a separate text editor, such as Notepad (Windows) or TextEdit (Mac). (In TextEdit, choose TextEdit⇨Preferences, and when the Preferences window appears, in the New Document Attributes section select Plain Text rather Rich Text.) Be sure to save the file with the .as suffix, which stands for ActionScript, of course.

To include the code from a separate ActionScript file in any part of your movie, simply add this ActionScript into the relevant frame, button, or movie clip:

```
#include your-filename-goes-here.as
```

This specifies an ActionScript file in the same directory as your .fla or .swf file. Or you can add this to specify an ActionScript file in a subdirectory:

```
#include some-subdirectory/your-filename-goes-here.as
```

Or add this to specify an ActionScript file in a directory that is at the same level as the directory containing your .fla or .swf file:

```
#include ../some-directory/your-filename-goes-here.as
```

Learning more

ActionScript gives you tremendous power over your Flash movies. If you enjoy using ActionScript, you may want to check out some of the great resources listed in Chapter 16. Another great reference is the *Macromedia Flash MX ActionScript Bible* by Robert Reinhardt and Joey Lott (by Wiley Publishing, Inc.).

Chapter 11

Extravagant Audio, High-Velocity Video

Silent movies have been gone for a long time now. Why should your Flash movies be silent?

You can create music and sound effects that play continuously or are controlled by your animation Timeline. You can also add sounds to buttons to liven things up a little. You can edit sounds and control when they start and stop. But be careful: Sound adds overhead to a movie, slowing down loading on a Web site. If you're careful about how you use sounds, however, you can get great results.

You can also easily include video clips in your Flash animations. You can import video clips in a variety of file formats and then scale them, rotate them, tween them, stack them up in layers, animate their transparency level, and do all the other creative things that you're used to doing in Flash, just as though the video clips were regular Flash animations.

Each new version of Flash continues to offer more support for video. In Flash MX 2004, you can now also edit your video clips while you're importing them into Flash.

Play It Louder!

To add a sound to your Flash movie, you must first import the sound. You can import AIFF, WAV, and MP3 sounds. Flash places these sounds in your Library. (Refer to Chapter 2 for more information about the Library.)

Sounds vary in sample rate — measured in kilohertz (kHz), bit rate, and channels. These statistics are important because they affect both the quality and the size of the sound file. Of course, the length of the sound also affects its size. Here's what you need to know:

- **Sample rate:** The number of times that an audio signal is sampled when it's recorded in digital form. Try not to use more than 22 kHz unless you want CD-quality music.

- **Bit rate:** The number of bits used for each audio sample. Sometimes called **bit resolution.** Sixteen-bit sound files are clearer with less background noise, but if you need to reduce file size, use 8-bit sound.

- **Channels:** Mono or stereo. In most cases, mono is fine for Flash files and uses half the amount of data.

Often, you need to take a sound as you find it unless you have software that can manipulate sounds. Luckily, you can set the specs of sounds when you publish your movie to an .swf file. You generally get best results by starting with high-quality sounds and compressing during publishing. (Refer to Chapter 13 for details on settings for publishing Flash files.)

You can check a sound's stats after you've imported the sound into Flash. The next section explains how to import a sound.

Importing sounds

Importing a sound is easy. To import a sound, follow these steps:

1. **Choose File⇨Import⇨Import To Stage (or choose File⇨Import⇨Import To Library) to open the Import dialog box.**

2. **Locate the sound that you want to import.**

3. **Click Open.**

Nothing seems to happen, but Flash has placed your sound in the Library. Choose Window⇨Library to check it out. To see the sound's stats, click the name of the sound in the Library window. Then click the Properties button at the bottom of the Library window.

The Flash libraries contain a number of sounds that you can use. Choose Window⇨Other Panels⇨Common Libraries⇨Sounds to see which sounds are available.

Sound can work to reinforce and enhance the message of your Flash movies. Check out www.soundrangers.com, which hosts thousands of inexpensive, original, royalty-free sounds that you can download in both .wav and .aif formats.

Placing sounds into a movie

After you import a sound into your movie, you need to place it and set its parameters. To place sounds in a movie, follow these steps:

1. **Create and name a new layer for the sound.**

   Click the Add Layer icon in the lower-left corner of the layer list to add a new layer. Each sound should have its own layer. Sounds are combined (mixed) when the movie is played.

2. **With the keyframe in the new layer selected, open the Library and drag the sound to the Stage.**

   Flash places the sound on the active layer. Flash extends the sound until the next keyframe, if there is one. The image of the sound waves appears in the Timeline between the keyframes.

3. **Choose Window⇨Properties to open the Property inspector if it's not already open.**

   If necessary, click the collapse arrow at the bottom-right corner of the Property inspector title bar to expand the inspector to its full size.

4. **From the Sound drop-down list, choose the sound that you want to place in your movie.**

   If necessary, click the keyframe where the sound starts. The Sound drop-down list shows all sounds that you've imported. Below the name of the sound, at the bottom of the Property inspector, the sound's stats are listed (kilohertz, channels, bits, duration, and file size), as shown in Figure 11-1.

Figure 11-1:
You can
set sound
parame-
ters in the
Property
inspector.

Frame	Tween: None	Sound: Beam Scan	
<Frame Label>		Effect: Fade Left to Ri... Edit...	
Type: Name		Sync: Start Repeat 0	
		22 kHz Mono 16 Bit 2.1 s 90.9 kB	

5. If desired, choose an effect from the Effect drop-down list.

These effects are fairly self-explanatory. For example, Left Channel plays the sound from only your left speaker. Fade In starts the sound softly and gradually brings it up to full volume. The default setting is None.

6. Choose a synchronization option from the Sync drop-down list.

- **Event:** Plays the sound when its first keyframe plays and continues to play the sound until it's finished, even if the movie stops. If the keyframe is played again before the sound is finished, Flash starts the sound again. Use this setting for button sounds when you want the sound to play each time that the button is passed over or clicked. (Refer to Chapter 8 for more information on adding sounds to buttons.) This setting is the default.

- **Start:** Plays the sound when its first keyframe plays and continues to play the sound until it's finished, even if the movie stops. If the keyframe is played again before the sound is finished, Flash doesn't start the sound again.

- **Stop:** Stops the sound. (Refer to Chapter 10 for details on the Stop All Sounds action.)

- **Stream:** Synchronizes the sound to the Timeline. Flash skips frames if it can't draw animation frames fast enough to keep up with the sound. The sound stops when Flash plays the last frame containing the soundwave. Use this option when you want to match the sound with a portion of the animation in your movie. You can insert an ending keyframe before placing the sound to control when the sound ends.

7. In the Loop text box, type the number of loops if you want to repeat the sound.

You can figure how many loops you need to play a sound throughout an animation by knowing how many seconds the sound is, how many frames your animation is, and the frame rate. If your animation is 48 frames and the rate is 12 frames per second (fps; the default), your animation is 4 seconds.

If your sound is 2 seconds long, loop it twice to play it throughout your animation. Use a high number of loops if you don't want to do the math, just to make sure.

8. **If you want, you can manually edit the sound, as we discuss in the "Editing Sounds" section, later in this chapter.**

After you place the sound, press Enter (Windows) or Return (Macintosh) or use the Controller to play your movie and hear the results.

Sounds can add significantly to file size and download time. You can place sounds in a shared library to reduce file size. See Chapter 12 for information on creating and accessing shared libraries.

Editing Sounds

After you place a sound, you can edit the sound to fine-tune its settings. You should delete unused or unwanted portions of a sound to reduce file size. You can also change the volume while the sound plays.

To edit a sound, follow these steps:

1. **Click a frame that contains a sound (or import a sound as described in the preceding section, "Placing sounds into a movie").**

2. **Choose Window⇨Properties to open the Property inspector if it's not already open.**

   If necessary, click the collapse arrow on the Property inspector title bar (Windows) or in the Property Inspector's lower right corner (Macintosh) to expand the inspector to its full size.

3. **Click the Edit button to open the Edit Envelope dialog box (see Figure 11-2).**

 To see a specific section of a sound in more detail, click the Zoom In button. Zoom in when you want to edit small details of a sound.

 To see more of a sound's timeframe, click the Zoom Out button. Zoom out to edit the sound as a whole.

  You can display sounds in terms of seconds or frames. Click the Seconds button to show sounds in seconds. Click the Frames button to display sounds by frames.

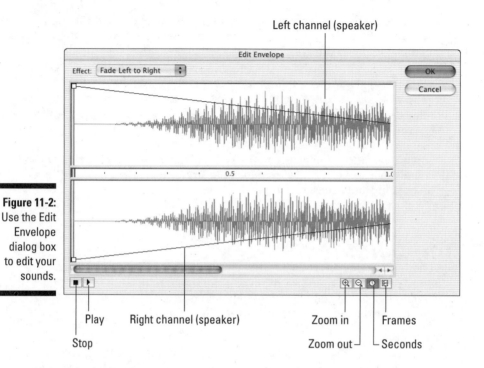

Left channel (speaker)

Figure 11-2:
Use the Edit
Envelope
dialog box
to edit your
sounds.

Play   Right channel (speaker)   Zoom in   Frames

Stop   Zoom out   Seconds

Deleting parts of a sound

Between the left (top) and right (bottom) channel display is a narrow strip that
controls the starting and ending points of a sound. By deleting the beginning
and end of a sound, you can eliminate unused portions of the sound. Along
this strip is a vertical bar at the beginning and end of the sound. These bars
control when the sound starts and ends. Use them to edit the sound as follows:

- **Time In control:** This bar, on the left edge of the sound, specifies the start
  of the sound. Drag the bar to the right to delete the beginning of the sound.

- **Time Out control:** This bar, on the right edge of the sound, specifies the
  end of the sound. Drag the bar to the left to delete the end of the sound.

Changing the volume

On both the left and right channel displays, Flash shows an envelope line to
indicate the approximate direction of the sound's volume. Where the volume

changes, Flash places small squares, called *envelope   handles.* To change the sound's volume, drag an envelope handle up (to increase volume) or down (to decrease volume).

You can click an envelope line to add a new envelope handle. This new handle enables you to create a new direction for the sound's volume at the handle's location.

When you finish editing a sound, click OK to close the Edit Envelope dialog box.

Managing Sound

Sound can increase the size of your movie by such a great extent that you need to be very careful how you use it. You should make every effort to compress the sound. You can also lower the sampling rate; however, your sound's quality is reduced. Nevertheless, you should try out all the possibilities until you get the best results.

The *sampling rate* is the rate at which the computer measures sound and converts it into numerical data. The computer makes these sample measurements many thousands of times per second. A higher sampling rate provides more information about the sound and, therefore, better audio quality. But all those extra measurements make for a much bigger data file.

Flash offers two ways to control the properties of a sound:

- ✔ **Use the Publish Settings dialog box to specify properties for all the sounds in a movie.** If you have only one sound or a couple of similar sounds, specifying settings this way is easy.

- ✔ **Use the Sound Properties dialog box to specify properties of specific sounds.** As long as you don't specifically override these properties when you publish, these settings stick. Use the Sound Properties dialog box when you want to specify different properties for each sound.

Because you specify the publish settings when you publish a movie, we discuss those settings in Chapter 13. In this section, we explain how to fine-tune sound properties in the Sound Properties dialog box.

To open the Sound Properties dialog box, open the Library (choose Window⇨ Library) and double-click the icon of the sound that you want to work with. Figure 11-3 shows the Sound Properties dialog box.

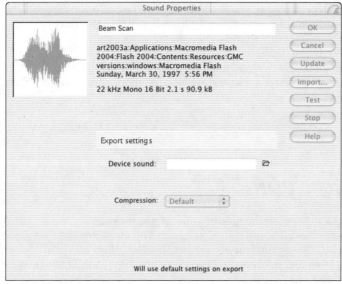

Figure 11-3:
Use the
Sound
Properties
dialog box
to set the
properties
of individual
sounds,
including
their com-
pression
and quality.

At the top of the dialog box, Flash displays statistics for the sound — its location, date, sample rate, channels, bits, duration, and file size. Use the Export
Settings section to specify how you want to export the file. For each compression type, Flash displays the settings available for that type. When you choose
settings, look at the bottom of the dialog box, where Flash displays the new
file size in kilobytes and in percentage of original size. Here are the options
available in the Compression drop-down list box:

- **Default:** This option leaves the sound as is, with no compression.

- **ADPCM:** You can convert stereo to mono to cut down file size. Available
  sampling rates are 5, 11, 22, and 44 kHz. You can choose from 2, 3, 4, or
  5 bits. Five bits results in the best sound; the Flash default is four bits.
  ADPCM is short for *Adaptive Differential Pulse Code Modulation*. This
  compression method produces files that take up less storage space than
  CD audio. It's used to store music on Sony Mini Discs.

- **MP3:** MP3 has been available since Flash 4 and is a popular and efficient
  compression method. You can convert stereo to mono and choose a bit
  rate, measured in kilobits per second. You can choose from 8 Kbps (poor
  quality) to 160 Kbps (near-CD quality). Generally, you want something
  between these two extremes. Try a bit rate between 20 and 84 Kbps for a
  good balance of file size and quality. You can also choose the quality —
  Fast, Medium, or Best. The Fast option optimizes the sound for faster
  download from your Web site but with some quality compromise.

✔ **Raw:** This option exports the sound with no sound compression. You can convert stereo to mono and choose the same sampling rates as for ADPCM.

✔ **Speech:** This option exports the sound with compression techniques specially designed for speech. You can choose the same sampling rates as for ADPCM. A good choice for speech is 11 kHz.

For music, MP3 provides the best compression, letting you keep your quality as high as possible. (*Note:* Around 1 percent of all Web users still have the Flash 3 player, which doesn't support MP3.)

After you specify a group of settings, click the Test button to see the results. This handy button lets you hear how your sound file sounds with each setting.

The Sound Properties dialog box also lets you update the original sound after you modify it with sound-editing software — just click the Update button. You can also click Import to import a sound file. The Stop button stops playing a sound that you're previewing.

When you're done, click OK to finalize your settings and close the dialog box.

Video Magic

The Flash Player has achieved more universal adoption than any other Web video technology, so Flash can be a great way to deliver video over the Web. Macromedia claims that 98 percent of Web surfers have the Flash Player, compared with 63 percent (at this writing) for Windows Media Player, 52 percent for Real Player and 37 percent for QuickTime. The Macromedia Web site provides more details — you can check it out at www.macromedia.com/software/player_census/flashplayer/tech_breakdown.html.

Flash can use a variety of video formats. If you have QuickTime 4 or later installed on your Mac or PC, you can import files in the AVI, MPG/MPEG, MOV, and DV formats. If you have DirectX 7 or higher installed on your PC, you can import files in the AVI, MPG/MPEG, and Windows Media File (WMV and ASF) formats. You can also use Flash to import Macromedia Flash Video (FLV) files, which are used in applications like video conferencing.

Embedding video into Flash

You can easily import video into your Flash movies, and now in Flash MX 2004, you can even do simple editing of your video within Flash.

In Flash MX 2004, importing video into your Flash movies is easier and more powerful with the new Video Import Wizard, which walks you through the complexities of compressing and embedding your video . . . and even enables you to edit your video clips before importing them into Flash.

To make a video clip part of your Flash movie, follow these steps:

1. **Click a keyframe (or create one by clicking a frame and choosing Insert⇨Timeline⇨Keyframe).**

2. **Choose File⇨Import⇨Import To Stage.**

   A file dialog box appears.

3. **Find and choose a movie file in the file dialog box and then click the Open (Windows)/Import (Mac) button.**

   The Video Import Wizard dialog box appears. If your movie is a QuickTime movie, the wizard now gives you a choice of embedding a video file in your Flash movie or linking to an external video file. We show you how to use the second option in the upcoming section, "Link to external video file."

4. **If your movie is QuickTime, choose Embed Video in Macromedia Flash Movie and then click Next. (If your movie isn't QuickTime, just keep reading.)**

   The Video Import Wizard window now gives you a choice of importing the entire video or editing it first. We show you how to use the second option in the next section of this chapter. If your movie's codec doesn't support editing, the edit option is not available. (The *codec* is the software that encodes the movie's images and sound into a computer file and then decodes it for playback. There are many codecs, and they use different techniques with varying advantages and disadvantages.)

5. **Select Import the Entire Video and then click Next.**

   The Encoding pane in the Video Import Wizard appears. This pane lets you select a compression profile and advanced compression settings.

6. **Click the pop-up menu under Compression profile and choose a suitable profile.**

   You can choose between profiles for users with modems, corporate local area networks (LANs), or different speeds of digital subscriber line (DSL) or cable modems. Higher speed connections like DSL and cable modems make it practical to use higher quality video that requires less compression.

7. **If you want to customize the Compression profile that you selected in the preceding step, click the Edit button to the right of the compression profile pop-up menu. Otherwise, skip to Step 16.**

   The Customized Encoding pane in the Video Import Wizard appears, as shown in Figure 11-4. This pane lets you specify the keyframe interval that you want for your video compression and the target bandwidth or quality desired.

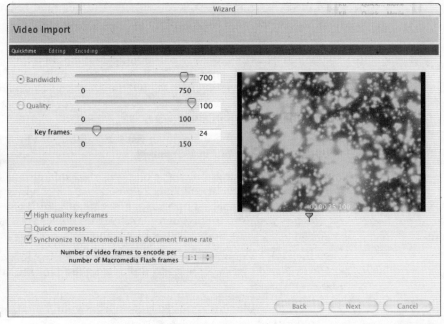

Figure 11-4:
In the Video
Import
Wizard,
you can
adjust the
quality
of your
video clip.

8. **Select either the Quality or Bandwidth radio button, and then drag the slider near either the Quality or Bandwidth radio button to choose the amount of compression that you want. If you choose the Bandwidth slider, select the High Quality Keyframes check box for more consistent image quality.**

Higher-quality video is less compressed and therefore requires a larger file size and higher bandwidth for speedy delivery. You may change the level of compression in your video by selecting either the Quality or the Bandwidth button — they are two ways of doing the same thing.

- **On the Quality slider:** 0 is the lowest quality, and 100 the highest.

- **On the Bandwidth slider:** You can choose approximate values between 0 and 750 Kbps. Most home modem users have modems that operate at 56 Kbps. DSL and cable modems typically are somewhere in the 256 Kpbs to 786 Kpbs range.

9. **Drag the Key Frames slider to choose the frequency of keyframes in your video clip.**

A keyframe stores the entire picture data for that frame, although the other frames store only the changes from the previous frame. Thus, fewer keyframes means smaller files. More frequent keyframes enable faster seeking in the video — for example, if the user wants to fast-forward or rewind.

10. **Select the Synchronize to Macromedia Flash Document Frame Rate check box if you want the video clip frame rate to match the frame rate of your Flash movie.**

    Usually, you want to choose this option. Sometimes, however, you may not want to choose it. For instance, if your Flash movie has a 30 fps frame rate and your video clip is NTSC (the American TV standard) with a 29.97 fps frame rate, you may want to avoid the hiccup effect caused by dropping frames from your video clip.

11. **Choose a ratio from the drop-down list for Number of Video Frames to Encode Per Number of Flash Frames.**

    If you choose 1:1, your movie plays one imported video frame for each Flash frame on your main Timeline. If you choose 1:2, your movie plays an imported video frame for every two Flash frames, and so on. The more frames you drop from your video clip, the smaller your file is, but it also can make your video playback look choppier.

12. **Select the Quick Compress check box if your video has lots of motion in it and you don't want to wait a long time for the video to be compressed.**

    This may reduce the time required to compress your video, but it also may decrease your video's image quality.

13. **Grab and drag the pointer below your video image in the Video Import Wizard window to preview the image quality of your compression settings at different locations in your video clip. Repeat any of Steps 8 through 12 to fine-tune your settings if you like.**

14. **Click Next.**

    The next pane in the Video Import Wizard appears. This pane lets you give a name and a description to your customized compression setting.

15. **Make any changes that you desire to the name and description of your customized compression setting, and then click Next.**

    In the Video Import Wizard, the pane again appears where you may select a compression profile and specify advanced compression settings.

16. **If you want to specify other compression settings, such as the color or dimensions of your video, click the pop-up menu under Advanced Settings and choose a suitable profile.**

17. **If you want to customize other compression settings, such as the color or dimensions of your video, click the pop-up menu under Advanced Settings and choose Create a New Profile at the bottom of the menu. If you've already chosen a profile and want to edit it, click the Edit button to the right of the Advanced Settings profile pop-up menu. Otherwise skip to Step 22.**

The Advanced Settings pane in the Video Import Wizard appears, as shown in Figure 11-5. This pane lets you apply color correction to your video, change its dimensions, and set other options.

18. In the Advanced Settings pane, specify any changes that you'd like.

Your color correction options include changing the hue, saturation, brightness, contrast, and gamma of your video.

- *Hue* is the color of an image, such as red or blue.

- *Saturation* is the purity of the color as measured by how much gray is mixed in with it.

- *Gamma* is a measure of the lightness levels in the image. With larger values of gamma, lighter parts of the image become even lighter.

In the **Dimensions section** of the window, you can reduce the size of your video by either entering a value less than 100 for the scale or by dragging the pop-up slider. Settings at less than 100 percent result in a smaller movie that may play more smoothly and require less file size. You can also crop your image by entering new values for the right, left, top, and bottom edges. Guides in the video image preview window show where your image is cropped.

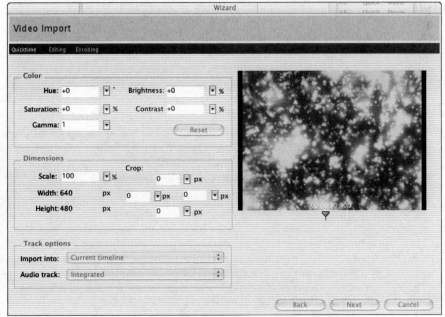

Figure 11-5:
In the Video Import Wizard, you can also color correct, scale, and crop your video clip.

In the **Track Options section,** you can choose whether to import your video as

- A video object on the current Timeline

- A Movie Clip on the first frame of your Flash document

- A graphic symbol on the current Timeline

In the Track Options section, you can also choose how to import the audio portion of your video:

- If you choose Separate, Flash imports the audio track as an audio object separate from the video file.

- If you choose Integrated, Flash imports the audio as part of the video file.

- If you choose None, Flash imports only the video portion, not the audio portion.

19. **Grab and drag the pointer below your video image in the Video Import Wizard window to preview effects of your changes at different locations in your video clip, and repeat Step 18 as desired.**

20. **Click Next.**

    The next pane in the Video Import Wizard appears. This pane lets you give a name and a description to your customized advanced settings.

21. **Make any changes that you desire to the name and description of your customized advanced settings, and then click Next.**

    In the Video Import Wizard, the pane again appears where you may select a compression profile and specify advanced compression settings.

22. **Click Finish.**

    A window with a progress gauge appears while your video is imported.

23. **If your video is longer than the span between keyframes into which you're placing it, a dialog box appears, asking whether you want to add to the span the number of frames required to play the entire clip. Choose Yes if you want to add the frames.**

    The video clip stops playing at the end of the span. If you chose No, then later you can still move the keyframe at the end of the span to add more frames.

Now you can scale, rotate, and tween your video clip. You can paint on top of it in other layers, you can tween its brightness and transparency — you can mangle it, destroy it, and bring it to life in all the usual Flash ways. (Refer to Chapter 9 for even more animation ideas.)

If you want to import a video clip as a reusable library, follow the preceding set of steps but choose File➪Import➪Import To Library in Step 1 rather than File➪Import➪Import To Stage.

Editing video in Flash

In the Editing pane in the Flash MX 2004 Video Import Wizard, you can chop up your video clips into multiple clips, trim the beginnings and endings of your clips, rearrange the order of your clips, and then combine them back into a single video sequence if you want.

To edit a video clip while importing it into your Flash movie, follow these steps:

1. **Click a keyframe (or create one by clicking a frame and choosing Insert⇨Timeline⇨Keyframe).**

2. **Choose File⇨Import⇨Import To Stage.**

   A file dialog box appears.

3. **Find and choose a movie file in the file dialog box and then click the Import button.**

   The Video Import Wizard dialog box appears. If your movie is a QuickTime movie, the wizard now gives you a choice of embedding a video file in your Flash movie or linking to an external video file. We show you how to use the second option in "Link to external video file," later in the chapter.

4. **If your movie is QuickTime, choose Embed Video in Macromedia Flash Movie, and then click Next. If your movie isn't QuickTime, just keep reading.**

   The Video Import Wizard window now gives you a choice of importing the entire video or editing it first

5. **Select the Edit the Video First radio button, and then click Next.**

   The Editing pane in the Video Import Wizard appears, as shown in Figure 11-6.

6. **To view your video in the preview pane, either click the Play button or drag the *playhead* (the triangle above the scrubber bar). Click the Stop button to stop playing the video. To zero in on a particular frame of video, you may want to move backward or forward a frame at a time by clicking the Backward or Forward buttons.**

7. **To change the beginning and ending frames of a video clip, drag the triangles below the scrubber bar. Or move the playhead to the desired frame and click the In button to make it the new beginning frame or the Out button to make it the new ending frame.**

   The beginning and ending frames are *In* and *Out* points, respectively.

8. **To see your video with the new In and Out points, click the Preview Clip button.**

   The video plays in the preview pane, starting at the new In point and ending at the new Out point.

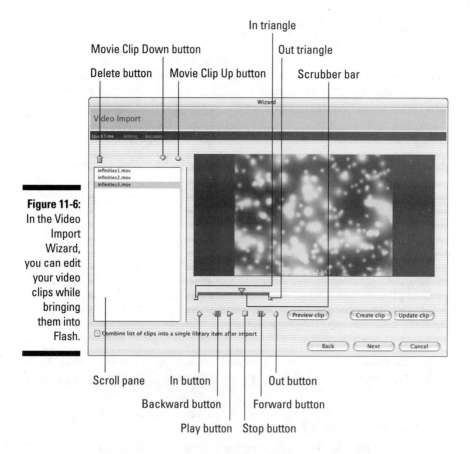

Figure 11-6:
In the Video Import Wizard, you can edit your video clips while bringing them into Flash.

9. **When you're happy with the In and Out points that you've set, click the Create Clip button to create a video clip with the current In and Out points.**

   The name of the clip appears in the scroll pane on the left side of the Video Import Wizard window.

10. **To rename the clip, click the name in the scroll pane and type a new name.**

    The new name appears in the scroll pane.

11. **Repeat Steps 6 through 10 to extract additional clips with new In and Out points from the same file.**

12. **To change the In and Out points in one of your new clips, click the clip's name in the scroll pane, move the In and Out points as we describe in Step 7, and then click the Update Clip button.**

13. **To change the order of the clips in the scroll pane, click the name of the clip to be moved. Then click the Move Clip Up or the Move Clip Down button at the top of the scroll pane.**

    The selected clip moves up or down to a new position in the list.

14. **To delete a clip from the scroll pane, click the name of the clip in the scroll pane, and then click the Delete button at the top of the scroll pane.**

    The selected clip disappears from the list.

15. **If you want to combine your clips back into a single video clip, select the Combine List of Clips into a Single Library Item After Import check box.**

    The clips are combined in the order that they appear in the scroll pane. This is handy if you want to use the clips bundled together in order, as a single movie clip.

    If you don't select Combine List of Clips into a Single Library Item After Import, the clips in your scroll pane are imported into your Flash document as separate items.

16. **Click Next.**

    The Encoding pane in the Video Import Wizard appears. This pane lets you select a compression profile and specify advanced compression settings.

17. **If you want to adjust your compression settings, you can do so now, as we describe starting in Step 6 of the previous section entitled "Embedding video into Flash." Otherwise, click Finish.**

    A window with a progress gauge appears while your video is imported.

18. **If your video is longer than the span between keyframes into which you're placing it, a dialog box appears, asking whether you want to add to the span the number of frames required to play the entire clip. Choose Yes if you want to add the frames.**

    The video clip stops playing at the end of the span. If you chose No, then later you can still move the keyframe at the end of the span to add more frames.

Linking to video in Flash

You can also include video in your Flash movies by linking to a separate Quick-Time movie file instead of actually embedding it in your Flash file. If you do this, you must publish your Flash file as a QuickTime movie — it doesn't work otherwise. (For more information on publishing your files, see Chapter 13.)

You can scale, rotate, and animate your linked video in Flash, but you can't tween it.

To link a QuickTime video clip into your Flash movie, follow these steps:

1. **Click a keyframe (or create one by clicking a frame and choosing Insert⇨Timeline⇨Keyframe).**

2. **Choose File⇨Import⇨Import To Stage.**

   A file dialog box appears.

   You can alternatively choose File⇨Import⇨Import To Library if you want the video clip to be in a Library.

3. **Find and choose a QuickTime movie file in the file dialog box and then click the Import button.**

   The Video Import Wizard dialog box appears. If your movie is a QuickTime movie, the wizard now gives you a choice of embedding a video file in your Flash movie or linking to an external video file. We show you how to use the first option earlier in this chapter.

4. **In the Video Import Wizard dialog box, select the Link to External Video File radio button. Click Next.**

5. **If your video is longer than the span between keyframes into which you're placing it, a dialog box appears, asking whether you want to add to the span the number of frames required to play the entire clip. Choose Yes if you want to add the frames.**

   The video clip stops playing at the end of the span. If you chose No, then later you can still move the keyframe at the end of the span to add more frames.

6. **View the linked video by choosing Control⇨Play.**

   It plays until the next keyframe.

You can't see the linked QuickTime video if you play your movie by choosing Control⇨Test Movie. To see the linked video, either choose Control⇨Play or publish the movie and then view the published movie. (See Chapter 13 for all the details on publishing your movies.)

Part V
The Movie and the Web

The 5th Wave   By Rich Tennant

@RICHTENNANT

SCREEEEEK

"Is this really the best use of Flash animation on our e-commerce Web site? A bad wheel on the shopping cart icon that squeaks, wobbles, and pulls to the left?"

In this part . . .

The not-so-secret desire of every Flash movie animation is to appear under the bright lights on the Web. In this part, we show you how to make that happen. We explain how to put all the pieces together to create a way-cool Flash-only site. You see how to build a Web site that contains a complete navigational system so that viewers can quickly get the information they need. We cover three techniques for creating a complete site.

We also discuss the nitty-gritty of publishing your Flash movie to a Flash Player file, the only kind of Flash file a Web browser can display. Besides the Flash Player file, Flash can create the HTML code you need and the alternative images you may want to use in case a viewer doesn't have the Flash Player. Flash makes it easy: Just specify your settings and click Publish.

Chapter 12

Putting It All Together

● ●

In This Chapter

▶ Creating slide presentations

▶ Offering your viewers a preloader

▶ Using shared libraries while your movie plays

▶ Enhancing navigation through your movie with named anchors

▶ Building user interfaces with components

▶ Putting together an entire Web site with Flash

▶ Checking out your viewers' Flash Player version

▶ Analyzing your movies with the Movie Explorer

▶ Making your site accessible to people with disabilities

● ●

*W*hen creating your Flash animation, you need to consider how you will integrate it with your entire Web site. Are you creating a small animation to insert into an existing HyperText Markup Language (HTML) site, or do you want your entire site to be *Flashed?* In this chapter, we cover techniques for creating entire presentations, Web pages, and sites by using Flash.

Building Slide Presentations — Fast!

Flash now comes in two versions: Flash MX and Flash MX Professional. In addition to including all the features of Flash MX, the Professional version of Flash has powerful features for programmers and production teams, such as capabilities for project file management and version control of Flash files as well as for connecting Flash to live external data sources and to Web services.

In this book, we focus on the features of Flash MX rather than Flash MX Professional because they're much more interesting to people who are new to Flash. There's one great feature of Flash MX Professional 2004 that we do want to introduce to you, though — Flash slide presentations.

With Flash MX Professional 2004, you can put together Flash presentations faster than ever with a new feature called *Screens mode*. In this mode, you can create a series of slides that are easy to shuffle around and rearrange, and you can easily add transitions between screens. Flash automatically connects the screens for you so that when you play your Flash movie to your audience, you (or your viewers) can advance from one screen to the next simply by pressing the keyboard's space bar or its forward arrow key.

On each slide, you can add layers of art, text, video, sound, and animation to your heart's content. It's easy to add new screens to your presentation, and you can nest screens like you do in an outline containing topics and sub-topics. To create a slide presentation, do the following steps:

1. **Choose File➪New.**

   The New Document dialog box appears, with two tabs — one labeled *General* and one labeled *Templates*.

2. **Choose the General tab in the New Document dialog box if it isn't already selected.**

   Below the General tab, a list of document types appears.

3. **Click the Flash Slide Presentation document type to select it and then click the OK button.**

   A new Flash document appears, with a Screen Outline pane to the left of the Stage.

4. **To add art to the currently selected slide, you can import graphics, video clips, or audio, or you can use the Flash drawing and text tools to create new art.**

   When you add or transform art on the Stage, the changes also appear in the thumbnail-sized image of the slide in the Screen Outline pane.

   See Chapter 2 for more on importing graphics and Chapter 11 for more on importing audio and video. See Chapter 3 for more on using the Flash drawing tools and Chapter 5 for more on adding text.

5. **To add another slide to your presentation, right-click (Windows) or Control+click (Mac) a slide in the Screen Outline pane and then choose Insert Screen from the contextual menu that appears. Or, better yet, just click the big plus (+) button at the top left of the pane.**

   A new blank slide appears in the Screen Outline pane under the slide that you clicked, and a new screen appears on the Stage.

6. **Repeat Steps 4 and 5 as desired.**

7. **If you want to add art that will be seen on every slide — a title, for instance — click the top slide in the Screen Outline pane and then import your graphics or use the Flash drawing and text tools to create your art.**

The topmost slide in the Screen Outline panel is the *master screen*. It can't be moved or deleted.

8. **If you decide that you want to change any of your slides, click the slide in the Screen Outline pane and edit it as in Step 4.**

9. **To view your presentation, choose Control⇨Test Movie.**

   Your presentation appears in a new window.

10. **To advance from one screen to the next, press your keyboard's space bar or its forward arrow key. To view the previous screen in the presentation, press your keyboard's back arrow key.**

You can facilitate the organization of your presentation into an outline of topics and subtopics by using nested slides. Each nested slide corresponds to a subtopic, and is indented in the Screen Outline pane. (In Figure 12-1, slides 1a and 1b are examples of nested slides. The Screen Outline pane shows that Slide 1b is the currently selected slide.) To add a nested screen to your slide presentation, right-click (Windows) or Control+click (Mac) on a slide in the Screen Outline pane and then choose Insert Nested Screen from the contextual menu that appears. The new nested slide will appear in the Screen Outline pane, below and slightly to the right of the parent slide.

By default, the art from parent slides automatically appears in the slides of their "children."

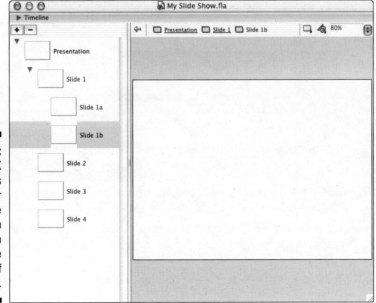

Figure 12-1: In Flash MX Pro Screens mode, your slides are shown in the Screen Outline pane to the left of the Stage.

You can easily add transition effects between your slides by using *Behaviors,* which is another powerful new feature of Flash 2004. (Check out Chapter 10 for more on Behaviors.) To add transition effects between two slides, follow these steps:

1. **In the Screen Outline panel, click the first of the two slides.**

   The selected slide is highlighted.

2. **If the Behaviors panel is not already open, choose Window⇨ Development Panels⇨Behaviors.**

   The Behaviors panel appears.

3. **Click the plus sign (+) in the Behaviors panel.**

   A pop-up menu appears.

4. **Choose Screen⇨Transition from the pop-up menu.**

   The Transitions dialog box appears, as shown in Figure 12-2.

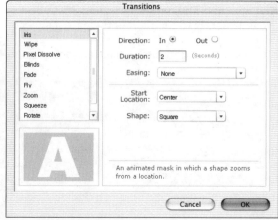

Figure 12-2: Use the Transitions dialog box to quickly create transition effects between your slides.

5. **Click the transition that you want in the list on the left.**

   An animated example of the transition appears below the list of transitions.

6. **Specify the direction, duration, and other parameters of the transition in the right-hand side of the dialog box.**

   Each time that you change the parameters, a new animated example of the transition appears again below the list of transitions, which gives you an idea of the effect of the parameters that you changed.

7. **Experiment with different parameter settings (direction, duration, and so on) until the example below the list of transitions looks good. When you finish setting parameters, click OK.**

   The Transitions dialog box disappears.

8. **Choose Control⇨Test Movie to watch the presentation.**

   Your movie includes the transition effect that you added.

You can also rearrange the order of your slides easily. Follow these steps to rearrange your slides:

1. **In the Screen Outline panel, press and hold the mouse button on a slide and drag that slide to a new position in the panel.**

   As long as you don't release the mouse button, the slide follows your mouse around in the Screen Outline panel.

2. **When you have the slide where you want it, release the mouse button.**

   The slide snaps into the new position.

 It's handy to give your slides logical names in the Screen Outline pane. These names won't be seen by viewers who use the Flash Player, but they can help you to organize the slides in your presentation if you have a lot of them, especially if you need to rearrange their order.

Here's what you do to rename a slide:

1. **In the Screen Outline pane, double-click the name of the slide.**

   The slide's name is highlighted.

2. **Type in the new name.**

   The name changes.

In Flash, it's a snap to add animation to your slide presentations, or to any other Flash documents, to give them more graphic impact. See Chapter 9 for extensive information on adding animation to your Flash documents.

Creating a Preloader

If you're very ambitious and create a huge Flash file, you may find that downloading it to a viewer's browser takes an unacceptable amount of time. Your audience won't wait forever. To solve this problem, you should create a *preloader,* which is a tiny movie that loads quickly and tells your viewers to wait. Often, all it says is loading. To create a simple preloader, follow these steps:

1. **Create two scenes — the second for your main movie and the first for the preloader.**

   The two scenes must be within the same movie. Refer to Chapter 9 for the lowdown on creating and changing the order of scenes.

2. **In the first scene (the preloader), create a small animation.**

3. **Click the first frame of your preloader scene and then choose Window⇨ Development Panels⇨Actions to open the Actions panel if it's not already open.**

   If necessary, click the collapse arrow on the Actions panel title bar to expand it.

4. **In the Script pane on the right side of the Actions panel, type in the following ActionScript code:**

```
if (_root._framesloaded>=_root._framestotal) {
gotoAndPlay("Scene 2",1);
}
```

   The ActionScript specifies that if the number of frames loaded is greater than or equal to the total number of frames in your movie (in other words, if the last frame of the main movie is loaded), the playhead of the Timeline should go to the first frame of Scene 2 and play it. Refer to Chapter 10 to read about ActionScript.

5. **Click the last frame of your preloader scene.**

6. **From the list of action types on the left side of the Actions panel, click the Global Functions category and then the Timeline Control subcategory; then double-click the gotoAndPlay action.**

   gotoAndPlay(); appears in the Script pane on the right side of the Actions panel.

7. **Type 1 in the Script pane.**

   Now your code should look like this:

```
gotoAndPlay(1);
```

   This ActionScript loops your preloader so that it plays over and over until your main movie is loaded.

 You can test your preloader by choosing Control⇨Test Movie, but your main movie may load so quickly that you don't even see the preloader. Choose View⇨Simulate Download to see how your preloader works while your main movie loads, as we explain in Chapter 13. You can also upload your file to a test page on your Web site to see how the preloader works. Make sure that your preloader is long enough for the human eye to see. Remember that one frame is displayed for only a fraction of a second.

 For examples of fancier preloaders, check out Go Figure v52-5.fla, which is also an example of an entire game created in Flash and liquidskydesign.fla in the Ch12 folder of the CD-ROM. *(Thanks to Chuck Miller for Go Figure, and to Radim Schreiber,* www.liquidskydesign.com, *for the Liquid Sky preloader.)*

Sharing Libraries on the Run

A *runtime shared library* is a library in a movie that has been posted to a Web site and is used by another Flash Player file (.swf). The movie using the shared library object doesn't contain the object but just uses it from the shared library. Shared libraries can help make your movies smaller. For example, you can share bandwidth-hogging elements, such as sounds and fonts.

Creating a shared library

A runtime shared library can be a movie clip, a button, a graphic symbol, or a font symbol. (See Chapter 7 for the lowdown on symbols.)

To share a font, you first have to create a font symbol, but that's easy. To create a font symbol, follow these steps:

1. **Choose Window⇨Library to open the Library panel.**

2. **Click the Options menu in the upper-right corner of the Library panel and then choose New Font.**

   The Font Symbol Properties dialog box appears.

3. **Select a font from the Font menu in the dialog box. Alternatively, type in the name of the font in the Font text box.**

4. **Type in a name for the font symbol in the Name text box.**

5. **Select bold or italic text (if you like) and then type in the font size that you desire in the Size box.**

6. **Click OK.**

   The dialog box disappears, and the name that you gave the font symbol appears in the Library panel.

You create a runtime shared library when you want to make an element in your movie available to other SWF player files. You do this by defining linked objects in a movie's library. To create a runtime shared library, follow these steps:

1. **With the Library panel open, select a movie clip, button, graphic symbol, or font symbol on the Library panel, right-click (Windows) or Control+click (Mac), and choose Linkage from the contextual menu that appears.**

   The Linkage Properties dialog box appears.

 2. **In the Linkage Properties dialog box, choose Export for Runtime Sharing.**

 3. **Type a name (no spaces allowed) for the symbol in the Identifier text box.**

 4. **Enter the Universal Resource Locator (URL; location on the Web) where you plan to upload the object in the URL text box.**

 5. **Click OK.**

    The Linkage Properties dialog box closes.

 6. **Save the file.**

 7. **Publish the file as an SWF player file. (See Chapter 13 for instructions on publishing files.)**

 8. **Upload the file to your Web site — to the URL (location) that you specified in Step 4.**

    In Step 3, you give the shared library a name; and in Step 4, you give the shared library an address (a location on the Web). The next section describes how you can use this name and address to link to the shared library from within a different movie.

Using a shared library

After you create a shared library, you can use it from within a different movie by specifying its name and URL or by dragging it into the destination movie. To use a shared library by specifying its name and URL, follow these steps:

 1. **In the destination movie, choose Window⇨Library.**

    The Library panel appears.

 2. **Select an object on the Library panel, right-click (Windows) or Control+click (Mac), and choose Linkage from the contextual menu that appears.**

    The Linkage Properties dialog box appears.

 3. **In the Linkage Properties dialog box, choose Import for Runtime Sharing.**

 4. **Type the movie clip, button, font, or graphic symbol name that you want into the Identifier text box (no spaces allowed).**

 5. **Enter the URL (the Web address) where the object is located.**

 6. **Click OK.**

    The Linkage Properties dialog box closes.

To use a runtime shared library by dragging it into your destination movie, follow these steps:

1. **Open your destination movie.**

2. **Choose File➪Open or File➪Open as Library.**

   The Open (or Open as Library) dialog box appears.

3. **In the dialog box, choose your *source* movie — the movie file whose runtime shared library you want to use — and click Open.**

   If you chose Open as Library, the source movie's library gets added to the Library panel.

   Otherwise, the source movie file opens, and you see both your source and destination movies. (If you can't see both movies, choose Window➪ Cascade.)

4. **Drag the linked object from its Library panel onto the Stage of your destination movie.**

   If you have the destination movie's Library open too, you can also drag directly from the shared library to the current library.

Working with shared libraries requires that all the pieces be in the proper place at the same time. We suggest checking a movie that contains an object from a shared library to verify that the object is displayed properly. You can do so by going online and viewing it in your browser.

Using Named Anchors

One complaint that people had about earlier versions of Flash is that their browsers' Forward and Back buttons don't allow them to navigate through Flash movies. When Flash takes over your Web page, suddenly your Forward and Back buttons can seem dead.

Flash fixed that problem by letting you insert *named anchors* into your movies. Your Web browser sees these anchors as though they're delineating separate Web pages within your Flash file. This makes it easy for a Web browser's Forward and Back buttons to work in your movies. When someone watching your Flash movie presses the Web browser's Back button, the browser simply moves to your movie's nearest previous frame containing a named anchor. If the previous named anchor is in an earlier scene, the browser moves to the named anchor point in the previous scene. The browser's Forward button enables you to undo the results of pressing the Back button.

Named anchors work only when you save your work as Flash Player 6 or Flash Player 7 movies and when they're viewed with Flash Player 6 or above.

To use named anchors in your movie, follow these steps:

1. **Choose Window⇨Properties to open the Property inspector if it's not already open. If necessary (Windows only), click the collapse arrow on the Property inspector title bar to expand it.**

2. **Click the keyframe where you want to add a named anchor.**

3. **In the upper-left corner of the Property inspector, type a name in the Frame Label text box.**

4. **Choose Anchor in the Type pop-up menu near the Frame Label text box.**

   An anchor icon appears in the keyframe that you clicked in Step 2.

Adding the Power of Components

Components in Flash are a group of sophisticated movie clips with special built-in methods and parameters that can be customized in many interesting ways. Components can be used to add interaction and navigation elements to your Flash movies, allowing you to use Flash to create surveys, forms, interactive art galleries, or even complete graphical user interfaces for your Flash movies. Among other things, components can also be used (with the help of some fairly sophisticated ActionScript) to access and manipulate data from the Web and other sources.

Flash MX 2004 ships with more than a dozen components, and you can download more components, built by Flash community members, from the Macromedia Exchange at www.macromedia.com/exchange/flash. Some of the components that ship with Flash MX 2004 are

- ✔ **Radio buttons:** These let you make one choice from several buttons.

- ✔ **Check boxes:** You can mark or clear each check box.

- ✔ **Push buttons:** Clicking one of these makes something in your movie happen.

- ✔ **Combo boxes:** These are drop-down menu lists.

- ✔ **Lists:** These are scrolling lists of choices.

- ✔ **Scroll panes:** These are scrollable (but not draggable) windows for your movie clips, JPEG images, and Flash Player files.

- ✔ **Windows:** These are draggable windows within your Flash movie that can display a movie clip, JPEG image, or Flash Player file. They also include a title bar, a border, and a Close button.

To add a component to your Flash movie, drag it from the Components panel (see Figure 12-3) onto the Stage.

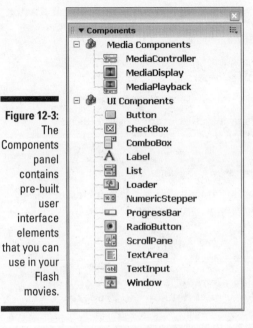

Figure 12-3:
The
Components
panel
contains
pre-built
user
interface
elements
that you can
use in your
Flash
movies.

In the following sections, we look at how you use several types of components. We skip push buttons because button symbols (which we describe in Chapter 8) are easier to use and do almost everything that you need.

Using radio buttons in a Flash movie

To use a set of radio buttons in your Flash movie, follow these steps:

1. **If the Components panel is not already visible, choose Window⟹ Development Panels⟹Components. If necessary, click the collapse arrow on the Components panel title bar to expand it, and click the plus (+) sign (Windows) or the right-pointing arrow (Mac) near the UI Components category in the Components panel to display all the components in the category.**

2. **Drag two or more radio buttons from the Components panel onto the Stage.**

   You need at least two radio buttons in every set of radio buttons. In a Flash movie, when you enable a radio button in a set, that button is turned on, and all the others in the set are turned off.

3. **Choose Window⇨Properties to open the Property inspector if it's not already open. If necessary (Windows only), click the collapse arrow on the Property inspector title bar to expand it.**

   The Property inspector appears with the Parameters tab set. The Property inspector lists five parameters.

4. **Select the radio button whose parameters you want to set.**

5. **To change the radio button's label, click in the label field on the Property inspector and type a new name for the radio button.**

   The radio button's label changes on the Stage.

6. **To change the radio button's initial state, click the Selected drop-down list on the Property inspector and choose True or False, depending on what you want.**

   If you choose True, the radio button is initially selected. If you choose False, the radio button is initially clear.

7. **To change the group to which the radio button belongs, type a new name in the Group Name text field on the Property inspector.**

   For example, type **myRadioGroup** into the Group Name text field.

   All the radio buttons with the same group name act as one group. Selecting one radio button in the group deselects all the other radio buttons with the same group name.

8. **To change the radio button's label placement, click the Label Placement drop-down list on the Property inspector and choose the right or left option to place the label to the right or left of its radio button.**

9. **To associate some additional information with the radio button, type in some information in the Data text field on the Property inspector.**

   Step 13 shows you how to use this data.

10. **Repeat Steps 4 to 9 for each radio button.**

11. **Decide which elements of your Flash movie will change when a radio button is selected; then add those elements to the Flash movie if you haven't already done so.**

   If for example, you decide that the contents of a dynamic text box will change when a radio button is selected, create a dynamic text box on the Stage and give it an instance name, such as myInfo. (See Chapter 5 to discover how to create dynamic text.)

12. **Choose Window⇨Development Panels⇨Actions to open the Actions panel if it isn't open already.**

13. **Select Frame 1 in the Timeline and enter this code in the Script pane of the Actions panel:**

```
myForm = new Object();
myForm.click = function(myEvent){
    myInfo.text = myEvent.target.selection.data;
}
myRadioGroup.addEventListener("click",myForm);
```

You can replace `myForm`, `myEvent`, `myInfo`, and `myRadioGroup` with any names that you like. `myInfo` in this example is the name of the dynamic text field that we mention in Step 11, and `myRadioGroup` is the group name of your radio buttons.

Line 1 of the code above creates a new little bundle of methods and properties named `myForm`. Line 5 adds an event listener to `myForm` so that when you select one of the radio buttons in `myRadioGroup`, the code in lines 2, 3, and 4 sets the text of the dynamic text field to whatever is in the data parameter of the radio button that you click.

The third line of code shows an example of how to change the contents of the dynamic text box that we describe in Step 11, but you can replace this line with other ActionScript code to do something else in your movie to respond to changes in which radio button is selected.

For example, if you want to set the text of the dynamic text field to be the label of the radio button that you click, replace this line:

```
myInfo.text = myEvent.target.selection.data;
```

with this line:

```
myInfo.text = myEvent.target.selection.label;
```

For radio buttons, the Property inspector has two tabs in the upper-right corner — one tab for properties, and one tab for parameters. If you have a radio button selected but its parameters don't show on the Property inspector, you probably clicked the Properties tab by accident. Click to select the Parameters tab in the upper-right (Windows) or lower-right (Mac) corner of the Property inspector; now it should display the radio button parameters. You can view even more of the radio button's parameters by choosing Window⇨Development Panels⇨Component Inspector.

Using check boxes in a Flash movie

To use check boxes in your Flash movie, follow these steps:

1. **Choose Window⇨Development Panels⇨Components to view the Components panel if it's not already open.**

2. **Drag a check box from the Components panel onto the Stage.**

3. **Choose Window⇨Properties to open the Property inspector if it's not already open. If necessary (Windows only), click the collapse arrow on the Property inspector title bar to expand it.**

   The Property inspector lists three parameters: Label, Label Placement, and Selected.

4. **To change the check box's label, click in the Label field on the Property inspector and type a new name for the check box.**

   The check box's label changes on the Stage.

5. **To change the check box's initial state, click the Selected drop-down list on the Property inspector and choose True or False, depending on what you want.**

   If you choose True, the check box is initially marked. If you choose False, the check box is initially cleared.

6. **To change the check box's label placement, click the Label Placement drop-down list on the Property inspector and choose either Right or Left.**

7. **To give the check box an instance name, click in the Instance Name field on the Property inspector and type a name.**

   For instance, you can enter **myCheckBox.**

8. **Decide which elements of your Flash movie will change when a check box is selected; then add those elements to the Flash movie if you haven't already done so.**

   For example, if you decide the movie will go to and play Frame 20 when a check box is marked, create a keyframe at Frame 20. (See Chapter 9 to discover how to create keyframes.)

9. **Choose Window⇨Development Panels⇨Actions to open the Actions panel if it isn't open already.**

10. **Select Frame 1 in the Timeline and enter this code in the Script pane of the Actions panel:**

```
myForm2 = new Object();
myForm2.click = function(myEvent2){
    if (myEvent2.target.selected){
    gotoAndPlay(20);
    }
}
myCheckBox.addEventListener("click",myForm2);
```

    You can replace myForm2, myEvent2, and myCheckBox with any names that you like. myCheckBox in this example is the instance name of your check box.

Line 1 of the code above creates a new little bundle of methods and properties named myForm. Line 7 adds an event listener to myForm so that when you mark the check box named myCheckBox, the code in lines 2, 3, 4, and 5 causes Flash to go to Frame 20 and starts playing there.

Lines 3 and 4 of the code show an example of how to move the Flash playhead to another section of the movie if the check box is selected. You can replace this line with other ActionScript code to do something else in your movie when the check box is selected.

Using combo boxes in a Flash movie

To use combo boxes in your Flash movie, follow these steps:

1. **Choose Window⇨Development Panels⇨Components to view the Components panel if it's not already open.**

   Refer to Figure 12-3 to see the Components panel in all its splendor.

2. **Drag a combo box from the Components panel onto the Stage.**

3. **Choose Window⇨Properties to open the Property inspector if it's not already open. If necessary (Windows only), click the collapse arrow on the Property inspector title bar to expand it.**

   The Property inspector lists four parameters: Data, Editable, Labels, and Row Count.

4. **Type a name in the Instance Name text field in the upper-left corner of the Property inspector.**

5. **To control whether the user can edit the items on the combo box's menu list, click the drop-down menu for the Editable parameter and then choose True or False.**

   Choosing True allows the user to rename each item on the menu list. Choosing False prevents that from happening.

6. **To create items on the menu list, double-click in the Labels text field.**

   The Values dialog box appears.

7. **In the Values dialog box, click the plus sign to add a menu item or click the minus sign to delete a menu item. Click the upward-pointing triangle to move an item up on the list, and click the downward-pointing triangle to move a menu item down on the list.**

   When you add an item to the list, it is excitingly named defaultValue.

8. **To change a menu item's name from defaultValue to something more interesting and meaningful, click the menu item in the Values dialog box and type a more useful name there.**

9. **Click OK.**

   The Values dialog box closes.

10. **To change the number of items that can be displayed in the combo box without a scroll bar, click the Row Count field on the Property inspector and type a new number.**

    The default number is 5.

11. **Choose Modify⇨Transform⇨Scale and change the size of the combo box if you want to make the combo box wider in order to make the menu items more legible.**

12. **Decide which elements of your Flash movie will change when a menu item in the combo box is selected and add those elements to the Flash movie if you haven't already done so.**

    If for example, you decide that the contents of a dynamic text box will change when a menu item in the combo box is selected, create a dynamic text box on the Stage and give it an instance name, such as myInfo3. (See Chapter 5 to learn about creating dynamic text.)

13. **Choose Window⇨Development Panels⇨Actions to open the Actions panel if it isn't open already.**

14. **Select Frame 1 in the Timeline and type in this code in the Script pane of the Actions panel:**

```
myForm3 = new Object();
myForm3.change = function(myEvent3){
    myInfo3.text = myComboBox.selectedItem.label;
}
myComboBox.addEventListener("change",myForm3);
```

    You can replace myForm3, myEvent3, myInfo3, and myComboBox with any names that you like. myInfo3 in this example is the name of the dynamic text field that we mention in Step 12, and myComboBox is the instance name of your combo box.

Line 1 of the code above creates a new little bundle of methods and properties named myForm3. Line 5 adds an event listener to myForm3 so that when you select one of the menu items in myComboBox, the code in lines 2, 3, and 4 sets the text of the dynamic text field to whatever is the label of the combo box menu item that you select.

The third line of code shows an example of how to change the contents of the dynamic text box that we describe in Step 12, but you can replace this line with other ActionScript code to do something else in your movie to respond to changes in which menu item in the combo box is selected.

Using list boxes in a Flash movie

To use list boxes in your Flash movie, follow these steps:

1. **Choose Window⇨Development Panels⇨Components to view the Components panel if it's not already open.**

2. **Drag a list box from the Components panel onto the Stage.**

3. **Choose Window⇨Properties to open the Property inspector if it's not already open. If necessary (Windows only), click the collapse arrow on the Property inspector title bar to expand it.**

   The Property inspector lists four parameters: Data, Labels, Multiple Selection, and Row Height.

4. **Type a name in the Instance Name text field in the left corner of the Property inspector.**

5. **To create items in the list box, double-click in the Labels text field.**

   The Values dialog box appears.

6. **In the Values dialog box, click the plus sign to add a list item or click the minus sign to delete a list item. Click the upward-pointing triangle to move an item up on the list, and click the downward-pointing triangle to move an item down on the list.**

   When you add an item to the list, it is cleverly named defaultValue.

7. **To change a list item's name from defaultValue to something more useful, click the menu item in the Values dialog box and type a more descriptive name there.**

8. **Click OK.**

   The Values dialog box closes.

9. **To set whether the user can select multiple items on the list, click the drop-down menu for the Multiple Selection parameter and choose True or False.**

   Choosing True allows the user to select multiple items on the list. Choosing False allows the user to select only one item on the list.

10. **To change the height (in pixels) of each item in the list, click the Row Height field on the Property inspector and type a new number.**

    The default height is 20 pixels.

11. **Choose Modify⇨Transform⇨Scale and change the size of the list box if you want to make the list box wider in order to make the menu items more legible.**

12. **Decide which elements of your Flash movie will change when a menu item in the list box is selected and add those elements to the Flash movie if you haven't already done so.**

    If for example, you decide that the contents of a dynamic text box will change when a list item is selected, create a dynamic text box on the Stage and give it an instance name, such as `myInfo4`. (See Chapter 5 to discover how to create dynamic text.)

13. **Choose Window⇨Development Panels⇨Actions to open the Actions panel if it isn't open already.**

14. **Select Frame 1 in the Timeline and enter this code in the Script pane of the Actions panel:**

```
myForm4 = new Object();
myForm4.change = function(myEvent4){
    myInfo4.text = myListBox.selectedItem.label;
}
myListBox.addEventListener("change",myForm4);
```

    You can replace `myForm4`, `myEvent4`, `myInfo4`, and `myListBox` with any names that you like. `myInfo4` in this example is the name of the dynamic text field that we mention in Step 12, and `myListBox` is the instance name of your list box.

Line 1 of the code above creates a new little bundle of methods and properties named `myForm4`. Line 5 adds an event listener to `myForm4` so that when you select one of the menu items in `myListBox`, the code in lines 2, 3, and 4 sets the text of the dynamic text field to whatever is the label of the list box menu item that you select.

The third line of code shows an example of how to change the contents of the dynamic text box that we describe in Step 12, but you can replace this line with other ActionScript code to do something else in your movie to respond to changes in which menu item in the list box is selected.

Using scroll panes in a Flash movie

Scroll panes allow you to put a movie clip, a JPEG image, or a SWF file inside a pane with scroll bars. This feature is useful if you want to display big movies or images without taking up lots of space on the Stage.

To add a scroll pane to your Flash movie, follow these steps:

1. **Choose Window⇨Development Panels⇨Components to view the Components panel if it's not already open.**

2. **Drag a scroll pane from the Components panel onto the Stage.**

3. **Choose Window⇨Properties to open the Property inspector if it's not already open. If necessary (Windows only), click the collapse arrow on the Property inspector title bar to expand it.**

   The Property inspector lists these parameters: Content Path, Horizontal Line Scroll Size, Horizontal Line Page Size, Horizontal Scroll Policy, Scroll Drag, Vertical Line Scroll Size, and Vertical Scroll Policy.

4. **To set the content of the scroll pane, click the Content Path field on the Property inspector and type the symbol linkage ID of the movie clip that you want to display. Alternatively, you can type the relative or absolute path to a JPEG image file or an SWF file.**

   For information on creating a symbol linkage ID, see the section on shared libraries in this chapter.

5. **To specify whether horizontal or vertical scroll bars are displayed, click the Horizontal Scroll Policy drop-down menu or the Vertical Scroll Policy drop-down menu and choose Auto, True, or False.**

   True means that the scroll bar will be displayed. False means that it won't. Auto means that the scroll bar will be displayed only if necessary. Therefore, Auto is usually a good choice.

6. **To specify whether the user must scroll in the window by grabbing and dragging the image or by grabbing and dragging the scroll bars, click in the Scroll Drag drop-down menu and choose True or False.**

   True means that the user must drag the image. False means that the user must drag the scroll bars. False is the default.

7. **To change the number of pixels that a scroll bar moves horizontally or vertically each time that you push one of the scroll bar's arrow buttons, click the Horizontal Line Scroll Size or Vertical Line Scroll Size field on the Property inspector and type the number that you want.**

   The default value is 5 pixels.

8. **To change the number of pixels that a scroll bar moves horizontally or vertically each time that you push the scroll bar track (above or below one of the scroll bar arrow buttons), click the Horizontal Page Scroll Size or Vertical Page Scroll Size field on the Property inspector and type the number that you want.**

   The default value is 20 pixels.

Using windows in a Flash movie

Windows allow you to put a movie clip, a JPEG image, or a SWF file inside a draggable window with a title bar, a border, and an optional Close button. The window appears inside your Flash movie. You can't drag the window outside your movie.

To add a window to your Flash movie, follow these steps:

1. **Choose Window⇨Development Panels⇨Components to view the Components panel if it's not already open.**

2. **Drag a window component from the Components panel onto the Stage.**

3. **Choose Window⇨Properties to open the Property inspector if it's not already open. If necessary (Windows only), click the collapse arrow on the Property inspector title bar to expand it.**

   The Property inspector lists three parameters: Close Button, Content Path, and Title.

4. **To set the content of the window, click the Content Path field on the Property inspector and type the symbol linkage ID of the movie clip that you want to display. Alternatively, type the relative or absolute path to a JPEG image file or an SWF file.**

   For information on creating a symbol linkage ID, see the section on shared libraries in this chapter.

5. **To specify whether the window has a close button, click the Close Button drop-down menu and choose True or False.**

   True means that the Close button will be displayed. False means that it won't. Some tricky ActionScript code is needed to make the window close when you click the Close button, so for now, choose False.

6. **To specify the name of the window that will appear in its title bar, click the Title field on the Property inspector and type a name.**

Creating an Entire Web Site with Flash

You can use Flash to create the complete user interface, along with all the graphics and text on your site. Typically, a fully Flashed site has the following structure:

✔ An HTML home page that contains these items:

   • Tests for the Flash Player and Player version

   • Automatic or user-controlled download of the Flash Player from Macromedia

   • A button that leads viewers to: an HTML site if they have a slow connection or don't want to download the Flash Player; or JavaScript that takes them there automatically

   • A Flash Player movie (perhaps requiring the latest Flash Player) including a preloader (if needed) and all the visual content of the page, with all text, graphics and navigation created in Flash

✔ Additional HTML pages, like the above page, for all the remaining pages in the Web site. (You may want these pages to also test for Flash in case your viewers don't enter the site via your home page.)

✔ An HTML page for those without the required version of Flash, suggesting that they download and install it.

✔ HTML pages that contains a non-Flash version of the Web site (if you want the site to be available to those who don't have and don't want to install the required version of Flash).

For information on creating an HTML page that tests for the Flash Player, see the "Testing for the Flash Player" section, later in this chapter.

The opening HTML page is the first thing that your viewers see. On the World Wide Web, first impressions are important if you want to your audience to stick around, so be sure to think carefully about what your goals are for this page. (See Chapter 15 for our top 10 tips on Web design.)

To match a Flash movie in a Web page to the rest of the page, match the background colors of the movie (by choosing Modify⇨Document) and the HTML page. (This technique doesn't work if your Web page uses an image for a background.) To set the background of the HTML page, edit the HTML file that Flash creates when you publish your movie. After determining the background color in hexadecimal code (by looking at the HTML code for the existing Web page), change the `BGCOLOR` tag in the HTML code in three places:

✔ In the background color where it reads `<BODY bgcolor="#99CCFF">` (for example)

✔ In the `OBJECT` tag where it reads `<PARAM NAME=bgcolor VALUE=#99CCFF>`

✔ In the `EMBED` code where it reads `BGCOLOR=#99CCFF`

After people get to your Flash page, you can do whatever you want. Some sites using Flash start with an intro, which is a preliminary movie that can either briefly explain what your site is for, or is used just wow your viewers. An intro is probably a bad idea. You probably want people to get to the main content of your site immediately. If the information in your intro is valuable, put that information in the main content of your site instead, where people won't feel annoyed that they are forced to view it.

Your site probably contains buttons that people can choose to navigate through your site, get more information, or contact you.

You can create the navigation structure in three main ways:

✔ Attach `On (mouse event)` or `Load Movie` actions to the buttons to display the content of movie clips or Flash Player movies (`.swf` files).

✔ Attach `getURL` actions to the buttons to link to other HTML pages or movies on your site. You can, of course, create the HTML pages with Flash.

✔ Use the buttons to display information or graphics located on other parts of your Timeline by using the `gotoAndPlay` or `gotoAndStop` action.

The `On (mouse event)` and `Load Movie` actions are described in Chapter 10. The `getURL` action is explained in Chapters 8 (with regard to buttons) and 10. You can use combinations of these methods. For example, you can use `On (mouse event)` to display information when the mouse cursor is over a button, along with `getURL` to link to another page when the button is clicked.

Creating navigation with getURL

When you attach a `getURL` action to a button, the button links to another HTML page in the same way that a button on a regular, non-Flash, HTML Web page does. For more information on the `getURL` action, refer to Chapter 10. Also, Chapter 8 explains how to add an action to a button.

Using the Timeline to store Web content

In most cases, you use the Timeline to display frames in sequence — in other words, animation. But the Timeline can also store static frames. You can create anything on the Stage in those frames, and you can display what is in those frames whenever you want.

Suppose that you have several buttons on the left side of your page. You want viewers to see different graphics and animation on the right side of the page when they click each button. Perhaps clicking one button displays information about a product. Clicking another button may display information about a second product.

To create a set of buttons that move the playhead to different sections of the Timeline, follow these steps:

1. **Place instances of your buttons in separate layers on the first frame of the Timeline of your movie.**

2. **On each layer, about 20 or so frames after the first frame, add a keyframe.**

   These 20 or so frames leave room to store static display frames or movie clips on the Timeline. The buttons continue to be displayed throughout the movie until the ending keyframe. If you have a lot of buttons, you may need to choose a keyframe greater than 20. The more buttons you want to provide descriptions for, the further out your ending keyframe needs to be.

3. **Create a new layer to display the right side of the page and give it a name, such as *Product Views*.**

4. **A few frames out (on Frame 10, for example) on the Product Views layer, create a keyframe.**

   This step starts a Timeline section for the product displayed when the user clicks your first button.

5. **Open the Property inspector if it's not already open (choose Window⇨Properties).**

6. **In the Frame Label text box on the left side of the Property inspector, type a label name.**

7. **On the Stage, create the graphics and words that you want to be displayed when a user clicks your first button. If you want to display animation when a user clicks your first button, drag a movie clip from the Library. (Refer to Chapter 7 for the scoop on creating movie clips.)**

   Place the graphics so that they don't cover your buttons when they appear.

8. **Repeat Steps 4 through 7 to create labels and displays on the Product Views layer for all your buttons, using subsequent sections of the Timeline until you reach the ending keyframe.**

9. **Select your first button.**

10. **Choose Window⇨Development Panels⇨Actions to open the Actions panel.**

11. **In the list on the left side of the Actions panel, choose the Global Functions category, then the Movie Clip Control subcategory, and then double-click** on.

    This code appears in the Script pane of the Actions panel:

    ```
    On () {
    }
    ```

    A list of suggested parameters also pops up.

12. **From the list of suggested parameters, choose Release.**

    The Release event causes the action to occur when your viewer presses and releases the mouse button.

13. **Click to reposition your cursor at the end of the current line.**

14. **In the list on the left side of the Actions panel, choose the Global Functions category, then the Timeline Control subcategory, and then double-click** gotoAndStop.

    gotoAndStop(); appears in the Script pane of the Actions panel.

15. **Type a quotation mark, then the name of the first label that you created on your Timeline in Step 6, followed by a quotation mark.**

    Your ActionScript should look like the one shown in Figure 12-4.

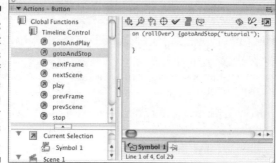

Figure 12-4: ActionScript that displays a section of the Timeline when the viewer presses a button.

16. **Repeat Steps 9 through 15 for the rest of your buttons and their respective frame labels.**

17. **Create a new layer and name it *Actions*.**

18. **Place a** Stop **action on the first frame.**

Refer to Chapter 10 for instructions on how to add an action to a frame.

If you don't do this final step, your movie simply plays through all the frames, displaying your descriptions one after another. You want viewers to see those frames only when they click a button.

Choose Control⇨Test Movie to try it out! When you press a button, the graphics, text, and movie clip animation on the appropriate frames appear.

If you choose Roll Over instead of Release in Step 12, you can display different information when the mouse cursor passes over each button. Figure 12-5 shows a Timeline with frames that are displayed when the mouse cursor passes over buttons.

Figure 12-5: You can use the Timeline to display different graphics and text when the mouse cursor passes over each button.

Look for HelpDesk-Timeline.fla in the Ch12 folder of the CD-ROM for an example of buttons that use the Timeline to display information about the purpose of the buttons. To test the move, choose Control⇨Test Movie. To see the ActionScript for the buttons, select a button and choose Window⇨ Development Panels⇨Actions to open the Actions panel. To see the ActionScript for a frame, click a frame with an *a* in it and choose Window⇨Development Panels⇨Actions to open the Actions panel.

Testing for the Flash Player

Although most people have the Flash Player installed, you may still have some viewers with totally out-of-date browsers. For viewers that don't have the Flash Player, it often downloads automatically as a result of the code that Flash places in the HTML file. If not, those viewers simply may not be able to view your site. You can test for the presence of the Flash Player and, even more, you can test to see which version of the Flash Player they have. If you're using features that exist only in Flash MX 2004, you want to make sure that viewers have Flash Player 7 player because people may still have Flash Player 6 (or an even earlier version) installed.

You can test for the Flash Player in several ways; we describe two possibilities in the following sections.

Letting the user decide

Some sites let the viewer simply choose between a Flash site and a non-Flash site. The problem with this method is that many users have no idea what Flash is, let alone whether they have the Flash Player.

A better method to let users determine whether they have the Flash Player is to place a small Flash animation that is also a button on an initial HTML Web page. Instructions tell them to click the button if they can see the animation, which links them to the main portion of your Flash site. If they cannot see the animation, you can offer an image with a link (or linked text) to the Macromedia Flash Player download site and another link to an alternative HTML site. (Refer to Chapter 8 for instructions on creating a Flash button.)

At the very least, you should offer users the opportunity to download the Flash Player. Do this with a link connecting them to the following URL:

```
www.macromedia.com/go/getflashplayer
```

Detecting the Flash Player version

A more sophisticated method is to automatically test for the version of the Flash Player. You can have one site for Flash Player 5 or later, one for Flash Player 7 or later, and a third HTML site for neither. Sounds complicated, no? But if you're very attached to effects that exist only in Flash MX 2004 (and Flash Player 7), you may have no other choice.

Here's an ActionScript that you can place in the first frame of a movie. In this case, the ActionScript finds any player greater than or equal to Version 4:

```
if (getVersion().substring(4, 5) >= 4) {
  gotoAndStop (10);
} else {
  gotoAndStop (15);
}
```

To be precise, this method can test for versions greater than 4.0r11. You cannot reliably use it to test for earlier versions. Also, it works only for users running Windows or Mac OS, not Unix or Linux.

Line 1 evaluates the portion of the text string returned by the `getVersion` function that gives you the version number. (Other portions return the platform — such as Mac or Windows — revision number, and so on.) It then tests whether the version is greater than or equal to 4. You can specify which version it tests. For example, in place of >=4, you can put ==7 (with two equal signs) to test whether your viewer has Flash Player 7.

Line 2 sends the movie to Frame 10 and stops. You can change this line to do anything that you want. For example, you can use the `getURL` action to send your viewer to another HTML page with your main Flash movie. You can also load a movie. (Refer to Chapter 10 for an explanation of the `gotoAndStop`, `getURL`, and `Load Movie` actions.)

Line 3 starts the alternative that happens if your test in Line 1 is not true — in this case, if the player version is not greater than or equal to 4.

Line 4 sends your viewer to Frame 15 and stops. Again, you can change this as we explain for the code of Line 2.

To test this code, follow these steps (we assume that you have Flash Player 7):

1. **Type the ActionScript just provided in your movie's first frame.**

   Chapter 10 explains how to place ActionScript in a frame.

2. **Add a keyframe in Frame 10 and place some text there that reads** `Frame 10.`

3. **Add a keyframe in Frame 15 and place some text that there that reads** `Frame 15.`

4. **Choose File⇨Publish Preview⇨Default.**

   This step creates an `.swf` Flash Player file from your movie.

   Because you have a Flash Player greater than or equal to Version 4, you should see `Frame 10` on your screen.

5. **Close the browser window and change** `>=4` **on Line 1 of the ActionScript to** `==5`.

6. **Save your movie and go to Publish Preview again.**

   This time, you should see `Frame 15` on your screen because the test in Line 1 was not true.

You can continue to play around with the ActionScript until you have something that works for you.

A more thorough way to detect a particular Flash Player version is to simply mark the Detect Flash Version check box in the HTML tab in Flash's Publish Settings before you publish your movie. (See Chapter 13 for the scoop on specifying Publish Settings.) This does a great job of detecting a particular Flash Player version but generates a lot of fairly fancy JavaScript code. This works really well if you don't need to customize the code, but the code is not easy for beginners to customize.

Creating alternative sites

However you direct viewers, you must create sites that they can see. Many Flash sites also include a complete set of non-Flash (HTML) pages for viewers who don't have the Flash Player and don't want to bother downloading it.

If you use features unique to Flash MX 2004, you can also create a Flash 5 site that uses only features available in Flash 5. The overwhelming majority of Web surfers have Flash Player 5 or later. But don't forget how much time you spend updating your Web site now. Imagine updating three sites! Make sure that you think through the consequences of having so many alternatives.

For detailed and up-to-the-minute information on how many computer users have which versions of the Flash player, check out the latest Macromedia statistics at `www.macromedia.com/software/ player_census/flashplayer`.

Using the Movie Explorer

The Movie Explorer is a great tool for analyzing an entire movie. When you start creating complex relationships among several Timelines, you may find that it's hard to remember what you've done. The Movie Explorer lays out the entire structure of your movie for you to see. The Movie Explorer is also a great tool for troubleshooting problems that may arise. By visually displaying your movie's components, you can more easily find where the trouble lies.

Another use for the Movie Explorer is to analyze other people's FLA files. When you open someone else's movie, you may wonder where the movie is. It may all be hidden in movie clips and actions that call other movies and movie clips. The Movie Explorer can help you ferret out the magic behind the animation.

To open the Movie Explorer, choose Window➪Other Panels➪Movie Explorer. The Movie Explorer is shown in Figure 12-6.

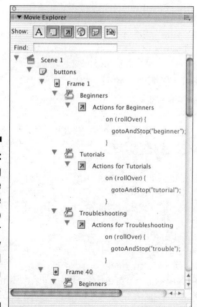

Figure 12-6:
Go exploring with the Movie Explorer to discover the many nooks and crannies in a movie.

You usually know what you're looking for when you open the Movie Explorer. For example, you may be looking for ActionScript or movie clips. Use the buttons at the top of the Movie Explorer to specify which movie elements are shown in the main window:

✔ **Show Text:** Displays all text objects in the movie.

✔ **Show Buttons, Movie Clips, and Graphics:** Displays a list of those objects.

✔ **Show Action Scripts:** Lists all ActionScript in the movie.

✔ **Show Video, Sounds, and Bitmaps:** Lists those objects.

✔ **Show Frames and Layers:** Shows each frame and each layer that contains objects.

✔ **Customize Which Items to Show:** Opens the Movie Explorer Settings dialog box, where you can indicate which items you want to show by marking or clearing them in a list of check boxes. You can also choose to display Movie Elements (scenes), Symbol Definitions (a separate listing by symbol), or both. Click OK to close this dialog box.

Movie elements are shown in a hierarchical manner in the Movie Explorer. For example, if a button has an action attached to it, you see a plus (+) sign (Windows) or a right-pointing triangle (Mac) next to the button. Click any plus sign (Windows) or right-pointing triangle (Mac) to expand the display, in this case to reveal the ActionScript for that button. Click any minus (–) sign (Windows) or downward-pointing triangle (Mac) to collapse the display.

In the Find text box, you can type any expression to search the entire movie. Suppose that you want to know whether a movie contains the getURL action. Just type **getURL** in the Find text box, and the Movie Explorer displays every instance containing that word.

The Find feature is not case-sensitive, but it finds only whole words. Therefore, if the movie contains *getURL* and you type **URL**, you don't get any result at all. You also don't get anything if you type **get URL** (two words).

You can use the Movie Explorer to select objects on the Stage or frames. Just click the item in the Movie Explorer, and Flash selects the object or frame. (If you select a frame, Flash also includes the frames up to the next keyframe.) If you select a scene, Flash selects the first frame of the scene.

The Movie Explorer contains an extensive menu that you can access by either clicking in the upper-right corner of the Movie Explorer panel or right-clicking (Windows) or Control+clicking (Mac) inside the Movie Explorer panel.

Some of the more useful features of this menu are

- **Find in Library:** Opens the Library (if it's not already open) and high-lights the object that you previously selected in the Movie Explorer.

- **Rename:** Lets you rename the selected object, such as a button instance.

- **Copy All Text to Clipboard:** Copies all the text in the Movie Explorer to the Clipboard (of course) so that you can paste it into another application.

- **Print:** Prints the entire contents of the Movie Explorer. All items, whether collapsed or not, are printed.

If you have difficulty understanding one of the more advanced Flash movies on the CD-ROM, try opening the Movie Explorer in the movie. Look for actions and movie clips. You may be surprised at what you can discover by using this tool.

If you're building a slide presentation using screens as we describe earlier in this chapter, the Movie Explorer works a little differently. It only displays the contents of the current screen — the screen selected in the Screens Outline pane. Also, Flash documents with screens don't contain scenes, so obviously for those documents, you can't view scenes in the Movie Explorer.

Making Your Site More Accessible

Flash includes capabilities that make it possible for you to make Flash more accessible to people with disabilities.

Most of the components in Flash MX 2004 are designed to be accessible to the visually impaired, through the use of screen readers, which generate a spoken description of the contents of your Flash screen. Screen reader software is widely available from a variety of companies.

Users can also navigate around most of Flash's components by using the keyboard rather than the mouse — this is automatically built into the components. Macromedia has also added some new features to ActionScript that can enhance the accessibility of Flash documents.

One of the easiest ways to make your Flash movie more accessible to people with disabilities is to use the Accessibility panel. When you add buttons, movie clips, text, Input Text fields, or components to your movie, you can use the Accessibility panel to make them accessible to screen readers. (Not all components can be made accessible, but most can.) To make a button, movie clip, text, Input Text field, or component accessible, follow these steps:

1. **Choose Window➪Other Panels➪Accessibility to open the Accessibility panel if it's not already open. If necessary (Windows only), click the collapse arrow on the Accessibility panel title bar to expand it.**

2. **Select the button, movie clip, text, Input Text field, or component on the Stage.**

3. **In the Accessibility panel, select Make Object Accessible.**

4. **If you selected a movie clip in Step 2, select Make Child Objects Accessible in the Accessibility panel if you want objects embedded within the movie clip to also be accessible. For example, select this if you want to allow text objects in the movie clip to be read by the screen reader software.**

5. **In the Accessibility panel's Name text field, type in a name for the symbol or component.**

   This name may be read aloud by the screen reader.

6. **In the Accessibility panel Description text field, type in a description of the symbol or component.**

   This description may also be read aloud by the screen reader.

7. **In the Accessibility panel Shortcut text field, type in a keyboard short-cut that viewers can use to select this object, if appropriate (if for instance, it's a radio button, and needs to be selected to receive input).**

   The screen reader can then use this information to read aloud something like, "The shortcut for this text field is Ctrl+K." (Not all screen readers support this feature.) Typing in information in the Shortcut text field doesn't actually implement keyboard shortcut functionality. You need to use ActionScript to detect and respond to any shortcut keypresses.

8. **In the Accessibility panel Tab Index field, enter the number of corre-sponding to this object's tab index value, if appropriate.**

    The *tab index* determines how users can use the Tab key to navigate through and select one the buttons, check boxes, and other controls in your movie. For example, suppose that you have three buttons with a tab index of 1, 2, and 3, respectively. When the movie starts, if the user presses the Tab key three times, the button with the tab index of 3 would be selected for input.

If you have the Accessibility panel open when nothing in your movie is selected, the panel offers you the option to Make Movie Accessible, which is selected by default. This allows screen readers to read the different objects in the Flash movie. You definitely want this option selected if you want to make your movie accessible to screen readers and other hardware and software for people with disabilities. Of course, you also have to name each object by using the Accessibility panel, as we describe above, for this to be useful.

Chapter 13

Publishing Your Flash Files

Y our Flash movie is done. Now you need to publish it in its final form —
most likely an `.swf` file that you can post on your Web site. In this chapter, we explain how to prepare a Flash movie for publishing and help you
determine the ideal publish settings for your needs. You also have the option
to publish to other graphic file formats (such as GIF, JPEG, QuickTime, AVI,
and others) in case you want to create a non-Flash site or use your material
in another program. We discuss these other file formats as well. We cover all
the bases so that you can get your animation up and running.

The filenames of Flash-published movies end with the `.swf` suffix. Note that
although the letters *SWF* originally stood for *Shockwave Flash,* Macromedia
no longer uses that term for Flash-published movies, although the letters
remain the same. So, to follow the Macromedia usage, we refer to SWF files as
Flash Player files. Flash converts your movie data into a highly compact and
efficient form in an SWF file, so that your SWF file contains only the information needed for playback of your movies. In contrast, when you save your

movies by choosing File⇨Save (or File⇨Save As), they are saved with the .fla suffix. They are saved in a format that can be read by the Flash MX 2004 application, but not the Flash Player. The .fla file contains lots of information about layers, Library items, your video source files, and so on, which you need when you are creating your movies and which the Flash Player doesn't need.

Optimizing Your Movies for Speed

Throughout this book, we offer suggestions for designing a Flash movie with speed in mind. In this section, we put them together so that you can review your movie as a whole before you publish it.

Simplifying artwork

By simplifying the artwork in your movie, you can greatly reduce the size of a Flash movie, thereby increasing its speed. Here are the most important techniques:

- **Use symbols for every object that appears more than once.** You can turn any object or group of objects into a symbol. Nest your symbols — for example, turn an object into a symbol and then use it in a movie clip or button. Remember that you can change the color of symbol instances — you don't need to create a new symbol. (Chapter 7 covers symbols in detail.)

- **Group objects whenever possible.** Groups are almost as efficient as symbols. (Chapter 4 explains how to create groups.)

- **Avoid bitmaps as much as possible.** If you must use bitmaps, use them only for still elements — don't animate them. (Chapter 3 explains how to import a bitmap and how to turn it into a vector graphic by tracing the bitmap.)

- **Optimize curves (choose Modify⇨Shape⇨Optimize).** Whenever possible, optimize curves to reduce the number of lines used to create a shape. (Refer to Chapter 4 for further explanation.)

- **Use solid lines rather than dashed, dotted, and other line types when possible.** Try to avoid custom line widths. (We explain line types in Chapter 3.)

- **Use the Pencil tool rather than the Brush tool whenever possible.** The Pencil tool uses fewer bytes in your movie.

✔ **Use the Web-safe color palette.** Avoid custom colors. (Refer to Chapter 3 for the lowdown on colors.) Custom color definitions are kept with the Flash Player file.

✔ **Use solid fills rather than gradients.** Gradients are more complex and make the Flash Player file bigger.

Optimizing text

Text can also consume lots of bytes. Here's what you can do to reduce the byte bite:

✔ **Reduce the number of fonts and font styles (bold, italic) as much as possible.** Use simpler sans serif fonts if you can. You get the best results size-wise with the device fonts (sans, serif, and typewriter), although you may find these device fonts boring. Flash doesn't need to store the outlines of device fonts in the .swf file, so these take up fewer bytes. (Refer to Chapter 5 for more information on fonts.)

✔ **If you create text fields, limit the text and specify any restrictions that you can in the Character Options dialog box.** (Choose Window⇨ Property to open the Property inspector if it's not already open, and then click Character in the Property inspector to open the Character Options dialog box.) For example, exclude unnecessary character out-lines, such as numbers.

If you have lots of text, consider which text really needs to be in the Flash file and which text can be created by using HyperText Markup Language (HTML). For example, you can insert a Flash file on part of your Web page and add HTML-based text on the other part of the page.

Using shared libraries

If you're using some of the same elements in more than one movie, you can put them into a shared library, and then your audience will need to download them only once. This can be especially useful for items that can be large, like music and fonts. Refer to Chapter 12 for the details on shared libraries.

Compressing sound

You can compress sounds to reduce file size. When you compress individual sounds in the Sound Properties dialog box, you can fine-tune settings for each individual sound in your movie. Later in this chapter, we review how to compress sound when you publish a Flash movie. Use the MP3 format whenever possible because it compresses well. If you need more information on compressing sounds, check out Chapter 11.

Here are some other ways that you can reduce the size of your sound files:

- ✔ Adjust the sound's Time In and Time Out points to prevent silent areas from being stored in your .swf file.
- ✔ Reuse sounds by using different In and Out points and by looping different parts of the same sound.
- ✔ Don't loop streaming sound.

Refer to Chapter 11 for more information on editing, looping, and streaming sound.

Animating efficiently

One of the most effective ways to reduce file size is to use tweens (refer to Chapter 9) whenever possible. Frame-by-frame animation creates larger files. Keeping animation localized in one area also helps. Small animations (animations where the objects don't move much) use less space than wide-area animations. Finally, place non-animated objects on different layers from animated objects.

Testing Movies

Before publishing your movie, you should test it. The first step is to simply play your animation, as we explain in Chapter 9. But playing the animation on the Stage doesn't provide you with enough information to determine the file size. Movie clips and certain actions that interface with other movies (such as Load Movie) don't function from within your .fla file. To find those kinds of bugs, you have to test your movie in a browser. This section tells you how to test both ways.

Flash MX 2004 is optimized for the tasks (such as drawing, adding keyframes, showing and hiding layers, typing in ActionScript code, and so on) that you perform when creating a Flash movie. It's not optimized for playing back your animation — the Flash Player is optimized for that. Your .fla file contains lots of information that you need when you're creating your movies and which the Flash Player doesn't need. The Flash Player only plays .swf files, which you can create when you choose File➪Publish.

Using the Test Movie command

After playing your animation, you want to use the Test Movie (or Test Scene) command. These commands provide estimates of downloading speed, so you can find bottlenecks that pause your animation. You can also see the results of movie clips and all actions.

To test a movie or scene, follow these steps:

1. **Choose Control⇨Test Movie (or Test Scene).**

   Flash publishes your movie to an .swf file by using the current settings in the Publish Settings dialog box (see the section "Publishing Flash Movies," later in this chapter) and opens a new window. You see your animation run. You can change the settings in the Publish Settings dialog box (choose File⇨Publish Settings) before using this command.

2. **Choose View⇨Download Settings and choose a downloading speed between 14.4 Kbps and 131.2 Kbps.**

   To specify your own settings, choose Customize, and in the Custom Modem Settings dialog box, enter the menu text that you want to appear on the menu and the bit rate in bytes per second. Click OK. Then open the Download Settings menu again and choose your customized setting, which now appears on the menu.

3. **Choose View⇨Bandwidth Profiler to see the graph showing downloading performance.**

   The bandwidth profiler (as shown in Figure 13-1) displays the byte size of each individual frame. Frames whose bars rise above the lower red, horizontal line cause loading delays.

Figure 13-1: When you test a movie, Flash displays tools to help you analyze the downloading performance of your movie.

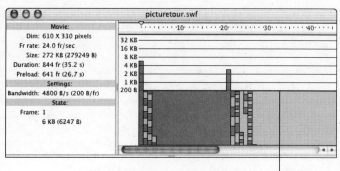

Frames with bars above this line cause loading delays.

4. **To see settings for any one frame, stop the movie by clicking the frame's bar.**

   To the left of the bandwidth profiler, Flash displays the movie's statistics — dimensions, frame rate, file size, movie duration, and the amount of animation to preload in frames and seconds. You also see the size of each individual frame.

5. **Choose View⇨Streaming Graph to see how the Flash movie streams into a browser.**

6. **Choose View⇨Frame by Frame Graph to see which frames contribute to delays. A frame whose bar extends above the red line may cause a bottleneck.**

   By default, Flash opens the SWF window in Streaming Graph mode.

7. **To close the SWF window, click its Close button.**

After you analyze your movie, you can go back and optimize it to eliminate delays. A short delay in the first frame is usually acceptable, but significant delays during the movie result in jerky animation or pauses.

If you have a long movie divided into scenes, you can save time by using the `Test Scene` command instead of the `Test Movie` command.

Testing a movie in a Web browser

The final steps of testing a movie are publishing it and viewing it in a Web browser. For a quick view, you can use the `Publish Preview` command. Flash publishes your movie to an `.swf` file, creates the appropriate HTML file, and opens the HTML file in your default browser. Viewing your Flash Player file in a browser reveals how the browser will display the movie when you upload it to a Web site.

Flash uses the current settings in the Publish Settings dialog box to create the preview, including the types of file formats that you have selected.

To preview your movie in a browser, follow these steps:

1. **Choose File⇨Publish Settings to open the Publish Settings dialog box and choose the desired file formats and publish settings.**

   See the "Publishing Flash Movies" section, later in this chapter, for more information on the Publish Settings dialog box.

2. **Choose File⇨Publish Preview and choose the desired format from the submenu.**

   Generally, you can use the first (default) HTML option, but if you have specified HTML settings, choose the second HTML option. Flash opens your browser and runs your movie.

3. **Close your browser to end the preview.**

As with any Web page material, you need to consider the following when testing a Flash Player file:

- ✔ **The browser that your audience is using:** Preview your Flash Player file in the current version of both Internet Explorer (IE) and Netscape Navigator, if possible. Ideally, you should try out at least one earlier version of each one, too. And you should test it in Safari on a Mac. Okay, so you probably won't do all this, but don't say that we didn't tell you.

- ✔ **The resolution of viewers' screens:** Test at least the following most common settings: 640 x 480, 800 x 600, and 1024 x 768. Remember that the amount of material that appears on the screen changes with the resolution. If you preview at 640 x 480, you can be sure that people with higher resolutions can see your entire movie.

- ✔ **The color settings of viewers' screens:** Common color settings range from 256 colors to 16 million. If you're using custom colors, some viewers may not see them accurately.

Professional Web site developers take this testing phase seriously. No matter how good an animation looks on your screen, if it doesn't translate well to a majority of viewers' screens, it's not a good animation.

Saving Your Work in Flash MX Format

If you're collaborating on a Flash project with a group of friends or co-workers and they're still using Flash MX (the predecessor of Flash MX 2004), there is still hope for them. You can save your work in Flash MX format.

To save your work in Flash MX format, follow these steps:

1. **Choose File⇨Save As.**

   The Save As dialog box appears.

2. **In the Save As dialog box, choose where you want to save your file and type the filename that you want.**

3. **In the Save As dialog box, click the Format pop-up menu and choose Flash MX.**

4. **Click Save.**

If you're using features new to Flash MX 2004, a window appears, listing the new features that won't be saved in the Flash MX file and asking whether you want to continue. Click the Save as Flash MX button if you want to continue.

Publishing Flash Movies

So you're finally ready to publish your Flash masterpiece. It's time to choose File⇨Publish Settings. Don't be overwhelmed by all the options. Usually, you use only a few of them. Start by specifying the settings. Then publish the movie to create the .swf file viewed on a Web page.

After you specify the settings, you can click OK rather than Publish if you want to go back to your Flash movie file and choose Control⇨Test Movie to see the results of your settings. You can try various settings until you're satisfied. Then click Publish to create the final SWF (Flash Player) file. Published files are in the same folder as your FLA movie file by default; you can specify another location if you wish. Of course, you can also move the files afterward.

The Publish Settings dialog box lets you easily specify all your settings in one place. Then you click the Publish button, and Flash creates the SWF (Flash Player) file according to your settings. Choose File⇨Publish Settings to open the Publish Settings dialog box, as shown in Figure 13-2, with the Formats tab on top.

Flash automatically names the files that it creates for you, using the Flash movie's name and adding the appropriate file extension, such as .html and .swf. You can see the names in the Publish Settings dialog box when you have the Formats tab on top. To specify your own name for a file, click in the File text box and type the name that you want. To revert back to the default filenames, click the Use Default Names button.

Most of the time, you need only the Flash (SWF) and HTML formats. But if you want other formats, select them on the Formats tab. When you mark an additional format, the dialog box adds a new tab for that format (except for the projector formats, which don't need one).

After you mark the formats that you want, click each tab to specify the settings for that format. The next few sections of this chapter explain each format, why you may want to use it, and how to specify the settings.

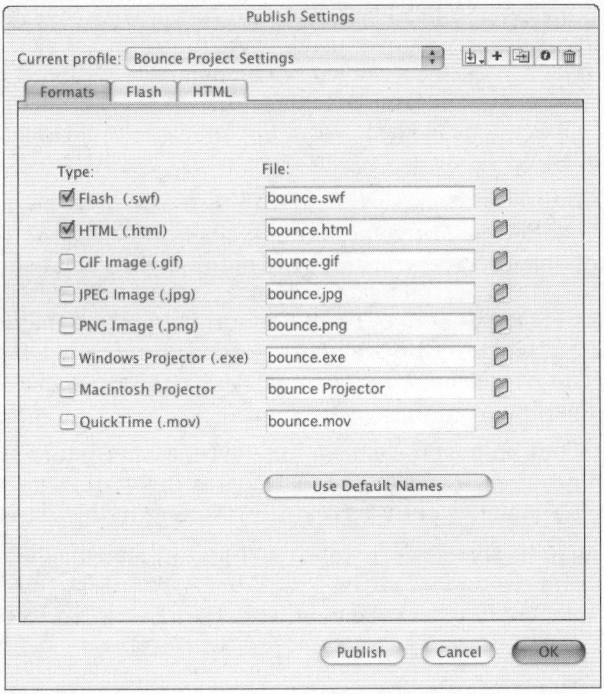

Figure 13-2:
The Publish
Settings
dialog box
is your
one-stop
place for
starting the
publishing
process of
your Flash
movie.

After you finish specifying all your settings, click the Publish button, and
Flash does your bidding, creating the files that you need to put your great
creation on the Web.

Publishing to SWF

The second tab in the Publish Settings dialog box is the Flash tab, which creates the Flash Player file, also called an .swf file. On this tab, as shown in
Figure 13-3, you specify settings that affect the .swf file.

Flash gives you the following options:

✔ **Version:** Allows you to save in previous version formats for backward com-
patibility. If you use new features but choose an old Flash Player version,
Flash warns you of potential problems when you publish your movie.

✔ **Load Order:** Specifies how Flash displays the first frame of the Flash
movie. Bottom Up (the default) loads layers from the lowest layer
upward. Top Down loads layers starting from the top layer and moving
downward. Your viewers will see the difference between these two settings only if the Flash movie is loading slowly (because of a slow Internet
connection, for instance).

✔ **ActionScript Version (for Flash Player 6 and 7 only):** Specifies whether your movie is using ActionScript 1.0 or ActionScript 2.0. ActionScript 2.0 is new in Flash MX 2004. It adds new commands to ActionScript that are mostly of interest to intermediate or advanced programmers who are building applications in Flash which implement new classes and sub-classes of objects.

ActionScript 2.0 is ActionScript 1.0 with powerful new programming contructs added to it. If you don't implement new classes and sub-classes of objects (and you certainly didn't if you're not sure what this means), then you can safely choose ActionScript version 1.0 in the Publish Settings above. Throughout this book, all the ActionScript features that we describe are part of both ActionScript version 1.0 and 2.0, and so we simply refer to ActionScript rather than the version number.

✔ **Generate Size Report:** Creates a .txt file that you can use to trou-bleshoot problem areas. The report relates the various parts of your movie to the number of bytes that they require in the .swf file.

✔ **Protect from Import:** Prevents the .swf files from being downloaded from the Web site and imported back into Flash. This feature isn't 100 percent safe, but it helps keep your work from being "borrowed."

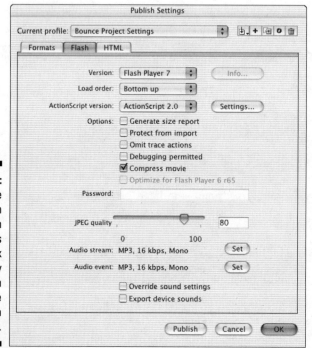

Figure 13-3:
Use the
Flash tab in
the Publish
Settings
dialog box
to specify
how Flash
creates the
SWF (Flash
Player) file.

✔ **Omit Trace Actions:** Omits special codes used by programmers. *Trace actions* insert into Flash movies the codes used to record and display technical information about a Flash movie's progress in a special window, named the Flash Debugger. Programmers use this information to debug their ActionScript programming. Mark the Omit Trace Actions check box to omit these codes from the .swf file, and your file will be smaller.

✔ **Debugging Permitted:** Lets you use the Debugger to debug a Flash movie from another computer. If you permit debugging, you can add a password to protect the movie file. Although this option is useful for ActionScript programmers, discussing it is beyond the scope of this book.

✔ **Compress Movie:** Compresses your movie file, especially text and ActionScript, so that it can download faster. This option is great except that your compressed file does not play in Flash Player versions earlier than Flash Player 6.

✔ **Optimize for Flash Player 6 r65:** This option appears if you choose Flash Player 6 when you choose the Flash Player version at the top of the dialog box. Flash Player 6 r65 was an updated version of Flash Player with significant bug fixes and performance enhancements.

✔ **Password:** Allows you to select a password for debugging, if you enable the Debugging Permitted check box. This option prevents viewers from debugging the movie unless they have the password.

✔ **JPEG Quality:** Sets the compression (size) versus quality of bitmaps, if you have any in your movie. You can set the quality anywhere from 0 (the lowest quality and highest compression) to 100 (the highest quality and lowest compression).

✔ **Audio Stream:** Displays and sets the audio compression for *stream sounds* (sounds that use the Stream Sync setting in the Property inspector when a frame with the sound is selected). This setting applies if you haven't set the compression for individual sounds in the Sound Properties dialog box. Also, if you enable the Override Sound Settings check box in the Publish Settings dialog box, this setting overrides the setting in the Sound Properties dialog box. To change the current setting, click Set. The options are the same as in the Sound Properties dialog box. (Refer to Chapter 11 for details on setting sound properties.)

✔ **Audio Event:** Displays and sets the audio compression for event sounds (as set in the Property inspector when a frame with the sound is selected). Otherwise, it's the same as Audio Stream.

✔ **Override Sound Settings:** Select this check box to override settings in the Sound Properties dialog box. Then the settings here apply to all sounds in your movie.

✔ **Export Device Sounds (Flash MX 2004 Pro only):** This gives you the option of exporting sounds in formats suitable for playback on mobile devices, such as the Sony CLIÉ NX series personal digital assistant (PDA). To do this you use proxy sound files, which are beyond the scope of this book.

Publishing to HTML

Web pages are created by using HTML. If you work on a Web site, you may write the HTML code from scratch or use an HTML editor. However, many people use a Web authoring program, such as Dreamweaver by Macromedia or FrontPage by Microsoft.

To place a Flash Player file on a Web page, you need the proper HTML code. Luckily, Flash creates this code for you, suitable for Internet Explorer and Netscape Navigator browsers. The HTML code simply tells the browser to look for and display your Flash Player file. Of course, you can write the HTML code yourself, but this method is easier.

Understanding the HTML code for a movie

Figure 13-4 shows the default HTML code created for a Flash movie, displayed in TextEdit on a Mac. (In TextEdit, before opening your HTML file, be sure to choose TextEdit⇨Preferences and then select the Plain Text radio button in the New Document Attributes section of the Preferences dialog box.) Windows users can use Notepad to view HTML code created by the Publish command.

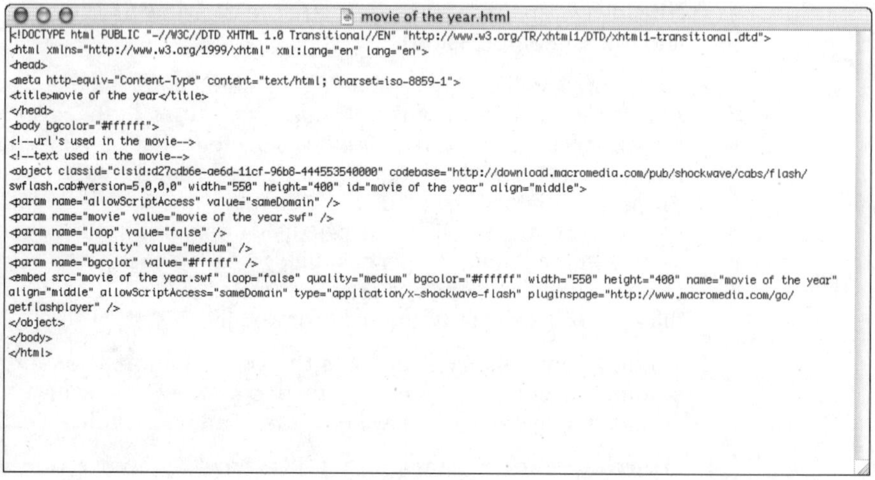

Figure 13-4:
Flash
creates
HTML code
that looks
like this
when you
publish a
movie to a
player file.

```
movie of the year.html
<!DOCTYPE html PUBLIC "-//W3C//DTD XHTML 1.0 Transitional//EN" "http://www.w3.org/TR/xhtml1/DTD/xhtml1-transitional.dtd">
<html xmlns="http://www.w3.org/1999/xhtml" xml:lang="en" lang="en">
<head>
<meta http-equiv="Content-Type" content="text/html; charset=iso-8859-1">
<title>movie of the year</title>
</head>
<body bgcolor="#ffffff">
<!--url's used in the movie-->
<!--text used in the movie-->
<object classid="clsid:d27cdb6e-ae6d-11cf-96b8-444553540000" codebase="http://download.macromedia.com/pub/shockwave/cabs/flash/
swflash.cab#version=5,0,0,0" width="550" height="400" id="movie of the year" align="middle">
<param name="allowScriptAccess" value="sameDomain" />
<param name="movie" value="movie of the year.swf" />
<param name="loop" value="false" />
<param name="quality" value="medium" />
<param name="bgcolor" value="#ffffff" />
<embed src="movie of the year.swf" loop="false" quality="medium" bgcolor="#ffffff" width="550" height="400" name="movie of the year"
align="middle" allowScriptAccess="sameDomain" type="application/x-shockwave-flash" pluginspage="http://www.macromedia.com/go/
getflashplayer" />
</object>
</body>
</html>
```

If you know some HTML, this page will look familiar to you. (And if you don't, you might want to check out *HTML 4 For Dummies*, 4th Edition, by Ed Tittel and Natanya Pitts, by Wiley Publishing, Inc.) It starts with the *tags* (codes) that all HTML documents contain, namely `<html>`, `<head>`, `<title>`, and `<body>`. Here's how to understand the rest of the codes, as much as is necessary:

- After `<body`, you see `bgcolor="#ffffff">`. This is the background color of the entire HTML page.

- After the comments (which start with `!–`), you see the `object` code. Microsoft Internet Explorer requires this tag in order to display your Flash Player files. The `object` code includes the following:

  - Detailed codes (which are required in order to tell Internet Explorer how to display your player file).

  - The specification of the version of the Flash viewer to look for and where to download it if necessary.

  - The width and height of the display in the browser.

  - The name of the file (`value="movie of the year.swf"`).

  - Parameter settings for quality and background color. You set the background color by choosing Modify⇨Document in Flash and choosing a background color in the Document Properties dialog box. (Refer to Chapter 2 for details on using this dialog box.)

- The `embed` code is for Netscape Navigator and accomplishes the same thing as the `object` code. Within this code, you see the following:

  - The name of the player file.

  - Parameters for quality and background color. (See the preceding comments for the `object` code.)

  - The width and height of the display in the browser.

  - The type of file (that is, a Flash Player file, called `shockwave-flash` in the HTML code).

  - Where to go to download the Flash Player if necessary.

- Finally, you see the closing `</object>` tag as well as the tags that end every HTML document: `</body>` AND `</html>`.

If you want to use the HTML document as is, you can. But if you want to place your Flash Player file in an existing HTML file, as you would for a Flash button, for example, you need to insert the `<embed>` and `<object>` codes into the desired location of your existing file. This process is easy: Copy the HTML code starting from `<object` through `</object>`, thus omitting the tags that are already on your existing HTML page. Then paste this code into your existing HTML document where you want your Flash Player file to be displayed on your page.

If you didn't change your default folder locations in the Formats section of the Publish Settings dialog box, your `.swf` file will be in the same folder as the HTML file that Flash creates when you publish your movie. In that case, the HTML `<object>` and `<embed>` tags created by the Flash publishing process reference the `.swf` file by simply mentioning the filename. For that to work, the `.swf` file must be in the same folder on your Web site's server as your Web page's HTML file.

If you usually keep images in a subfolder and want to place your `.swf` file in that subfolder, you can specify them in the Formats tab of the Publish Settings dialog box. Or you can edit the HTML code in a text editor to change the references for *both* the `<object>` and `<embed>` tags to add the path to the subfolder. If you already do this for other images, the process is the same for the `.swf` file. For example, if you keep your images in a subfolder named images and the current code refers to `tulip.swf`, change the reference for both the `<object>` and `<embed>` tags to `images/tulip.swf`.

Specifying Flash Player detection and other HTML settings

To create the HTML file, you need to specify the HTML settings from the HTML tab of the Publish Settings dialog box, as shown in Figure 13-5.

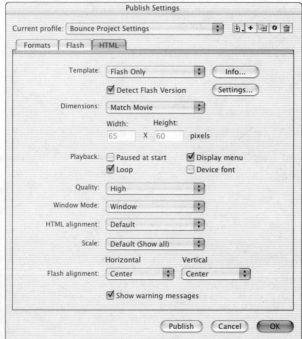

Figure 13-5:
Use the HTML tab of the Publish Settings dialog box to specify how Flash creates HTML code to display your movie.

Templates

The first setting chooses a template. The *template* determines the format and contents of the HTML file. To keep matters simple, choose the default, Flash Only. Table 13-1 explains the other template options. For more information, refer to Chapter 12.

Table 13-1	HTML Template Options
Option	**Comments**
Flash for Pocket PC 2003	Creates an HTML file with `<object>` and `<embed>` tags and with Pocket PC-specific alignment. Can be used with Pocket IE and with desktop Internet Explorer and Netscape browsers.
Flash HTTPS	Creates an HTML file with `<object>` and `<embed>` tags, using the HTTPS protocol to specify where to go to download the Flash Player if that's necessary. *HTTPS* is a method that is designed to send data over the Web more securely than the standard method (HTTP).
Flash Only (Default)	Creates an HTML file, as we describe in the previous section, with `<object>` and `<embed>` tags.
Flash with AICC Tracking	Includes support for AICC (Aviation Industry CBT Committee) tracking when using Macromedia Learning Components.
Flash with FSCommand	Used when you have added an `FSCommand` action to your movie to interface with JavaScript. The HTML file also includes the `<object>` and `<embed>` commands.
Flash with Named Anchors	Adds browser scripting and HTML anchors so that viewers can bookmark Flash content in Flash Player 6 and later.
Flash with SCORM Tracking	Includes support for SCORM (Sharable Content Object Reference Model) tracking when using Macromedia Learning Components.
Image Map	(If you don't know what an image map is, don't worry about this option.) Rather than display an SWF player file, uses a GIF, JPEG, or PNG image (which you need to choose from the Formats tab) as a client-side image map coded in your HTML page.
QuickTime	Creates `<embed>` and `<object>` tags in an HTML page to display a QuickTime Flash movie based on your Flash movie. You need to mark the QuickTime check box on the Formats tab. A QuickTime Flash movie plays with only QuickTime 4 or later. QuickTime 4 can recognize only Flash 3 features. QuickTime 5 can also recognize Flash 4 features.

Beneath the Template combo box is the Detect Flash Version check box. (This option is only available if you choose Flash Player 4 or later in the Flash tab of the Publish Settings dialog box and you don't choose the QuickTime or Image Map template.) Mark this check box to add browser scripting to detect the Flash Player for the version of Flash you specify in the Flash tab. When this check box is enabled, the Settings button to the right is also enabled. To further specify version detection settings, follow these steps:

1. **Choose File⇨Publish Settings.**

2. **When the Publish Settings dialog box appears, click the Settings button on the HTML tab.**

   The Version Detection Settings dialog box appears.

3. **Type revision numbers in the Major Revision and Minor Revision text fields if you want to more exactly specify the minimum version required.**

4. **Type in new names for the detection file, the content file and alternate file if you don't want to use the default names.**

   The detection file is an HTML file that also contains an SWF file. (Flash creates both of these for you, and together they detect the user's Flash version.) The content file is the HTML template file that contains your Flash content. The alternate file is an HTML file (with no SWF file) for users who don't have the version of Flash you require.

5. **Mark the Use Existing radio button if you want Flash to automatically create the alternate file. Or if you create an HTML file as the alternate file, mark the Use Existing radio button and then click Browse to select your HTML file.**

6. **Click OK.**

   The Detection Settings dialog box closes.

Dimensions

The Dimensions options control the size allotted to your Flash Player movie on your Web page. You have three options:

- **Match Movie** matches the width and height that you set in the Movie Properties dialog box (choose Modify⇨Document).

- **Pixels** lets you specify, in pixels, the Width and Height. Type the desired values in the text boxes.

- **Percent** lets you specify the area used by the Flash Player movie as a percentage of the browser window size. The 100% setting is ideal for pages that are designed to take up the entire page. Type the desired values in the text boxes.

Playback

The Playback section determines the values of parameters in the HTML code. You have four options:

- **Paused at Start** creates a PLAY parameter whose value is FALSE. The viewer must start the movie by clicking a button in the movie — the button's instance needs to have a Play action in it. Alternatively, viewers can right-click (Windows) or Control+click (Mac) the movie and choose Play from the shortcut menu, but they may not be aware of this. By default, this check box is not marked, so movies start to play automatically.

- **Loop** creates a LOOP parameter whose value is TRUE. The movie repeats over and over. By default, this check box is marked, so make sure to clear it if you don't want to loop your movie!

- **Display Menu** creates a MENU parameter set to TRUE. This option enables viewers to right-click (Windows) or Control+click (Mac) the movie and choose from a menu. The menu options in Flash Player 7 are Zoom In/Out, Show All, Quality (High, Medium, or Low), Settings, Print, Debugger, and About Macromedia Flash Player. Without this option, Settings and About Flash Player are the only items on the shortcut menu. By default, Display Menu is marked.

- **Device Font** applies to Windows playback only. When this check box is enabled, the HTML file includes a DEVICE FONT parameter set to TRUE, and Flash substitutes *anti-aliased* (smoothly curved) system fonts for fonts not available on the viewer's system. By default, this item is not marked.

Quality

The Quality section determines the quality parameter in the <object> and <embed> tags of the HTML code. Quality refers to the level of *anti-aliasing,* which means the smoothing of the artwork so that it doesn't have jagged edges. Of course, the lower the quality, the faster the playback. Usually, you want to find a middle ground between quality and speed. You have six options:

- **Low** doesn't use any anti-aliasing.

- **Autolow** starts at low quality but switches to high quality if the viewer's computer, as detected by the Flash Player, can handle it.

- **Autohigh** starts at high quality but switches to low quality if the viewer's computer can't handle the playback demand. This option should provide good results on all computers.

- **Medium** applies some anti-aliasing but doesn't smooth bitmaps. This option is a good middle ground between low and high.

✔ **High** always uses anti-aliasing for vector art. Bitmaps are smoothed only if they're in a tween. This setting is the default. (See Chapter 9 for the scoop on tweens.)

✔ **Best** always uses anti-aliasing, including for animated bitmaps.

Window Mode

Window Mode specifies how the player movie's window interacts with the rest of the page. The Window setting plays your movie in its own window. The Opaque Windowless setting creates an opaque background for the movie so that other elements in the Web page don't show through when they're behind the movie. The Transparent Windowless setting makes the Flash background color transparent so that other elements on your Web page show through. The latter setting can slow down playback. The Windowless settings embed window-related attribute in the `<object>` and `<embed>` tags. The code for Windowless only has an effect in more recent browsers running on Windows or Mac OS X — Internet Explorer version 5 (most versions) and later, Netscape version 7 and later, Mozilla 1 and later, and Opera 6 and later.

HTML Alignment

The HTML Alignment setting specifies the `ALIGN` attribute and specifies how the Flash Player movie is aligned within the browser window. You have five options:

✔ **Default** centers the Flash movie. If the browser window is smaller than the movie, this option crops the edges of the movie.

✔ **Left** aligns the movie along the left side of the browser window. If the browser window is too small, this option crops the other sides of the movie.

✔ **Right** aligns the movie along the right side of the browser window. If the browser window is too small, this option crops the other sides of the movie.

✔ **Top** aligns the movie along the top of the browser window. If the browser window is too small, this option crops the other sides of the movie.

✔ **Bottom** aligns the movie along the bottom of the browser window. If the browser window is too small, this option crops the other sides of the movie.

Scale

The Scale setting defines how the movie is placed within the boundaries when (and only when) you set a width and height different from the movie's original size, using the Pixels or Percent options in the Dimensions section of the Publish Settings dialog box. You have four options:

- ✔ **Default (Show All)** displays the entire movie without distortion but may create borders on both sides of the movie.

- ✔ **No Border** scales the movie to fill the dimensions without distortion but may crop portions of the movie.

- ✔ **Exact Fit** fits the movie to the dimensions, distorting the movie if necessary.

- ✔ **No Scale** stops the movie from changing its scale if the viewer resizes the Flash Player window.

Flash Alignment

Flash Alignment determines how the movie fits within the movie window (as opposed to the browser window). It works together with the Scale and Dimensions settings. In other words, it determines how the Flash movie fits within the dimensions that you specify. For the Horizontal setting, you can choose Left, Center, or Right. For the Vertical setting, you can choose Top, Center, or Bottom.

At the bottom of the Publish Settings dialog box is the Show Warning Messages check box, which is not marked by default. When it's enabled, you see warning messages during the publishing process. Nevertheless, the publishing process continues, but you know that you may have made an error. For example, if you have chosen a template that requires a GIF or JPEG image but you haven't selected either format on the Formats tab, you see a warning message.

After you choose your settings, click OK to return to your movie or click Publish to publish it.

Publishing to Other Formats

As we explain in the preceding section, you can choose an HTML template that requires other formats, or you can use other formats to create still images or create QuickTime movies. Although you have many options, after you try a few out, you generally find a satisfactory solution that doesn't require much fiddling.

Creating GIF graphic files

Create a GIF graphic when you want to give viewers without the Flash Player an alternative image, or for any reason you like. You can also create animated GIFs. To specify the settings, mark GIF Image on the Formats tab and then click the GIF tab, as shown in Figure 13-6.

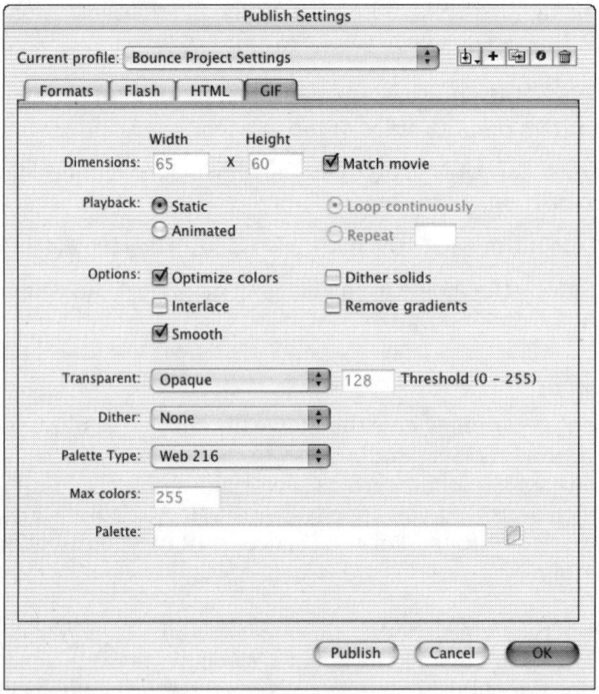

Publish Settings

Current profile: Bounce Project Settings

Formats | Flash | HTML | GIF

Width   Height
Dimensions: 65   X   60   ☑ Match movie

Playback: ⦿ Static   ⦾ Loop continuously
          ◯ Animated   ◯ Repeat

Options: ☑ Optimize colors   ☐ Dither solids
         ☐ Interlace   ☐ Remove gradients
         ☑ Smooth

Transparent: Opaque ▾   128   Threshold (0 – 255)

Dither: None ▾

Palette Type: Web 216 ▾

Max colors: 255

Palette:

Publish   Cancel   OK

Figure 13-6:
The GIF tab
of the
Publish
Settings
dialog box.

You can also create static GIF images by choosing File➪Export➪Export Image, as we explain in the section "Exporting Movies and Images," later in this chapter.

Flash publishes the first frame of your movie unless you label a different frame with the label #Static. (To create a label, click the frame and choose Window➪Properties to open the Property inspector. In Windows, if necessary, click the collapse arrow on the Property inspector title bar to expand it. Type a label name in the Frame text box on the left side of the Property inspector.)

On the GIF tab, you can specify the following settings:

✔ **Dimensions:** Mark the Match Movie check box to match the settings in the Movie Properties dialog box (choose Modify➪Document). Clear the Match Movie check box to specify a different Width and Height. If you change the Width and Height settings, you need to calculate proportional measurements to avoid distorting the image.

✔ **Playback:** This section determines whether you create a static or an animated GIF:

 • **Static** creates a single still image GIF. By default, Flash uses the first frame. To specify a different frame, create a frame label of #Static on the frame that you want to use. (To create a label, click the frame and choose Window➪Properties to open the Property inspector. In Windows, if necessary, click the collapse arrow on the Property inspector title bar to expand it. Type a label name in the Frame text box on the left side of the Property inspector.)

- **Animated** creates an animated GIF. If you choose this option, select either the Loop Continuously or the Repeat radio button, entering the number of times that you want to repeat the GIF. To save only some of your frames, create a frame label of #First on the first frame that you want to save and #Last on the last frame.

✔ **Options** specifies how the GIF appears:

- **Optimize Colors** removes unused colors from the file's color table in order to reduce the size of the file.

- **Interlace** causes a static GIF to load in incremental resolutions, so the image first appears fuzzy and then successively sharper. Some people like this option because viewers may be able to click the image before it fully downloads, thus reducing their waiting time.

- **Smooth** anti-aliases (smoothes) the artwork. Text usually looks better (and file size is larger), but occasionally you may get an undesirable halo effect around your art. In that case, turn off smoothing.

- **Dither Solids** does just that — it dithers solid colors as well as gradients and images. *Dithering* is a way to approximate colors not available on the color palette by using a range of similar colors. See the Dither option, which we describe a couple of paragraphs from now.

- **Remove Gradients** turns gradients into solids. Gradients may not look good in a Web-safe color table. Nevertheless, Flash uses the first color in the gradient, which may not be the color that you want.

✔ **Transparent** determines how your movie's background and colors with alpha (opacity/transparency) settings are translated into the GIF format. You have three options:

- **Opaque** makes the background of the movie opaque.

- **Transparent** makes the background of the movie transparent.

- **Alpha** lets you set a threshold below which all colors are transparent. You can specify any number from 0–255. A value of 128 is equivalent to an alpha setting of 50%. Any colors whose alpha setting is below the number that you set disappear because they become transparent.

✔ **Dither** enables dithering, as we define in the earlier Dither Solids bullet in the Options descriptions. Dithering helps to create more accurate-looking colors but increases file size. Choose one of the three options:

- **None** disables dithering.

- **Ordered** provides a medium amount of dithering and a corresponding medium increase in file size.

- **Diffusion** provides the best-quality dithering and increases file size the most. It works with only the Web 216-color palette. (Refer to Chapter 3 for a description of color palettes.)

✔ **Palette Type** determines the color palette for the GIF image. (Refer to Chapter 3 for a discussion of colors in Flash.) The GIF file format can't have more than 256 colors. You have four options:

- **Web 216** uses the standard 216-color palette that includes only Web-safe colors (those that look good on all Web browsers). You can usually get good results for Flash artwork without increasing file size.

- **Adaptive** creates a unique color table for your GIF, based on the actual colors present. You get more accurate color, although these colors may not be Web safe. Also, file size may be larger. Use this option if the accurate representation of colors is most important, as in a photographic bitmap image. You can use the Max Colors text box to specify how many colors that you want in the table. The default is 255. Use fewer colors to reduce file size.

- **Web Snap Adaptive** works like the Adaptive option but optimizes the color palette for the Web. Colors close to the 216 Web-safe colors are turned into one of the colors on that palette. Other colors function like the Adaptive option. As with the Adaptive option, you can specify the number of colors on the palette in the Max Colors text box.

- **Custom** lets you specify a palette in the ACT format. Click the ellipsis (...) button to browse for a color palette file. (Read the section in Chapter 3 on solid colors for an explanation on how to create a color palette and save it in ACT format.)

After you specify your settings, click OK to return to your movie or click Publish to publish the GIF file as well as the other formats that you chose.

Creating JPEG graphic files

JPEG files can display many more colors than GIF files and therefore produce more realistic photos and other complex drawings. JPEG graphics are compressed to reduce file size. But they decompress when downloaded, using more memory.

To create a JPEG image, mark JPEG Image on the Formats tab. Flash then creates a JPEG tab in the Publish Settings dialog box, as shown in Figure 13-7.

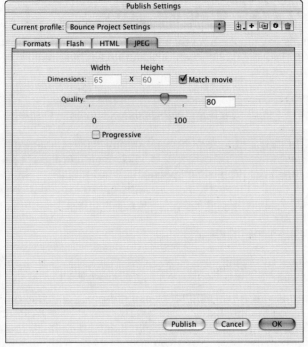

Figure 13-7:
JPEG
images
are easy
to create
because
there are
few settings
to specify.

Flash publishes the first frame of your movie unless you label a different frame with the label #Static. (To create a label, click the frame and choose Window⇨ Properties to open the Property inspector. In Windows, if necessary, click the collapse arrow on the Property inspector title bar to expand it. Type a label name in the Frame text box on the left side of the Property inspector.)

You have the following options:

✔ **Dimensions:** By default, Flash matches the dimensions of the movie. Clear the Match Movie check box to specify your own width and height preferences.

✔ **Quality:** You can choose the quality by using the slider bar or the text box. A lower setting means lower image quality but a smaller file. A higher setting produces a better-quality picture, but file size is larger. For your first effort, try the default of 80 and then adjust the setting based on the results.

✔ **Progressive:** This displays the image in increments of greater resolution. This option is equivalent to using the Interlaced option for GIF files, as we explain in the preceding section.

After you're done, click OK to return to your movie or click Publish to publish the JPEG and other formats that you specified.

Creating PNG graphic files

PNG files can display more colors than GIF files and support transparency. They offer some of the advantages of both GIFs and JPEGs, but not all browsers support them completely.

To create a PNG image, choose PNG Image on the Formats tab. Flash creates a PNG tab in the Publish Settings dialog box, as shown in Figure 13-8.

Flash publishes the first frame of your movie unless you label a different frame with the label #Static. (To create a label, click the frame and choose Window➪ Properties to open the Property inspector. In Windows, if necessary, click the collapse arrow on the Property inspector title bar to expand it. Type a label name in the Frame text box on the left side of the Property inspector.)

You have the following options:

- ✔ **Dimensions:** By default, Flash matches the dimensions of the movie. Clear the Match Movie check box to specify your own Width and Height settings.

- ✔ **Bit Depth:** Controls the number of bits per pixel, which in turn means how many colors the image contains. You can choose 8-bit for 256 colors (like a GIF), 24-bit for 16.7 million colors, or 24-bit with Alpha, which allows for transparency. When you choose 24-bit with Alpha, the image's background becomes transparent.

- ✔ **Options:** See the Options settings for GIF images that we explain earlier in this chapter.

- ✔ **Dither:** See the Dither settings for GIF images that we explain earlier in this chapter. *Note:* This option applies only if you choose an 8-bit depth.

- ✔ **Palette Type:** See the Palette Type settings for GIF images that we explain earlier in this chapter. *Note:* This option applies only if you choose an 8-bit depth.

- ✔ **Max Colors:** See the Palette Type settings for GIF images that we explain earlier in this chapter.

- ✔ **Palette:** See the Palette Type settings for GIF images that we explain earlier in this chapter.

- ✔ **Filter Options:** The PNG format filters an image line-by-line in order to compress it. You have these options:

  - • **None:** Applies no filtering. The resulting file is larger than with the other options.

  - • **Sub:** Filters adjoining pixel bytes (working horizontally). Works best when the image has repeated horizontal information.

  - • **Up:** Filters in a vertical direction. Works best when the image has repeated vertical information.

- **Average:** Uses a mixture of horizontal and vertical comparison; a good first-try option.

- **Path:** Uses a more complex method that uses the three nearest pixels to predict the next one.

- **Adaptive:** Creates a unique color table for your PNG file, based on the actual colors present. You get more accurate color, although these colors may not be Web safe. The file size may also be larger. Use this option if accurate representation of colors is most important, as in a photographic bitmap image.

After you specify your settings, click OK to return to your movie or click Publish to publish your PNG image and create the other files that you have chosen.

Creating QuickTime movies

QuickTime is a format for digitized movies. QuickTime movies are played on the QuickTime Player. Flash lets you import, export, and publish QuickTime movies. (Refer to Chapter 3 for instructions for importing QuickTime movies as well as other graphic images.) Exporting images and movies is covered in the section "Exporting Movies and Images," later in this chapter.

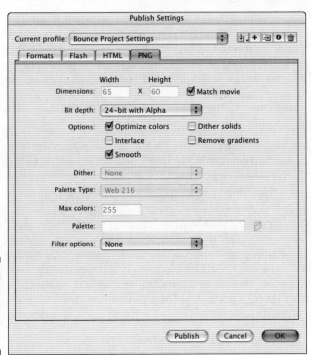

Figure 13-8:
Use the PNG tab to create PNG images.

You can import a QuickTime movie, add a Flash movie, and then publish the results as a Flash or QuickTime movie, thereby combining the two. (You can also import Flash Player files directly into the QuickTime player of QuickTime 4 or later.) When Flash creates the QuickTime movie, it places the Flash movie in a separate Flash track within the QuickTime movie.

To publish a QuickTime movie from Flash, mark the QuickTime check box on the Formats tab of the Publish Settings dialog box and click the QuickTime tab that appears, as shown in Figure 13-9.

Use these settings to configure your QuickTime movie:

- **Dimensions:** Match Movie sizes the QuickTime movie according to the size of your Flash movie. If you clear the Match Movie check box, you can specify your own Width and Height settings.

- **Alpha:** This option determines the opacity and transparency of the Flash track within the QuickTime movie. This setting makes sense only if you've combined QuickTime and Flash movies into one QuickTime movie. Use the Layer option, which we describe next, in conjunction with this option. Auto, the default, makes the Flash track transparent if it's on top of other tracks, but opaque if it's on the bottom or is the only content in the movie. Alpha-Transparent makes the Flash track transparent. You can see other content in tracks below the Flash track. Copy makes the Flash track opaque.

- **Layer:** Layer specifies how the Flash track is layered with QuickTime content. Auto places the Flash track in front of other tracks if Flash artwork appears on top of the QuickTime movie at any time. Otherwise, it places the Flash movie on the bottom layer. Top places the Flash track on top of other tracks. Use Top when you want your Flash movie to appear in front of the QuickTime movie. Bottom places the Flash track on the bottom. Use Bottom when you want your Flash movie to be a background to the QuickTime movie.

- **Streaming Sound:** Mark the Use QuickTime Compression check box to export all your streaming audio to a QuickTime soundtrack. Click Settings to specify how you want the audio compressed. (Refer to Chapter 11 for a description of streaming sound.)

- **Controller:** A *controller* is a control panel that lets you play back the movie. QuickTime has a controller similar to the Flash controller (described in Chapter 9). Choose None if you have created your own controller within your Flash movie to enable viewers to view the movie or if you want your movie to play automatically. Standard displays the QuickTime controller. Choose QuickTime VR for a specialized controller for QuickTime VR movies that creates panoramic and 3-D viewing effects.

✔ **Playback:** This option specifies how the movie plays. Enable the Loop check box to replay the movie over and over. Mark Paused At Start if you don't want the movie to play automatically when it opens. (If you choose a controller, the movie is automatically paused and the user uses the controller to start the movie.) Select Play Every Frame to display every frame, even if it means slowing down playback. (Otherwise, the QuickTime movie skips frames as necessary to maintain the timing.) The Play Every Frame option also silences the QuickTime audio track.

✔ **File:** Mark the Flatten (Make Self-Contained) check box to combine the Flash movie with other content into one QuickTime movie. If this check box is not marked, Flash creates a QuickTime movie that references the Flash SWF file and any other QuickTime content that you may have previously imported into your Flash movie. The file size is smaller, but you need to make sure that these related files are available in the same folder when played back on a Web site. If you don't mark the Flatten check box, be sure to enable Flash (.swf) on the Formats tab of the Publish Settings dialog box.

After you specify your settings, click OK to return to your movie or click Publish to publish your QuickTime movie and the other file formats that you chose.

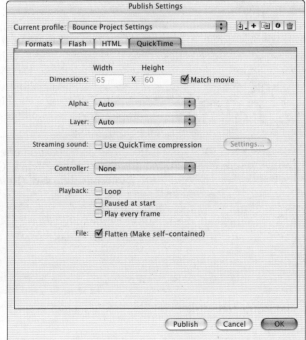

Figure 13-9: Use the QuickTime tab to specify how your QuickTime movie plays.

Creating self-playing movies

You can also create projectors in the Publish Settings dialog box. A *projector* is a self-playing Flash movie that doesn't require the Flash Player. You can use a projector for a Flash movie that you want to place on a CD-ROM or even on a floppy disk.

You can create a Windows or Mac version from either platform. But if you create a Mac version in Windows, you need to use a file translator, such as BinHex, so that the Mac Finder recognizes it as an application.

To create a projector, follow these steps:

1. **Choose File➪Publish Settings.**

   The Publish Settings dialog box opens.

2. **On the Formats tab, mark the Windows Projector or Macintosh Projector check boxes, or both.**

3. **Click Publish.**

4. **Click OK or Cancel to close the Publish Settings dialog box.**

For Windows, Flash creates an EXE file. For the Mac, Flash creates a compressed BinHex file (HQX).

Don't forget to test your movie after you place it on a CD-ROM or floppy disk. Try it out with a variety of processor speeds if possible.

Using Publish Profiles

In Flash MX 2004, you can now save all the settings that you configure in the Publish Settings dialog box as a *publish profile*. You can then duplicate, modify, export, import, and delete your publish profiles and trade them with your collaborators. This makes it easy for you to repeatedly use any collection of settings that you need. You can create standard publish profiles, which you use to make sure that all your files are published uniformly, and you can create specialized publish profiles that are specific to a single project.

To create a publish profile, follow these steps:

1. **Choose File➪Publish Settings.**

   The Publish Settings dialog box appears.

2. **Click the Create New Profile button in the upper-left part of the dialog box.**

   The Create New Profile dialog box appears.

3. **Type in a name for your profile and click OK.**

   The Create New Profile dialog box disappears, and the name of your new profile appears in the Current Profile pop-up menu of the Publish Settings dialog box.

4. **Specify the publish settings for your document in the Publish Settings dialog box, as we describe in the previous sections of this chapter, and then click OK.**

To duplicate a publish profile, do the following steps:

1. **Choose File⇨Publish Settings.**

   The Publish Settings dialog box appears.

2. **Select the publish profile that you want to copy in the Current Profile pop-up menu (near the top of the dialog box).**

3. **Click the Duplicate Profile button in the upper-left part of the dialog box.**

   The Duplicate Profile dialog box appears.

4. **Type in a name for your duplicate profile and click OK.**

   The Duplicate Profile dialog box disappears. The name of your duplicated profile appears in the Current Profile pop-up menu of the Publish Settings dialog box.

To modify a publish profile, follow these steps:

1. **Choose File⇨Publish Settings.**

   The Publish Settings dialog box appears.

2. **Select the publish profile that you want to modify in the Current Profile pop-up menu (near the top of the dialog box).**

3. **Choose the publish settings that you want for your document in the Publish Settings dialog box, as we describe in the previous sections of this chapter, and then click OK.**

To delete a publish profile, follow these steps:

1. **Choose File⇨Publish Settings.**

   The Publish Settings dialog box appears.

2. **Select the publish profile that you want to delete in the Current Profile pop-up menu (near the top of the dialog box).**

3. **Click the Delete Profile button in the upper-left part of the dialog box.**

   A dialog box appears asking you to confirm that you want to delete the profile.

4. **Click OK.**

To use a publish profile in a different document, first you export it from the document in which you created it. Then you import it into the new document.

To export a publish profile, follow these steps:

1. **Choose File⇨Publish Settings.**

   The Publish Settings dialog box appears.

2. **Select the publish profile that you want to export in the Current Profile pop-up menu (near the top of the dialog box).**

3. **Click the Import/Export Profile button (in the upper-left part of the dialog box) and choose Export from the pop-up menu.**

   The Export Profile dialog box appears.

4. **In the dialog box, choose a location where you want to save the file and Click Save.**

To import a publish profile, follow these steps:

1. **Choose File⇨Publish Settings.**

   The Publish Settings dialog box appears.

2. **Click the Import/Export Profile button (in the upper-left part of the dialog box) and choose Import from the pop-up menu.**

   The Import Profile dialog box appears.

3. **In the dialog box, browse to find the publish profile that you want to import and click Open.**

   The name of the imported publish profile appears in the Current Profile pop-up menu of the Publish Settings dialog box.

Using Publish Preview

If you want to specify Publish Settings, see the results, and then go back to tweak your settings, you can use Publish Preview rather than Publish. Publish Preview creates the files specified in the Publish Settings dialog box, just as the Publish command does. The only difference is that Publish

Preview automatically displays the requested file, usually the SWF file. The value is in simply saving the steps of manually opening your files in your browser — helpful when you're doing lots of tweaking and going back and forth between your publish settings and your browser several times to see what works best.

To use Publish Preview, follow these steps:

1. **Specify your settings by using the Publish Settings dialog box (as we explain earlier in this chapter) and click OK.**

2. **Choose File⇨Publish Preview.**

3. **From the Publish Preview submenu, choose the file format that you want to preview.**

4. **When you're done, close the window or browser.**

Posting Your Movie to Your Web Site

After you finish publishing your movie, post it on your Web site or place it on a CD-ROM or other media.

To put your movie on a CD-ROM, copy your published HTML and SWF files onto a CD-ROM by using CD burner software. Also copy any image files and QuickTime movies that you published in Flash.

Refer to the section "Understanding the HTML code for a movie," earlier in this chapter, for instructions on modifying the HTML code if you want to place your SWF file on an existing page or place your SWF file in a subfolder.

To post your movie to a Web site, upload both the HTML and the SWF file. If you also created other image files or a QuickTime movie, you need to upload them as well.

Open your browser and load the page containing your Flash movie. Hopefully, it works perfectly and looks great! If not, check out the HTML code, check your publish settings, and make sure that the necessary files are in the proper location on your Web site's server.

Exporting Movies and Images

In addition to publishing, Flash lets you export QuickTime movies and image files. Export a Flash file when you want to use it in another application. For example, you may want to export a frame as a GIF file and insert it into a word processing document. Use Export Movie to export to a QuickTime movie or to create a still image of every frame. You can also use Export Movie to export to an SWF file. This method is a shortcut compared with publishing if you already have the HTML code that you need and you just want to update an SWF file.

To export a movie or image, follow these steps:

1. **To export to an image, select the frame that you want to export.**

2. **Choose File⇨Export⇨Export Image or File⇨Export⇨Export Movie.**

3. **In the dialog box, navigate to the desired location and type a name for your image or movie.**

4. **Choose a type of file from the Save as Type drop-down list box.**

5. **Click Save.**

6. **Depending on the format that you choose, a dialog box may appear. If so, specify the settings and then click OK.**

   These settings are similar to or the same as the ones that we describe earlier in this chapter for publishing movies and images.

Table 13-2 lists the types of files that you can export.

Table 13-2		Export File Types	
File Type	*Windows*	*Mac*	*Comments*
Adobe Illustrator (AI)	X	X	A vector format.
Encapsulated PostScript (EPS)	X	X	A vector format used in Adobe Illustrator and recognized by many other applications.
Drawing Exchange Format (DXF)	X	X	A format that causes you to lose fills when importing into AutoCAD.
Windows Bitmap (BMP)	X		A raster (bitmap) format. Many applications recognize it. Offers variable bit-depths and transparency support. File size is large.
Metafile (EMF/WMF)	X		A vector format supported by many applications. Creates smaller files than EPS.

File Type	Windows	Mac	Comments
FutureSplash Player (SPL)	X	X	The original version of Flash, before Macromedia bought it.
Graphics Interchange File (GIF)	X	X	A raster format, limited to 256 colors.
Joint Photographic Experts Group (JPEG/JPG)	X	X	A raster format that sup ports 24-bit color.
QuickTime (MOV)	X	X	A QuickTime 4 format movie.
QuickTime (Macintosh)		X	On Macs only, uses the Video QuickTime 3 format, bitmapping all content.
PICT (PCT)		X	A raster format that can be used with most Mac and many PC applications. Variable bit-depths. Transparency support.
Portable Network Graphic (PNG)	X	X	A raster format that sup ports variable bit-depth and transparency.
Video for Windows (AVI)	X		A raster video format. Files can get large.
Windows Audio (WAV)	X		Exports just the sound.

After you export a movie or image, you can then import it into the desired application for further editing or display. Note that when you choose to export a movie to a format such as GIF, JPG or PNG, you export a sequence of individually numbered images.

Creating Printable Movies

Suppose that you want your Web site viewers to be able to print a form on your Web site that you created in Flash. Or perhaps you want them to print your contact information so that your Web page can become your business card. The Flash Player printing features enable your viewers to print receipts, information sheets, coupons, or whatever else helps you do business on the

Web. You can specify certain frames in a movie — including frames in the main Timeline, a button, or a movie clip — to be printable from the Flash Player shortcut menu. Viewers right-click (Windows) or Control+click (Mac) to access the Print command.

Your viewers need instructions on how to print, so place some text somewhere telling them what to do.

Of course, viewers can use their browser's Print command to print. The result, however, isn't nearly as controllable. When we tried it, our browser printed only the first frame, which was useless in our example. The browser also added the Uniform Resource Locator (URL), the name of the movie, the date, and the page number.

By default, the Flash Player shortcut menu lets viewers print the entire movie, frame by frame. This feature is fairly useless for most purposes. But by specifying which frames are printed and the print area, you can use the Player's Print command to make specific information or forms available to your viewers.

Preparing your movie for printing

If you want a nice, clean result, you need a nice, clean frame. The Flash Player prints all objects on all layers of the movie. If you want to create a form, for example, put it in its own frame and make sure that objects on other layers don't continue into that frame.

Alternatively, you can specify the print area so that you include only the area that you want printed, excluding other objects on the Stage in the frame. But if you specify a small area, this area becomes the entire page size when printing, so the objects in that small area are enlarged to take up the entire printed page. You can control the layout by changing the dimension, scale, and alignment HTML settings (on the HTML tab of the Publish Settings dialog box).

Make sure that everything you want to print is on the Stage. For example, if you want to print from a movie clip, it must be on the Stage and have an instance name.

You can make a movie clip invisible by setting its `_visible` property to `false`. (Use the Actions panel.) This capability enables you to instruct viewers to print a form that they don't see on the screen.

If your movie displays text instructing users how to print from the printable area, you may want to exclude this text from the printable area. They probably don't want to print the instructions on how to print, right?

Specifying printable frames

To specify which frame or frames you want to print when your viewers choose Print from the Flash Player shortcut menu, follow these steps:

1. **With the movie open, choose Window⇨Properties to open the Property inspector.**

   The shortcut is Ctrl+F3 (Windows) or ⌘+F3 (Mac).

   If necessary (in Windows only), click the collapse arrow on the Property inspector's title bar to expand it.

2. **Select from the Timeline the frame that you want printed.**

3. **If the frame that you selected is not a keyframe, make it a keyframe by choosing Insert⇨Timeline⇨Keyframe. (Refer to Chapter 9 for the low-down on keyframes.)**

4. **In the Property inspector, type #p in the Frame text box, as shown in Figure 13-10.**

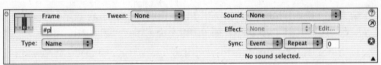

Figure 13-10: Use the Property inspector to label frames for printing.

For each additional keyframe that you want to specify for printing, select the frame and label it #p.

Specifying the print area

Unless you specify the print area, the Flash Player prints the entire Stage. If you have loaded other movies, the Flash Player uses their Stage size. You may, however, want to specify a different area. As we mention earlier in this chapter, you may want to include instructions on how to print, but you may not want the instructions to be printed. You can exclude other objects on the Stage as well.

Choosing a very small print area results in an output of very big objects. The Flash Player sizes your objects to take up the entire printed page.

You create an object, usually a rectangle, to specify the print area.

To specify the print area, follow these steps:

1. **Click a frame that you have labeled #p (as we describe in the preceding section).**

2. **Create a rectangle around the area that you want to be printed.**

   You may have to experiment with different sizes of rectangles. See the instructions in the section "Printing movies from the Flash Player," a little later in this chapter, to test the printing of your movie.

   Use the No Fill feature for the rectangle so that you can see the material that you want to print.

3. **Select the rectangle and choose Edit⇨Cut to cut it to the Clipboard.**

4. **Click a frame without a #p label but on the same layer.**

   Using the next frame may be a good choice in order to keep the printing area rectangle conveniently close to the frame that you've specified for printing.

5. **Choose Edit⇨Paste in Place.**

   You now have a rectangle of the right size, but in its own frame — a frame without a #p label.

6. **With the frame containing the rectangle that you selected, choose Window⇨Properties to open the Property inspector.**

   If necessary (in Windows only), click the collapse arrow on the Property inspector's title bar to expand it.

7. **In the Frame text box on the left side of the Property inspector, type #b to signify that the shape in this frame will be used as the boundary for the print area.**

You can have only one #b label in a Timeline. Also note that if you use a #b label, it must be on the same layer as the #p label.

You can place a `Print` action in a frame. A `Print` action offers options that are unavailable when you use the procedure that we just explained. You can print frames in other movie clips as well as on the main Timeline. You can also specify vector or bitmap printing. Vector printing is clearer, but you lose transparency. For more information on creating actions, refer to Chapter 10.

Printing movies from the Flash Player

Before uploading your printable movie to your Web site, you should test the printing function. To do so, use the Publish Settings dialog box to specify the publish settings that you want, as we explain throughout this chapter. Then choose File⇨Publish Preview⇨Default. Your browser opens, and you see your movie play.

To test-print your movie, right-click (Windows) or Control+click (Mac) in the browser. From the Flash Player shortcut menu, choose Print.

Choose the print range to select which frames to print or choose All. In Windows, you can also choose Selection to print the current frame. If only one frame has been made printable, the Pages option appears dimmed. Any option that you choose prints the frame that you've specified for printing. Click OK (Windows) or Print (Mac) to print.

After you upload your movie onto your Web site, viewers use the same procedure to print your movie.

Place on your page some text giving your viewers instructions on how to print your movie. Many viewers don't even know that the shortcut menu exists.

Part VI
The Part of Tens

The 5th Wave   By Rich Tennant

"Remember — if you're updating the family web site, no more animated GIFs of your sister swinging from a tree, scratching her armpits!"

In this part . . .

In the famous *For Dummies* Part of Tens, we answer the ten most-asked questions — or at least the seven questions we most wanted to answer. We fill you in on the top ten Web design tips so that your Flash Web site looks great and draws crowds. In this part, you find some cool techniques for creating drag-and-drop objects and simulating 3-D effects in Flash. In the chapter on the ten best Flash resources, we manage to give you dozens of Flash resources, such as the many Flash resource Web sites (while convincing our publisher that only ten exist). Finally, to top off the book, we give you our vote for ten great Flash Web sites. Surf all ten and be amazed and inspired by the possibilities!

Chapter 14

Frequently Asked Questions

• •

*I*n this chapter, we answer some frequently asked questions about Flash while explaining how to create some very cool effects and streamline the process of creating Flash movies.

How do I make drag-and-drop objects?

You can create draggable movie clips to use for games, drag-'n'-drop interfaces, or slider bars. Although creating draggable movie clips is an advanced function, it's too much fun to leave out of this book. The secret is to create a button inside a movie clip and to attach the actions to the button.

To create a draggable movie clip, follow these steps:

1. **Choose Insert⇨New Symbol to create a new symbol.**

2. **Name your new symbol, click the movie clip behavior, and click OK.**

3. **On the Stage, create an object that you want to be draggable.**

4. **With the object selected, choose Modify⇨Convert to Symbol to open the Convert to Symbol dialog box.**

5. **Name the symbol, choose the button behavior, and click OK.**

   You now have a button inside a movie.

6. **Choose Window⇨Development Panels⇨Actions to open the Actions panel if it's not already open.**

   If necessary, click the collapse arrow on the Actions panel title bar to expand it.

7. **On the list on the left side of the Actions panel, click the Global Functions category and then the Movie Clip Control subcategory, and then double-click the function on (it's below** getproperty **in the list).**

   The on action appears on the right side of the window. A list of suggested event types also pops up.

8. From the list of suggested event types, choose Press.

The code in the Script pane of the Actions panel should now look like this:

```
On (press) {
}
```

Choosing Press makes the drag function work when you press the mouse button.

9. Click to reposition your cursor at the end of the current line.

10. On the list on the left side of the Actions panel, in the Global Functions category and the Movie Clip Control subcategory, double-click startDrag.

Flash adds the startDrag() ; statement on the right side of the Actions panel, and a small yellow box with code hints appears.

The code in the Script pane of the Actions panel should now look like this:

```
On (press) {startDrag();

}
```

11. Type in the word this and then click to reposition your cursor at the beginning of Line 4 (which is a blank line).

this refers to the button that is your target for dragging. The code in the Script pane of the Actions panel should now look like the following:

```
On (press) {startDrag(this);

}
```

12. On the list on the left side of the Actions panel, in the Global Functions category and the Movie Clip Control subcategory, double-click the function on. (It's below getproperty in the list.)

The on action appears on the right side of the panel, and a list of suggested event types also pops up.

13. From the list of suggested event types, choose Release.

The code in the Script pane of the Actions panel should now look like this:

```
On (press) {startDrag(this);

}
On (release) {
}
```

14. **Click to reposition your cursor at the end of the current line.**

15. **On the list on the left side of the Actions panel, in the Global Functions category and the Movie Clip Control subcategory, double-click** stopDrag.

Flash adds the stopDrag(); statement on the right side of the Actions panel. The code in the Script pane of the Actions panel should now look like this:

```
On (press) {startDrag(this);

}
On (release) { stopDrag();

}
```

Now when you release the mouse button, the drag effect stops.

16. **Click the collapse arrow on the Actions panel title bar to collapse it.**

17. **Choose Edit⇨Edit Document to return to the main Timeline.**

18. **Drag the movie clip that you created from the Library to the Stage.**

To open the Library, choose Window⇨Library.

19. **Choose Control⇨Test Movie and then click and drag your movie clip.**

The movie clip follows your mouse!

You can constrain the movement of the movie clip to certain areas. For example, on a slider bar, you don't want the movie clip going all over the page — only along the bar. See *startDrag* in the ActionScript Dictionary for more details. (Choose Help⇨ActionScript Dictionary to view it.)

Look for drag and drop tree.fla in the Ch14 folder of the CD-ROM. Open the movie and choose Control⇨Test Movie. Drag the decorations onto the tree. Have fun! Also look for draganddrop_ex.fla in the same folder of the CD-ROM. This example includes some more complex ActionScript. *(Thanks to Craig Swann, of Crash!Media, at* www.crashmedia.com, *for this file.)*

Why is motion tweening not working?

For motion tweening to work, you need to make sure that several pieces are in place. (Review Chapter 9 for the basic instructions on motion tweening.)

Motion tweening problems can arise from any number of sources, a few of which follow:

- Make sure that you've created a group, text, or an instance of a symbol. Motion tweening doesn't work reliably on anything else.

- If you have a dashed line rather than a solid line indicating your motion tween on the Timeline, you didn't properly create an ending keyframe. Undo the steps that created the tween, create an ending keyframe, and try again.

- If you're having trouble changing the length of the tween by dragging on one of the keyframes, that keyframe wasn't included when you created the motion tween. Select the offending keyframe by itself (press Ctrl for Windows or ⌘ for Mac while you select, if necessary), and choose Motion from the Tweening drop-down list of the Property inspector.

- If you can't figure out why your motion tweening isn't working, you may have some action or setting that you don't even remember. Movies can get very complex, and comprehending all the relationships and interconnections can be difficult. Try copying to the Clipboard the object that you're animating and pasting it into a new, "clean" movie. You can copy and paste frames as well. In the new movie, you should be able to analyze the situation more clearly.

- If the animation worked previously, try undoing your last several actions. You can also try removing any recently created objects or ActionScript. If you can revert to the time your animation worked, you can start again from there.

- Only the simplest ActionScript and button behaviors work on the Stage. If you're trying to run your animation by using the Controller or pressing Enter, try Control⇨Test Movie instead. If your movie has more than one scene, try Control⇨Test Scene to try to isolate the problem to one scene.

- If you have more than one object on a layer, place each object on its own layer. (Refer to Chapter 6 for a discussion of working with layers.) Animate only one object on a layer.

How can I sync sound with motion?

Suppose that you want certain parts of your animation synchronized with specific sounds. For example, each time that a ball bounces, you want it to make a sound. Without specifically synchronizing the sounds, the sound and the animation may play at different speeds. A faster computer may play the animation faster but doesn't adjust the length of the sound. (For basic information on adding sound to Flash, refer to Chapter 11.)

To synchronize animation with the sound, you need to use a stream sound. When you add the sound file to a frame, choose Stream from the Sync drop-down list in the Property inspector. Then adjust the keyframes so that the animation and the sound end at the same time.

 To be more precise, you can synchronize your animation with specific parts of the sound. To accomplish this task, choose Modify➪Timeline➪Layer Properties and choose 200% or 300% from the Layer Height drop-down list. You can also click the little button in the upper-right corner of the Timeline and choose Medium or Large for the size of the frames from the option menu that appears. Now you can see the shape of your sound wave more clearly so that you can adjust the keyframes of your animation to match certain parts of the sound.

One way to pinpoint which frame to use for placing an animation event is to drag the playhead (the red rectangle) just above the Timeline. This technique lets you control the speed of the animation. You can drag left or right until you find the exact frame that you want to work with. You can then move a keyframe to that frame, for example, to move an animation event to a frame containing a specific portion of your sound.

What is the best way to import bitmaps?

The quick answer to the question of the best bitmap formats is that there *isn't* any best bitmap format. The best formats to import into Flash are vector formats because they're smaller, they scale perfectly, and they load more quickly.

Okay, sometimes you just *have* to use a bitmap. Maybe you need to put into the animation your boss's photograph or a photo of the product that you sell. Maybe you want an effect that you can create only in Photoshop. What do you use?

You may not have a choice of format. If your information systems department hands you a logo in JPEG format, you probably have to use it.

 A trick for changing a file's format is to open an existing bitmap file in an image-editing program. Most let you save that file in another format.

At other times, you can choose your format. For example, when you scan a photo, most scanner software lets you choose from among several formats. A digital camera may also let you choose the format. Of course, if you create the bitmap in an image-editing program, you can choose from any format that the program supports. (Refer to Chapter 3 for instructions on importing bitmap images. *Hint:* Choose File➪Import➪Import to Stage or File➪Import➪Import to Library.)

Here are some commonly used bitmap formats:

- The **GIF file** format, which generally displays well in a browser, can't have more than 256 colors. Use the GIF format for simple drawings that have a limited color palette.

- **JPEG files** can display many more colors than GIF files and therefore produce more realistic photos and other complex drawings. Although JPEG graphics can be highly compressed to reduce file size, they lose some fidelity as a result. Also, when Flash recompresses the file during export or publishing, you may end up with an unfocused mess.

- **BMP** doesn't lose quality when compressed, but the BMP format results in larger file sizes. If you want the lowest file size but do not want to compromise quality, the BMP format can be the best choice. The Flash image compressor works best and most efficiently with images that have not been compressed using techniques that may lose some image quality.

- **PNG** is also a nice compromise between file size and image quality. The PNG format doesn't lose quality when compressed and allows many more colors than the GIF format (and provides the capability for transparency).

Your final result is the .swf file that you publish. Flash compresses bitmaps (as well as the entire movie) when the movie is exported to an .swf Flash Player file. Therefore, you need to think about the entire round-trip journey that your bitmap will make. You may have to test varying bitmap formats and publish the movie for each one to see the exact results.

When you export, you can set the JPEG quality on the SWF tab of the Publish Settings dialog box. You also set the overall quality on the HTML tab. For that quality setting, only the High and Best settings *smooth* (anti-alias) the bitmaps in the movie. (Refer to Chapter 13 for more information about publishing your Flash movie.)

When you import a bitmap image into Flash, you can take the following steps to ensure good-looking results:

- Save your graphics in the highest quality possible. If you have a photograph, don't import it as a GIF file.

- Don't overcompress your original bitmaps, but don't import 100K files, either. Find a happy medium. Try saving an image in several formats to see the difference in quality and size.

- Set the compression type and quality in the Bitmap Properties dialog box. After you import the image, open the Library (choose Window➪Library) and right-click (Windows) or Control+click (Mac) the image and choose Properties to open the Bitmap Properties dialog box, as shown in Figure 14-1.

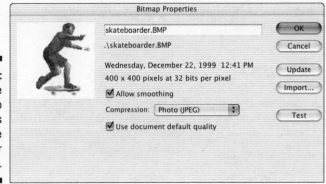

Figure 14-1:
Use the
Bitmap
Properties
box to fiddle
with your
bitmaps.

How do I rescale my movie's size?

You create a beautiful Flash movie that takes up the entire page. But then your boss says that you need to fit it into an existing HTML page, which translates into reducing the size of the whole thing by 25 percent. What do you do? Get a new boss, if possible.

Barring that, you can rescale the size of the movie by following these steps:

1. **Decide the amount of the reduction you need to achieve, such as 25 percent.**

2. **If you have any hidden layers, right-click (Windows) or Control+click (Mac) any layer and choose Show All from the contextual menu that appears.**

    This step ensures that all layers are considered in the reduction.

 3. **Click the Edit Multiple Frames button (just below the Timeline).**

4. **Drag the onion skin markers to the beginning and ending frames of your animation.**

    Refer to Chapter 9 if you need more information on how to use the onion skin markers.

5. **Choose Edit➪Select All.**

6. **Choose Window➪Design Panels➪Info to open the Info panel.**

    You see the Width (W), Height (H), and X and Y coordinates.

7. **Multiply all the numbers in the Info panel by the reduction percentage.**

    Write down the results of your calculations, just to be safe.

 8. **Click in the W (Width) text box and type the new number for the reduction percentage; then press Tab to move to the next box.**

 9. **Repeat Step 8 for the H (Height), X, and Y text boxes.**

You're done! Flash scales your entire movie by the percentage you specified.

Size requirements are key pieces of information that you need to nail down before building a Flash movie so that you can (you hope!) avoid any need to rescale your movie's size.

What are the best movie creating tips?

Every Flash user collects a number of techniques that make creating a Flash movie easier. The following items are a few ideas to help you get started.

- ✔ Save multiple versions of your movie by choosing File⇨Save As. If a problem arises, you can always go back to a previous version and start again.

- ✔ As soon as you have an overall structure, test your movie in a variety of browsers (for example, Internet Explorer, Netscape Navigator, and Apple's Safari) at various resolutions, if possible. You can more easily fix problems early, before you develop a complex situation. Use Control⇨Test Movie as soon as you develop your animation and continue to test in this way for each new significant change.

- ✔ Add comments (refer to Chapter 10) to your ActionScript so that you can figure out what you did when you go back to your movie after your vacation.

- ✔ Use consistent names for symbols. Many Flash users add the type of symbol after the name, so a button could be called *Contact_btn*, and a movie clip could be called *Intro_mc*. When you start creating movie clips inside buttons, you may get confused if you don't name your symbols intelligently.

- ✔ Use meaningful names for your instances. If you have three instances of a button symbol, you need to be able to distinguish which is which. You can name them by their purpose, such as E-mail, Services, and Clients.

- ✔ When you complete work on a layer, lock the layer to avoid making unwanted changes.

You're sure to discover other techniques as you become more experienced in Flash.

Can Flash do 3-D?

You can't really create 3-D in Flash. Flash is decidedly a 2-D program. But, not to be deterred, Flash users have created many tricks to make you think you're seeing 3-D.

One simple approach is to rotate a 2-D object in what appears to be 3-D space. For example, you can draw a circle and scale it in one dimension so that it becomes progressively more of an oval until all you see is a straight line. Continue to expand it from the line through fatter and fatter ovals until you have a circle again. You've just apparently rotated the circle 180 degrees. Continue until you're finished. You can select a group of frames and copy them or reverse them. (Refer to Chapter 9 for more details.) You can see a simple example in Figure 14-2.

You can use shape tweening to create this 3-D effect. You can shape tween a circle into a line and back again to make it look like it's rotating.

For fancier results, you can use software packages, such as Swift 3D, which are designed for creating 3-D animation for Flash. Also, some high-end 3-D animation packages such as Maya, have Flash export capabilities built-in.

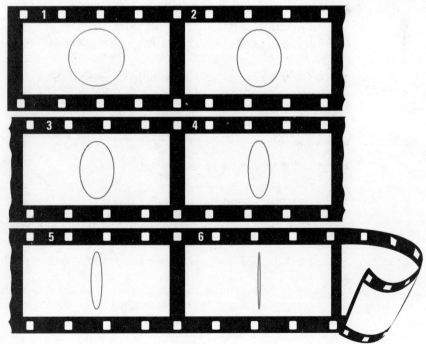

Figure 14-2: The circle is 2-D, but looks like it's rotating in 3-D; here, you see the first quarter revolution.

Another technique for simulating 3-D is to import an object from a 3-D program, such as 3D Studio Max, AutoCAD, or Maya.

In the following steps, we use AutoCAD as an example. To import an object from AutoCAD, follow these steps:

1. **Within AutoCAD, create the 3-D object, display the view that you want to start with, and then choose File⇨Export.**

   The Export Data dialog box opens. The Files of Type drop-down list should read Metafile (*.wmf).

2. **In the File Name text box, enter a name for the file. Add a 1 after the filename. Click Save and select the object when prompted.**

3. **Rotate the 3-D model slightly.**

   In AutoCAD 2000 and later, you can use the 3-D Orbit command for this step.

4. **Save this new view as a .wmf file as we explain in Step 2, consecutively numbered from the first file.**

   For example, if the first file is 3d1.wmf, name the second file 3d2.wmf.

5. **Repeat Steps 2 through 4 until you've rotated the model 360 degrees.**

6. **In Flash, choose File⇨Import⇨Import to Stage.**

7. **Choose Windows Metafile (*.wmf) from the Files of Type drop-down list, select the first WMF file that you created, and then click Open.**

8. **When Flash asks whether you want to import all the files in the sequence, click Yes.**

   Flash imports all the files, placing them in consecutive keyframes. The WMF file may be imported with a border as well as the lines that make up the object.

9. **For each keyframe, do the following:**

   a. *If your graphic has a border:* Click anywhere outside the objects, select just the border, and press Delete.

   b. *If your graphic is imported as one object:* Select all the objects and then choose Modify⇨Break Apart.

   c. Select the objects and then choose Modify⇨Convert to Symbol.

You can now play your animation. Note that you lose any shading or materials that you created in AutoCAD, so your model has a wire-frame look. You can use fills to modify your 3-D object in Flash to create the appearance of solidity.

For an example of creating a simple 3-D animation using this technique, look in the Ch14 folder of the CD-ROM for 3d rotation.fla.

What if you don't have a 3-D program? Well, do you have Microsoft Word? Yes, folks, you can create 3-D objects in your lowly word processing program.

To create a 3-D object by using Microsoft Word, follow these steps:

1. **Open Microsoft Word and, in a new document, open the Drawing toolbar if it isn't already open by choosing View⇨Toolbars⇨Drawing.**

2. **On the Drawing toolbar, click the AutoShapes drop-down arrow and choose any shape that you want.**

   You can even draw your own shape by using the Scribble tool (one of the options on the Lines submenu, under AutoShapes).

3. **Click in your blank document to place the shape.**

   If you want, use the Fill Color tool to change the fill. Select the shape and then, from the Fill Color drop-down list, choose Fill Effects and create a cool gradient on the Gradient tab.

4. **Click the 3-D button at the right end of the Drawing toolbar and choose from the box that opens a 3-D perspective that you like.**

   You may need to try out a couple of choices until you get the best effect.

5. **Click the 3-D button again and choose the 3-D Settings button at the bottom of the box to open the 3-D Settings toolbar.**

   Use the Tilt Left, Right, Up, or Down button to tilt the object until it looks perfectly flat so that you don't see any of the 3-D effect. Keep the 3-D Settings toolbar open.

6. **Choose Edit⇨Copy to copy the shape to the Clipboard.**

7. **Return to Flash and choose Insert⇨New Symbol; specify a movie clip behavior for the symbol and then name it.**

8. **Click OK.**

9. **Choose Edit⇨Paste to paste the shape into the first frame.**

10. **Go back to Word and decide which way you want your shape to rotate.**

    You can choose from up, down, left, or right.

11. **Select your 3-D shape in the Word document and click twice on Tilt Left (or Right or Up or Down) in the 3-D Settings toolbar.**

12. **Copy the shape to the Clipboard.**

13. **Go to Flash and create a keyframe in the next frame.**

14. **Paste the shape from the Clipboard.**

15. **Repeat Steps 11 through 14 until you're looking at your shape on edge.**

16. **Select all the frames except the first and the last and then choose Edit➪Timeline➪Copy Frames.**

17. **Click the first empty frame (the one after your last frame) and then choose Edit➪Timeline➪Paste Frames.**

    You now have the quarter revolution twice and need to modify the second set so that it becomes the second quarter revolution.

18. **Select all the frames that you've pasted and choose Modify➪Timeline➪Reverse Frames.**

    If you play the animation now, it looks as though the shape is revolving one quarter and then back again.

19. **Select the first of the frames that you pasted and choose Modify➪ Transform➪Flip Horizontal (if you used Tilt Left or Right in Word) or Flip Vertical (if you choose Tilt Up or Down in Word).**

20. **Repeat Step 19 with the remaining frames that you've pasted.**

    You now have a half revolution.

21. **Select all but the first and last frames and then choose Edit➪Timeline➪Copy Frames.**

22. **Click the first empty frame after the last frame and choose Edit➪Timeline➪Paste Frames.**

23. **Select all the frames that you've pasted and choose Modify➪Timeline➪Reverse Frames.**

You're done! Play your animation and watch your shape roll.

This method does have some disadvantages. First, all your images from Word are imported as bitmaps, not vector images. Second, you're animating frame by frame. As a result, your file is larger and downloads slower. If you use this method for just a small animation, however, it beats learning how to use a fancy 3-D program (and paying for it, too). Test the results and see whether it works for you.

Look in the Ch14 folder for `rotating star.fla`, which is an example of using Word to create 3-D objects. The animation is in a movie clip, so choose Control➪Test Movie to see the results (or open the `.swf` file directly).

Chapter 15

The Top Ten Web Design Tips

● ●

*T*he vast majority of Flash movies end up on Web sites. To help ensure that your Web site is as attractive and useful as possible, this chapter offers ten Web design tips. Some of these tips apply to all Web sites, and others are specific to those sites that use Flash movies.

Set Your Goal

A general principle of Web design is to know why you have a Web site. Write out one main goal and perhaps one or two secondary goals. For example, the main goal of your site may be to sell used music CDs. A secondary goal may be to provide viewers with music reviews so that they can decide which CDs they want to buy. Another secondary goal can be to attract viewers to your site (so that they can buy your CDs). Avoid putting material on your site that doesn't help you reach your goal.

How does your Flash movie help you attain your Web site's goal? Perhaps your movie displays the covers of your most widely sold CDs and plays some of the music, giving viewers an instant understanding of your site's purpose. On the other hand, if your Flash movie just displays an animated logo, it may even distract viewers from the important features of your home page.

By default, the Flash HyperText Markup Language (HTML) file loops your files. Looped short animations tend to look like the animated GIFs that we all know and hate — and ignore. Avoid looped animation unless you have a good reason for it, especially if it moves across the Web page in a banner. Viewers may assume that it's advertising and ignore it, which is probably not your goal.

Make Thumbnail Sketches First

This may be the most radical, life-altering advice in this book: After you articulate the goals for your Web site, try out several different designs for each type of page in your site by drawing small sketches of them. For your home page, try out at least a dozen designs.

Keep the sketches really small, so they're the size of a postage stamp. This makes it easier for you to try a lot of different designs quickly.

It also forces you to think of the overall design of your site before you jump into the details. You can easily see the words on your pages as blocks of text as well as how the big shapes on your pages relate to each other. This gives you a chance to pick a strong overall design that graphically supports your goals for the site. Try it — you may be amazed at how this can improve your Web page designs.

Connect the Parts to the Whole

You've found a compelling overall graphic design by drawing your thumbnail sketches as we describe in the preceding section. Now while you fill in the details of your page, see how you can organize the details of your page so that they fit well into its main graphic theme as captured in your thumbnail sketch. This will help you avoid clutter and will make your pages easier to understand, more powerful, and more attractive.

Unlike television, the Web is an interactive medium. Viewers need to understand the purpose of your site and how to navigate it. Clutter and complex structures are usually counterproductive. You can use Flash to create a simple, compelling navigational system. But you must be careful when mixing and matching HTML and Flash elements to avoid confusion. For example, let all your buttons look similar — don't create five different shapes and colors of Flash buttons just because you can.

Keep It Simple

Simplicity can be powerful. Sketch out the map of your site and make sure that the lines of navigation are short and simple. Don't use long explanations when a short one will do. Don't use lots of images when one will suffice.

Your Flash movies should also be as simple as possible. Animation goes by fast. If too many objects are moving at once, viewers don't know where to focus their attention.

Use Fewer Than Four Fonts

To create a Web page design with maximum coherence and impact, you should probably restrict your page design to two or three fonts at most. It makes visual sense to use one font for the body of your text and one font for the headlines. You could perhaps use a third font for a logo or for some other special item, but this may look best if it has some kind of strong visual harmony with the other fonts that you're using.

Use four fonts, and people may start to think that you're designing a ransom note, not a Web page.

Be Consistent

Each page on your site should have the same logo. Certain links should go on each page (such as a link to your home page) and be in the same place on each page. If you have other links, such as Search or E-Mail, they should also be consistent throughout your site.

Text color, fonts, hyperlinks, backgrounds, buttons, and other elements should all be consistent to avoid confusion and error.

Your URLs and page headings should also have a consistent theme. URLs should be as simple as possible, and headings need to be complete and clear. Viewers often see headings out of context, such as in the results of a search engine or in your table of contents. For example, if you're selling used CDs, don't use *Jazz* at the top of one page and *Looking for Some Classical Music?* at the top of another. Instead, put *Used Jazz CDs* on the first page and *Used Classical CDs* on the next. These headings are simple, complete, and consistent.

If you're combining HTML and Flash content, use consistent fonts and colors for both.

Make It Lean and Fast

Viewers don't like to wait for a page to download. Throughout this book, we discuss ways to make your Flash movies smaller so that they download faster. More and more Web surfers have cable modems or digital subscriber line (DSL) connections, giving them higher-speed Internet access. (A study by comScore Media Metrix in early 2003 reported at `cyberatlas.com` showed that 34 percent of the U.S. online population had broadband access, and 54 percent of the Canadian online population had broadband.) But many still don't. You don't want potential viewers to give up on your site because it takes too long to load. So any time that you find a way to make your Flash movie smaller without sacrificing important content, go for it.

The same advice applies to the rest of your Web site: Keep the graphic images as small as possible and use as few as possible.

Know Who's Watching and How

Many Web site hosts provide you with information on the browsers (including which version) and the resolutions used by your viewers. You may not be able to cater to every browser and monitor resolution out there, but you should try to create a Web site that your target audience can see.

Many sites that use Flash offer a non-Flash alternative rather than force viewers without the Flash Player to download it. The non-Flash alternative has non-animated graphics in place of the Flash movie.

Remember that viewers on a screen with lower resolution see much less than do viewers on screens with a higher resolution. Those with lower resolution may miss important parts of your Web page and Flash animation. You may want to consider that the percentage of Web surfers with 640 x 480 screen resolutions has dropped dramatically — statistics from `www.thecounter.com` as of this writing show the percentage is down to 2 percent of Web surfers. But they're not gone completely, and the number of viewers with even smaller screens is rising as the number of personal digital assistants (PDAs) with wireless Internet access increases.

Ensure Your Viewer Has the Flash Player

As we explain in Chapters 12 and 13, you can choose to publish an HTML file that detects whether the Flash Player is installed on the viewer's computer. If not, it displays an image file. (You need to publish to one of the image formats at the same time for this technique to work.)

The default HTML text doesn't check for the Flash Player, but it includes the location to download the player. In some situations, the Flash Player downloads automatically if it's not already installed where your Web browser can find it — or a window pops up, offering the viewer the chance to download it. Many sites include a button that says `Can't see the animation? Download the Flash Player here` or something to that effect. The button links to the Macromedia download center at `www.macromedia.com/go/getflashplayer`.

Many Web surfers have no idea how Web sites are created and have never heard of Flash. Therefore, giving viewers a choice of Flash and non-Flash sites may not be meaningful. (Of course, if you're a Web site designer and you think that potential clients viewing your site may be savvier than most viewers, you may have no problem in this regard.) In most situations, using the words *animated* and *non-animated* may work better. Of course, feel free to use the word *Flash* along with some explanation. (You want the world to know what Flash is, don't you?) See Chapter 12 for more information on how to detect whether your viewer has the Flash Player.

Test and Then Test Again

As we describe in Chapter 13, you undoubtedly need to test your Web site with several browsers, not just the latest version of Internet Explorer. Testing at various screen resolutions (probably at least 800 x 600 and 1024 x 768) is also extremely important. Depending on your target audience, you should probably also test your Web site at various Internet connection speeds, such as 28.8 Kbps and 56 Kbps, as well as at faster speeds (for DSL and cable modem connections). Test your Web site on a system that doesn't have the Flash player as well as one that does.

Finally, have a few friends review your site and navigate through it. Ask them to write down their impressions, moments of confusion, questions, and comments. (Of course, they can also write down profuse praise.) When you work on a Web site, you get so involved in it that you need someone objective and without your inside knowledge to provide a fresh perspective.

Chapter 16

The Ten Best Flash Resources

Flash is such a flexible program that you never stop learning. And just when you think you've got it, out comes a new version! In this chapter, we point you to the many resources that you can turn to when you want to increase your knowledge about Flash.

Of course, we think that this book is a great resource on Flash. But you're already using this book, and much more about Flash is out there, readily available to help you become a truly great Flash animator.

Take the Feature Tour and Do the Tutorials

When you start Flash, you're given the option of taking a quick Flash tour. Take the tour; your Web browser will appear with the Flash MX 2004 tour at the Macromedia Web site. What a great way to see an animated overview of the main features of Flash.

Flash also comes with a few tutorials on the basics of Flash. You can find it by choosing Help⇨How Do I. You may find it useful to go through each lesson that interests you.

If your computer is connected to the Internet, you can get the latest updated version of Help from Macromedia by clicking the green arrow labeled Update in the upper-right hand area of the Help window.

Take a Course

Many colleges and universities offer courses in Flash. Sometimes these courses are part of a Web design or graphic art course, or they may stand alone. To find these courses, call local educational institutions and ask!

The advantage of a course led by a teacher is that you have a chance to ask questions — and receive answers. A teacher also guides the learning process and possibly even gives you lots of tips and hints!

You might also consider taking courses from Macromedia University, which offers both self-paced and instructor-led courses in the use of Flash and other Macromedia products. Go to www.macromedia.com/university/ for more information, including free sample lessons.

Look on the Flash Web Page

Macromedia maintains a large resource on its Web site. Go to www.macromedia.com/support/flash, where you can find learning tips, tutorials, support, technical notes, news, and updates. Macromedia also has a wonderful gallery of great Flash Web sites. Looking at these sites and wishing that you could do the same is lots of fun. Someday, you will! Go to www.macromedia.com/software/flash/ and click the Showcase link.

Join a Flash Discussion Group

Macromedia maintains several Flash newsgroups where anyone can ask questions and get expert answers. The two main newsgroups are

- ✔ **Flash:** For technical issues relating to Flash and Flash Player.
- ✔ **Flash Site Design:** For discussing techniques as well as technical issues.

To read messages from and send messages to these groups, just point your Web browser to webforums.macromedia.com/flash/.

If you have software for reading newsgroups on your computer, you can alternatively go to news://forums.macromedia.com/macromedia.flash and news://forums.macromedia.com/macromedia.flash.sitedesign to read messages from and send messages to the two main groups.

Several other excellent active discussion groups reside on Web sites. The best way to tell whether a discussion group is active is to see how many messages have been posted in the past one or two days. You can also check out how many different people are participating. See the section "Check Out the Flash Resource Sites," later in this chapter.

You can also subscribe to electronic mailing lists for ongoing discussion sent by e-mail. With more than 30,000 members, the Yahoo! FLASHmacromedia list is one of the largest such lists specifically for users who want to discuss Flash techniques. You can ask questions and get answers from the community of Flash users. To sign up or to view the Web archive of messages, go to groups.yahoo.com/group/FLASHmacromedia. You can also subscribe by sending a blank e-mail to FLASHmacromedia-subscribe@yahoogroups.com.

Another busy and informative mailing list is the flasher list. You can subscribe (for free of course) or search its archives at `www.chinwag.com/flasher`.

You can find more than 200 other Macromedia Flash e-mail discussion groups at Yahoo! alone. Find them by surfing the Web over to `groups.yahoo.com` and typing **Macromedia Flash** into the Search box.

Check Out the Flash Resource Sites

A huge Flash community is on the Internet . . . so vast, in fact, that you'll probably never be able to participate in all its offerings. These Web sites offer news, tutorials, discussion groups, tips, and links to other Flash resources.

Some of these sites are more up-to-date, lively, and complete than others. The quality of the tips and tutorials varies widely. Some specialize in tips for beginners; others are geared toward advanced users. This section briefly reviews the ones that we find most useful, in alphabetical order.

`www.actionscript.org`

This site is a well-designed, comprehensive resource on ActionScript. It includes extremely active discussion forums (with tens of thousands of messages); more than 100 tutorials on ActionScript at beginning, intermediate, and advanced levels; a library with more than 400 ActionScripts, more than 700 Flash movies, and more than 25 components; links; a Flash bookstore; and downloadable software tools.

`www.artswebsite.com`

This site includes lots of great examples and downloads from a Flash teacher. You also find tutorials on some great, popular effects.

`www.bestflashanimationsite.com`

This site showcases Flash sites that have been voted the best by viewers. This is a good place to find top-notch examples of Flash in 11 categories: Artwork, Cartoons/Anime, Corporate, Experimental, Flash 3D, Games, Motion Graphics, Navigation, Original Sound, Technical Merit, and Typography.

`www.flash99good.com`

This well-designed site is dedicated to providing information about how to make Flash sites more usable. It presents excellent tips on usability, case studies of sites that make bad use of Flash, tutorials, and links to more Flash usability information on the Web.

`www.flashfilmmaker.com`

The Flash Filmmaker site is for everyone interested in using Flash for cartooning and creating movie entertainment. The site includes forums, some tips and tricks, and links to lots of Flash movies, organized by genre.

`www.flashfruit.com`

At Flash Fruit, you can find a carefully selected group of links to interviews, tutorials, ActionScript, online magazines, and more. The Flash Fruit editors have done a good job of picking some of the best resources for Flash users.

`www.flashgallery.co.uk`

Flashgallery is a nicely designed showcase of inspiring Flash sites. The gallery displays a thumbnail-size view of each showcased site, accompanied by a succinct description of its best features and a rating by the editors on a scale from 1 to 10.

`www.flashkit.com`

Flash Kit is probably the largest Flash site, and it's up-to-date. (We define *up-to-date* as having Flash MX 2004 material within days after it has shipped.) Thousands of FLA files for you to download and study, hundreds of tutorials, numerous active discussion groups (including Flash MX 2004 topics, one for newbies, and many more), links, sounds, more than a thousand downloadable fonts — if you can think of it, you can find it here.

`www.flashmagazine.com`

This site includes up-to-date technical Flash information, including lessons on ActionScript. You also find links, reviews, articles, and an interesting list of applications that can output Flash Player files.

`www.flashthief.com`

Flash Thief is a very useful site with .fla movies, tutorials, sounds, fonts, articles, and a gallery of inspirational Flash sites. One unique feature of this site is its "e-naked" section, in which high-quality sites are critiqued, taken apart piece by piece, and analyzed from a technical viewpoint.

`www.moock.org/webdesign/flash`

Colin Moock is a master Flash designer, and his Web site contains tons of advanced technical information, Flash industry news, his weblog, annotated links, and more. You can generally find lots to chew on here.

```
www.popedeflash.com
```

This is a resource for sharing information about combining Flash and 3-D. Here you find a very useful weblog, tutorials, a gallery of sites that combine Flash and 3-D, and an online forum.

```
www.ultrashock.com
```

Ultrashock, another multifaceted site, includes tutorials, downloads of `.fla` files, discussion forums, and links to more than 1,000 sites, including links to Flash games, Flash cartoons, and cool sites that use Flash.

```
www.were-here.com
```

At We're Here Forums, you find a wealth of resources: an extensive forum, daily news about Flash, dozens of tutorials, and more than 100 FLA file downloads.

Check Out Sites That Use Flash

In Chapter 17, we list ten great sites that use Flash. And many resource sites have galleries of great sites, as does Macromedia. You can get ideas by looking at what others do. (It's interesting, for instance, that simple Flash sites are sometimes the most beautiful and practical.)

Attend a Flash Conference

Attending a conference on Flash is an exciting way to learn much more about Flash from an array of experts, see award-winning Flash movies, participate in workshops and seminars, hear the latest news from Macromedia, make contacts with others interested in Flash, and generally immerse yourself in the world of Flash. Even just visiting the Web sites of some of these conferences can be quite instructive. Conferences you might consider attending include

- **Flashforward** (including the Flash Film Festival): Held in the spring in San Francisco and in the summer in New York City. For information, visit `www.flashforward2004.com`.

- **Macromedia MAX Conference:** A four-day conference in the fall, designed by Macromedia for professional developers and designers who use Macromedia software. For information, visit `www.macromedia.com/macromedia/conference`.

- **Macromedia Flash Kit Conference:** A two-day conference in the summer produced by Jupitermedia in association with the popular Flash Web site, www.flashkit.com. For information, visit www.jupiterevents.com, and click the link to the Flash Kit Conference.

Look at Our Sites

Check out the *Macromedia Flash MX 2004 For Dummies* page on the Wiley Web site. You can find the site by surfing to www.dummies.com and typing **Flash** in the Book Search box. And check out Ellen Finkelstein's site, at www.ellenfinkelstein.com. It contains tips and tutorials for beginners. We hope that you find these sites helpful!

Collect Flash Movies

Many Flash resource Web sites let you download .fla movies. You can also trade movies with others who you know use Flash. Analyzing movies is a great way to see how effects are created. In Chapter 14, we explain how to use the Movie Explorer to ferret out all the hidden details of a movie.

Be sure to check out the Library of a movie — most of the secrets lie there. Select objects with the Actions panel open to see the actions attached to objects. You'll soon be on your way to adapting the techniques that you see to your own projects.

Reuse Your Best Stuff

After you've created some great Flash movies, you can reuse your best stuff. *Fadeouts* (changing transparency), *glows* (soft edges), and masks are simple effects that you can use again and again. You can also reuse ActionScript on new objects. After you get a technique down, you don't need to re-create the wheel. If you've created an animated logo, you may be able to use it over and over. Certain simple animations can be created in new colors, using the same original symbols.

You can import items from the Library of any movie into your current movie. Choose File➪Import➪Open External Library and choose the Flash file that contains the Library that you want to use. Then drag the items that you want from the imported movie Library onto the Stage or into the Library of your current movie.

Chapter 17

Ten Great Web Sites That Use Flash

● ●

Trying to choose the ten best Web sites that use Flash is almost absurd — so many good ones are out there. In addition, by the time you read this book, who knows whether these sites will still be around? Nevertheless, we want to give you a shortcut to finding top-quality Flash sites so that you can get ideas and see the possibilities.

How did we choose? Certainly, many wonderful sites we just missed. But we created a list of more than 100 sites and looked at them all. We chose them based on

- ✔ **Beauty:** We want to show you sites that are beautiful examples of artistic Web design.
- ✔ **Creativity:** We chose only sites that seem to have a real spark of inspiration and originality, in order to show you Flash's tremendous range.

Note that many of these sites can take a really long time to load if you don't have a broadband connection to the Web.

www.bit-101.com

This is the personal site of Flash experimenter Keith Peters. Here in his online laboratory, you'll find the results of more than 500 of his explorations with Flash, in which he uses various principles of math and physics to take Flash into interesting new realms.

www.chipotle.com

This is a graphically striking, refreshingly offbeat, and funny site devoted to a chain of gourmet burrito shops. Flash is used in every aspect of this site, yet it doesn't look in any way like a typical Flash site.

www.habitat.net

The Web site for Terrence Conran's renowned chain of furniture stores features some great Flash design, including lots of cool little people pushing text around. The site includes a catalog of furniture as well as a gallery of interiors, and both are easy and interesting to browse through. It's interesting that the site hasn't changed much over the years, yet still seems fresh and appealing.

www.lego.com/hahli

This is an animated adventure game (in Flash of course) that's part of Lego's site for toys based around the game Bionicle. The graphics are fun and evocative.

www.lfs.nl

Ellen Pronk's personal Web site is her visual diary and sketchbook in which she records her doodles, photos, and mostly abstract Flash animations. Each animation does one thing simply but well. *Lfs* is a kind of shorthand for *liefs,* which translates to *with love.*

www.miniusa.com

The MINI USA site has style, a great sense of humor and loads of interactivity that makes the Mini seem like a very charming car to own.

www.organicselections.com

Here's another site that's loaded with charm. Natural Selections sells organic cotton clothing in the authors' hometown. The site uses a lot of hand-drawn Flash vector grapnics for a homegrown look that's relaxing and appealing, which provides an interesting contrast to a lot of the hard-edge, in-your-face Flash animation that you see on the Web.

www.typorganism.com

...t.y.p.o.r.g.a.n.i.s.m... is an intriguing series of interactive typographic experiments based on the metaphor that type is an organism. Here Flash is put to use for a variety of striking typographic effects which respond to user interaction and which evolve over time.

www.velocityworks.com

The Velocity Works Web design firm has built entirely in Flash an amazingly complete, sophisticated, and appealing user interface for its Web site. The interface includes draggable windows, customizable wallpaper, sound effects, and interactive forms.

www.whoswestudios.com/flashsite.html

This site is a stunning antithesis to the Natural Selections site described previously. It's a very high-tech, tour-de-force of Flash animation of photographic objects, and it also manages to be very funny. Like many of the previous sites, it possesses a clarity and strength of vision that gives it a lot of power.

Part VII
Appendixes

The 5th Wave   By Rich Tennant

©RICHTENNANT

"Why don't you try blurring the brimstone and then animating the hellfire."

In this part . . .

In the Appendixes, we dump everything that we couldn't fit elsewhere but thought too useful to forget. We explain how to install Flash (it's a snap), customize your preferences, and create your own keyboard shortcuts. One Appendix shows you all the Flash MX panels and labels them carefully so that you know what they do. We also offer a glossary of need-to-know terms and tell you what's on the CD-ROM (lots of stuff!).

Appendix A

Installing Flash and Setting Your Preferences

· ·

*I*nstalling Flash is simple; nevertheless, sometimes a few pointers can help. After you're up and running, you may want to customize how Flash works. You can set quite a number of preferences. You can also create your own keyboard shortcuts.

Installing Flash

Installing Flash is a cinch, although you have a couple of options. Here's the lowdown on getting started.

You can install Flash in four different ways:

- ✔ Install from a CD (onto a PC).
- ✔ Download it to a PC.
- ✔ Install from a CD (onto a Mac).
- ✔ Download it to a Mac.

We discuss these methods separately in the next four sections.

Installing Flash onto a PC from a CD

So you went out and bought "Flash in the box," and you have a CD-ROM drive on your PC. To install Flash from the box, follow these steps:

1. **Exit all Windows programs.**

2. **Insert the CD-ROM.**

   In most cases, the setup program starts automatically. If not, choose Start⇨Run and click Browse. Then find and double-click Setup.exe on your CD-ROM drive. Click Run.

3. **Follow the instructions on the various screens that appear.**

   Unless you want to save space by not installing the lessons and samples, choose the typical installation. Other than that, the most significant choice that you have is where you install Flash. You can browse to change the location or accept the default, which is `C:\Program Files\Macromedia\Flash MX 2004`.

4. **After you follow the screen instructions, the setup program starts copying files; when it is completed, click Finish.**

5. **Read the ReadMe file offered on the last screen.**

   Although we guarantee that most of the stuff in the file is irrelevant to you, sometimes this file has just the weird detail that applies to your situation, so take the two minutes to read it.

Installing Flash by downloading it to your PC

If you like, you can download the Flash trial directly from the Macromedia Web site. You can then pay for it within 30 days. Follow these steps:

1. **Go to** `www.macromedia.com/software/downloads/`.

2. **On the list of Macromedia products, choose Flash.**

   You need to complete or create a password and answer a few questions.

3. **Follow the instructions for downloading the installation file.**

   When you download the file, you choose the location on your hard drive. Remember this location.

4. **When the download is complete, double-click the installation file.**

   Here's where you need to remember where you saved it. The installation program guides you through the process of installing Flash.

5. **Unless you want to save space by not installing the lessons and samples, choose the typical installation.**

   Other than that, the most significant choice that you have is where you install Flash. You can browse to change the location or accept the default, which is `C:\Program Files\Macromedia\Flash MX 2004`.

After you install Flash, you can play with it! You can buy it at any time by clicking Buy Now on the first screen when you open Flash.

Installing Flash onto a Mac from a CD

If you bought Flash in a box, you have a CD-ROM that you can use to install Flash.

To install Flash on your Mac from a CD, follow these steps:

1. **Insert the CD-ROM. Find and double-click the Flash MX 2004 Installer icon.**

2. **When a window appears, displaying a software license agreement, click the Accept button so that you can continue the installation.**

3. **Unless you want to save space by not installing the lessons and samples, choose Easy Install, which is the default.**

   Other than that, the most significant choice that you have is where you install Flash. You can browse to change the location or accept the default location, which is on the startup disk drive.

4. **Click Install.**

   The installer program starts copying files. When it's done, you see the Macromedia Flash MX 2004 folder displayed on your computer screen, containing the Flash MX 2004 program, a few documents, and a bunch of other folders. One of the documents is the `ReadMe.html` file. You can view the contents of this file by simply double-clicking it. Although we guarantee that most of the stuff in the file is irrelevant to you, sometimes this file has just the weird detail that applies to your situation, so take the two minutes to read it.

Installing Flash by downloading it to your Mac

In this ultramodern day and age, you can now install Flash on your computer without ever leaving your Web browser. To download Flash, follow these steps (or something like them, assuming that the Macromedia Web site doesn't change too much):

1. **Go to** `www.macromedia.com/software/downloads/`.

2. **On the list of Macromedia products, choose Macromedia Flash MX 2004.**

   You need to complete or create a password and answer a few questions.

3. **Follow the instructions for downloading the installation file.**

4. **When the download is complete, double-click the installation file.**

    The installation program guides you through the process of installing Flash.

    The most significant choice that you have is where you install Flash. You can browse to change the location or accept the default, which is the startup disk drive.

After you install Flash, you can play with it! If you download the trial version, you can buy it at any time by clicking Buy Now on the first screen when you open Flash.

Setting Your Preferences

Flash offers a number of ways to customize how you work. Why not make Flash suit you?

The main location for setting preferences is the Preferences dialog box, as shown in Figure A-1, with the General tab on top. To open the Preferences dialog box, choose Edit⇨Preferences (Windows) or Flash⇨Preferences (Mac).

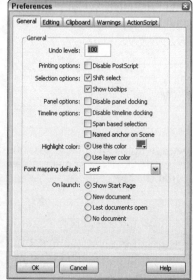

Figure A-1:
Use the
Preferences
dialog box
to bend
Flash to
your will.

The following sections describe how to use this dialog box.

General tab

On the General tab, you can set the following options:

- **Undo Levels:** Set to 100 by default; you can enter any value from 2 to 9,999. The higher the value, the more memory Flash takes to remember all those steps. You may be surprised by how many commands you give in half an hour, so 100 is probably a good setting. However, if you want to save commands from the History panel that you executed half an hour ago, make it higher.

- **Printing Options — Disable PostScript:** For Windows only; enabling this check box disables PostScript output when you print to a PostScript printer. Mark this check box only if you have trouble printing to a PostScript printer. This option is not marked by default.

- **Selection Options — Shift Select:** Enabled by default, which means that you have to press Shift to select more than one object (by clicking). If you don't press Shift, the first object is deselected. Clearing this option means that you can click as many objects as you want in order to select them. This method is an efficient way to work, but most people aren't familiar with it. If you select something by accident, press Shift and click the object to deselect it.

- **Selection Options — Show Tooltips:** By default, shows short explanations of Flash interface features (such as toolbars and buttons) when you pass your cursor over them. You can make the ToolTips go away by clearing this check box.

- **Panel Options — Disable Panel Docking: (Windows only)** Prevents you from docking panels at the edge of the Flash window.

- **Timeline Options — Disable Timeline Docking:** Prevents the timeline from docking at the top of the window.

- **Timeline Options — Span Based Selection:** Lets you click between two keyframes to select the entire section between them, à la Flash 5.

- **Timeline Options — Named Anchor on Scene:** Automatically creates a named anchor at the beginning of each scene. For more information on anchors, see Chapter 12.

- **Highlight Color:** Lets you specify the color of the box around selected symbols and groups. Select the Use This Color radio button and pick a color to specify your own color. Otherwise, you can select Use Layer Color to use the layer's outline color.

✔ **Font Mapping Default:** Lets you choose which font you want to use when you open a movie in Flash that contains a font you don't have.

✔ **On Launch:** Defines what happens when you open Flash. The default, Show Start Page, displays a window where you can choose to start a new document or open recently used documents. Instead, you can choose to open a new blank document, to open the documents that were open the last time you used Flash, or to start with no document at all.

Editing tab

On the Editing tab, you can set the following items:

✔ **Pen Tool — Show Pen Preview:** Displays a preview of the line or curve segment before you click the next point. Recommended!

✔ **Pen Tool — Show Solid Points:** When marked, shows filled points at vertices.

✔ **Pen Tool — Show Precise Cursors:** Displays a small crosshair rather than the pen-shaped cursor, for more precise placement of points.

✔ **Vertical Text — Default Text Orientation:** Sets vertical text as the default. Use this option for some Asian fonts.

✔ **Right to Left Text Flow:** Sets the default for vertical text so that new vertical lines flow from right to left.

✔ **No Kerning:** Removes kerning from vertical text.

The drawing settings are covered in Chapter 3.

Clipboard tab

The Clipboard tab enables you to set preferences for displaying, exporting, and importing certain objects. Here are your choices:

✔ **Bitmaps — Color Depth:** Specifies the color depth for bitmaps copied to the Clipboard. This setting applies to Windows only. You can choose to match the screen or set a color depth from 4-bit to 32-bit with alpha. You can use this setting to reduce the size of bitmaps that you paste into Flash from the Windows Clipboard.

✔ **Bitmaps — Resolution:** Sets the resolution of bitmaps copied to the Clipboard. This setting applies to Windows only. Choose Screen to match your screen resolution or choose 72, 150, or 300. You can use this setting to reduce the size of bitmaps you paste into Flash from the Windows Clipboard.

✔ **Bitmaps — Size Limit:** Applies to Windows only; lets you specify a size limit in kilobytes for the amount of RAM (memory) that is used for a bitmap on the Windows Clipboard. If you have large images, you may need to increase this number, which is set to 250K by default.

✔ **Bitmaps — Smooth:** Applies to Windows only. This box, marked by default, applies anti-aliasing to bitmaps. *Anti-aliasing* smoothes the appearance of bitmaps so that they don't appear so jagged. You can affect the smoothing of bitmaps during publishing by choosing the quality of the output, which we explain in the discussion of the HTML tab in Chapter 13.

✔ **Gradients:** Applies to Windows only and lets you specify the quality of gradients that you copy to the Clipboard for use in other applications. Choose from None to Best.

✔ **PICT Settings:** Applies to Macintosh only. Lets you specify the method and resolution used to copy art to the Clipboard. From the Type menu, choose Objects to copy art as vector graphics or one of the bitmap settings to copy it as a bitmap. In the Resolution input box, type in the resolution that you desire in dots per inch. If you want to include PostScript data, select the Include Postscript check box. In the Gradients menu, choose the Gradient quality you want when you paste the clipboard into a document outside of Flash. (When pasting within Flash, this setting is ignored, and you always get the full gradient quality.)

✔ **FreeHand Text:** By default, the Maintain Text as Blocks check box is marked so that text pasted from FreeHand can be edited in Flash.

Warnings tab

The Warnings tab lists ten situations in which Flash will display a warning message. All are enabled by default, so you're safe. If you find these warnings annoying or unnecessary, you can clear the appropriate check box.

ActionScript Editor

The ActionScript Editor lets you customize how ActionScript looks and functions on the Action panel:

✔ **Automatic Indentation/Tab Size:** By default, any ActionScript that you type is automatically indented. The tab size (amount of indentation) is four spaces. You can remove the automatic indentation or change the tab size.

✔ **Code Hints/Delay:** Code hints provide pop-up text in the Actions panel that helps you complete your code based on what you're typing. You can remove these hints and set a time delay for the display of the hints.

- ✔ **Open/Import:** This specifies the encoding used for fonts when opening or importing. The default, UTF-8, provides Unicode encoding that supports multiple languages.

- ✔ **Save/Export:** This specifies the encoding used for fonts when saving or exporting. The default, UTF-8, provides Unicode encoding that supports multiple languages.

- ✔ **Text (Font and Font Size):** You can set the font and size of text in the ActionScript Editor.

- ✔ **Syntax Coloring:** By default, ActionScript is colored based on the syntax of your code. For example, comments are highlighted in gray. You can remove coloring completely or change the colors for each syntax type.

- ✔ **Language:** In Flash MX 2004, you can put ActionScript in frames, buttons, movie clips, and multiple separate ActionScript text files. If you click the ActionScript 2.0 Settings button here, you can modify the places that Flash searches when your ActionScript in one place references certain kinds of ActionScript (called *classes*), which may be elsewhere. If you're just starting out with Flash, you almost certainly are not defining new class definition files in ActionScript, in which case you definitely don't have to worry about this.

Customizing Keyboard Shortcuts

You can create a shortcut for any menu item and change existing shortcuts. (See the Cheat Sheet at the front of this book for commonly used keyboard shortcuts.) Besides the standard set of shortcuts, Flash MX 2004 comes with some built-in shortcuts based on other programs, such as FreeHand 10, Illustrator 10, and Photoshop 6, so that you can use those same familiar shortcuts in Flash MX 2004.

To create shortcuts, choose Edit⇨Keyboard Shortcuts (Windows) or Flash MX 2004⇨Keyboard Shortcuts to open the Keyboard Shortcuts dialog box, as shown in Figure A-2. (The figure shows the Windows version; the Mac version is nearly the same.)

You can't change the original set of shortcuts. Instead, create a duplicate set of shortcuts and modify the duplicate. Give the duplicate a new name, such as *MyWay,* and then use these shortcuts:

 To duplicate a shortcut set, click Duplicate Set at the top of the Keyboard Shortcuts dialog box.

 To rename a set of shortcuts, click Rename Set at the top of the Keyboard Shortcuts dialog box.

 To delete a set of shortcuts, click Delete Set at the top of the Keyboard Shortcuts dialog box.

Figure A-2:
The Keyboard Shortcuts dialog box enables you to use your fingers the way *you* want.

After you have a new set of shortcuts, choose from the Commands drop-down list the types of commands that you want to change. You can change all six (Windows) or seven (Mac) types of commands, but only one at a time:

- **Drawing Menu Commands:** Changes shortcuts for commands from the menu.

- **Drawing Tools:** Changes shortcuts for the tools in the Tools panel.

- **Test Movie Menu Commands:** Changes shortcuts for commands from the menu that appears when you choose Control⇨Test Movie.

- **Script Edit Commands:** (Macintosh only.) Changes shortcuts for commands from the menu that appears when you are using the Script window. This is the editor window that appears when you choose File⇨New (or File⇨Open) and then choose a script file to edit, such as an ActionScript (.as) file or a Flash JavaScript (.jsfl) file.

- **Timeline Commands:** Changes shortcuts for commands that move and select frames on the Timeline.

- **Workspace Accessibility Commands:** Changes shortcuts for commands that change the focus to the Stage or the Timeline, select panels, and select objects within a panel.

- **Actions Panel Commands:** Changes shortcuts for working in the Actions panel.

For each type of command set, click the plus (+) sign (in Windows) or the right-pointing arrow (on the Mac) on the list to display all the commands and their current shortcuts. Here's how to create a new shortcut:

1. **Select the command that you want to customize.**

2. **Click the Add Shortcut button.**

   Flash adds a new shortcut, named `empty`.

3. **Press the keyboard combination that you want to use.**

   You must include Ctrl (Windows)/⌘ (Mac), Alt (Windows)/Option (Mac), or Shift before the second key. Flash tells you whether that combination is already assigned to another shortcut.

   • If you want to use that shortcut, click Change. Flash alerts you if the shortcut is already taken and lets you reassign the shortcut.

   • If you don't want to use that shortcut, select the `empty` shortcut on the Shortcuts list and click Remove Shortcut.

4. **Repeat Steps 2 and 3 to change as many shortcuts as you want.**

5. **Click OK when you finish changing shortcuts.**

Until you get used to your new shortcuts, create a list and tape it to the side of your monitor for easy reference.

Appendix B

The Property Inspector and the Panels

• •

Several panels have been added in Flash MX 2004, and others have been changed. In this Appendix, we help you discover these features in more detail. The panels often have unlabeled buttons and menus that hold hidden treasures — or at least hidden features — if you know where to look.

The Tools Panel

The Tools panel contains all the drawing tools as well as many editing tools. Most drawing tools have their own *modifiers* that control how the drawing tool works. In this figure, you see only one set of modifiers. Refer to Chapter 3 for the full scoop.

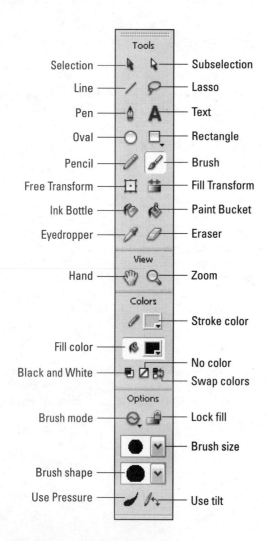

The Property Inspector

The Property inspector is *context sensitive,* which means that it displays information useful to what you're doing at the time. In this section, you see some variations on this theme.

Property inspector with no selection

When no object is selected and the cursor is on the Stage, you see document properties, as shown here.

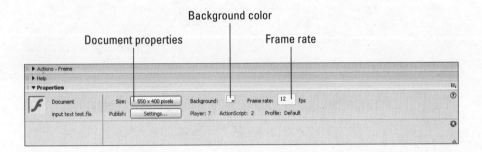

Property inspector with a shape selected

When you select a shape, the Property inspector displays properties of the shape so that you can edit them, as you see here.

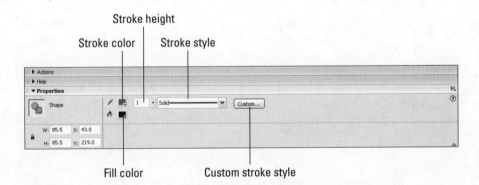

Property inspector with keyframe selected

When you click a keyframe on the Timeline, the Property inspector displays properties of the frame, as you see here.

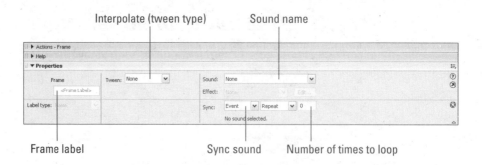

Interpolate (tween type) Sound name

Frame label Sync sound Number of times to loop

Property inspector with a symbol instance selected

When you select an instance of a symbol, the Property inspector displays properties of the instance so that you can edit them, as in the variation shown here.

Instance name

Symbol behavior Swap symbols Color styles

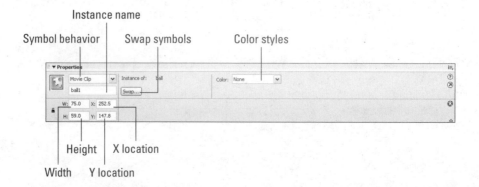

Height X location

Width Y location

The Align Panel

The Align Panel gets your objects in line, where they ought to be. For more information, refer to Chapter 4.

Distribute objects evenly

Align objects horizontally   Align objects vertically

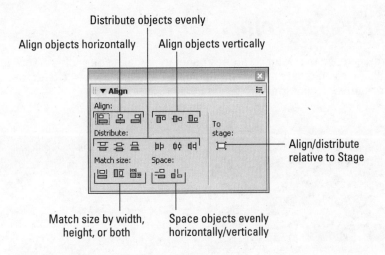

Align/distribute
relative to Stage

Match size by width,   Space objects evenly
height, or both   horizontally/vertically

The Color Mixer Panel

The Color Mixer panel is similar to an artist's palette. You can create your
own colors for both strokes (lines) and fills.

Stroke color

No color   Fill color   Transparency (alpha) value

Default colors   Swap colors   Color specification mode

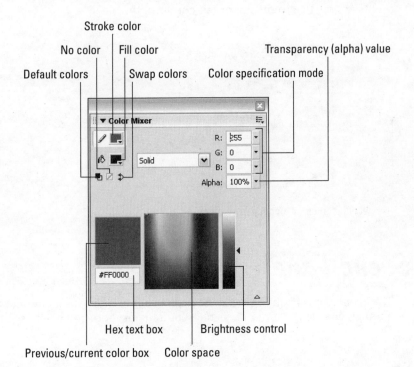

Hex text box   Brightness control

Previous/current color box   Color space

The Color Swatches Panel

You can use the Color Swatches panel to manage your colors. New colors and fills that you create appear on this panel for easy access. (Refer to Chapter 3 for more information.)

The Info Panel

The Info panel lets you control the precise size and location of objects. (Refer to Chapter 4 for more information on using this panel.) The X and Y measurements are relative to the upper-left corner of the Stage.

Width of instance   X location of instance

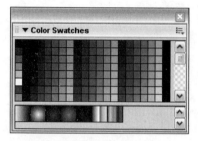

Height of instance   Y location of instance

The Scene Panel

The Scene panel is quite simple. You can use it to move from one scene to another, change the order of scenes, and rename, add, and delete scenes.

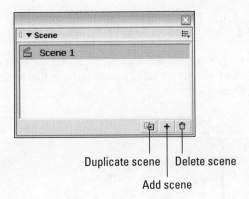

Duplicate scene | Delete scene

Add scene

The Transform Panel

Use the Transform panel to scale, rotate, and skew objects with precision. You scale by percentage, and you rotate and skew by degrees (increasing degrees going clockwise). To use the Copy and Apply Transform button: Select an object and specify any transform settings that you want. Then click Copy and Apply Transform. Flash creates a new object with the new settings on top of the old object. You can leave the new object there to create a composite object or immediately move it to a new location. Use the Reset button to return a transformed object to its original properties. Refer to Chapter 4 for more information about this panel.

Width   Height   Skew vertically

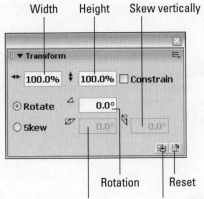

Rotation   Reset

Skew horizontally   Copy and Apply Transform

The Actions Panel

The Actions panel is where all the action is — the ActionScript, that is. On this panel, you write or insert code that makes your movies interactive. Refer to Chapter 10 for more information.

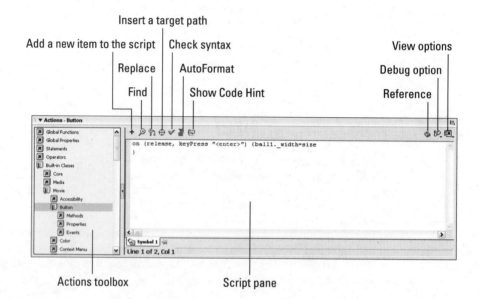

Insert a target path

Add a new item to the script   Check syntax   View options

Replace   AutoFormat   Debug option

Find   Show Code Hint   Reference

Actions toolbox   Script pane

The Debugger Panel

The Debugger panel contains features to help you debug your ActionScript code. You can set *breakpoints,* which are points where the ActionScript stops, to help you find out where the bugs are. You can also step through your code bit by bit to find those elusive bugs. You use the Debugger panel while movies are playing in the Flash Player, on your hard drive, or even on a Web server. To use the Debugger panel with an .fla movie on your hard drive, choose Control⟹Debug Movie.

The Movie Explorer Panel

Explore the depths of your movie with the Movie Explorer. Refer to Chapter 12 for details.

Remove all breakpoints

Toggle breakpoint   Step over

Stop debugging   Step in

Continue   Step out

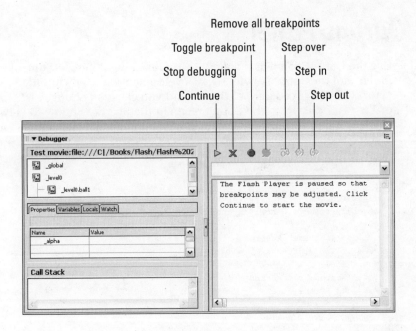

Show video, sounds, and bitmaps

Show buttons, movie clips, and graphics   Show frames and layers

Show text   Customize which items to show

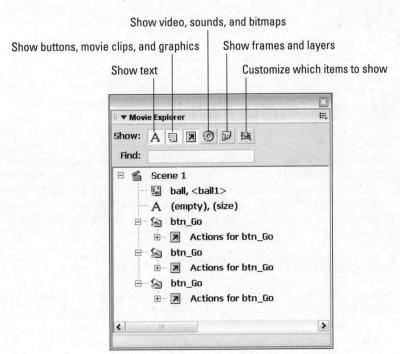

The Output Panel

Use the Output panel as a way to test your movie. Choose Control⇨Test Movie and then choose Window⇨Development Panels⇨Output. Some errors are displayed automatically, and you can also choose List Objects or List Variables from the Debug menu in the Player window to view a list of objects and variables.

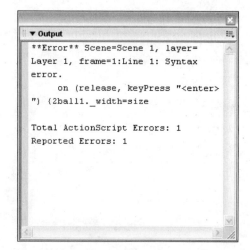

The Accessibility Panel

Accessibility features make your movies more accessible to people with certain disabilities or limitations — for example, limited sight or no sight. You can display or hide objects, depending on the needs of your viewers. These features make some of the nongraphical objects in your movie available to screen readers, which read parts of the screen out loud.

The Components Panel

Components are pre-built movie clips that come with predefined parameters that you can set to alter their appearance and behavior. They allow you to build complex Flash applications even if you don't have an advanced understanding of ActionScript. Some components are non-visual and allow you to do such things as manipulate information from data sources (for a Flash movie with a news ticker, for instance). Other components are interface elements, such as check boxes, radio buttons, and drop-down lists (combo boxes), which you can add to your movies to create interactivity. For more information, refer to Chapter 12.

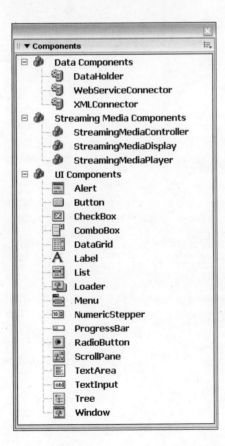

The Component Inspector

Use this panel to assign labels and parameters to components, such as check boxes, lists, and other interface elements.

The History Panel

The History panel stores all your commands. You can review them, repeat them, or save them to use again later. See Chapter 4 for details.

The Strings Panel

Use the Strings panel to create strings of text in various languages. These can be used for Web sites in multiple languages. Click the Settings button to set up the languages.

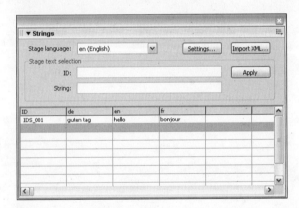

Appendix C

What Those Obscure Terms Really Mean

● ●

absolute path: A complete description of the location of a file. On the Internet, it usually starts with `http://` and continues with the complete Universal Resource Locator (URL) and filename (for example, `http://www.ellenfinkelstein.com/index.html`). On a computer, an absolute path starts with the disk drive, such as C, and continues with the folder and filename.

action: An expression in ActionScript, the Flash scripting language, for controlling objects and creating interactivity in a movie (see Chapter 10).

ActionScript: The Flash scripting language. Uses a syntax similar to JavaScript for animating objects and creating interactivity in a movie.

ActiveX controls: Software building blocks that are often small enough to be downloaded over the Internet and that can provide extra functionality inside Windows applications. For example, one Flash ActiveX control enables you to play a Flash Player movie from within Microsoft Office documents.

AIFF sound: A sound stored in the Audio Interchange File Format, developed by Apple. Flash can import AIFF sounds (see Chapter 11).

alpha: Opacity. Flash can change the opacity of colors so that you can create see-through objects (see Chapter 3). Technically, alpha and opacity aren't exactly the same thing, but for all practical purposes, in Flash they are.

anchor point: A point that you specify when creating a Bezier curve or line segment with the Pen tool. An anchor point helps define the shape of the object (see Chapter 3).

anti-aliasing: A method of displaying objects so that they appear smoother. *Aliasing* is the jaggedness that you get when you try to draw a diagonal line on the checkerboard-like grid of the computer screen.

authoring environment: The place where you create Flash movies (the Stage and the Timeline).

AVI: The Windows bitmap-based movie format. Flash can export to AVI format (see Chapter 13). AVI stands for *Audio/Video Interleaved*.

behaviors: Prewritten collections of ActionScript code that you may add to your movie from the Behaviors panel (see Chapter 10).

bit: A *bi*nary digi*t*. The binary world deep inside computers, where memory switches are either on or off; uses just two digits: 0 and 1.

bit rate: A measurement of the quality of a sound, measured in kilobits per second, or Kbps (see Chapter 11).

bit-depth: The number of binary digits (ones and zeros) of information per dot of color. A bit-depth of 8 gives you a palette of 2^8 colors (256 colors). A bit-depth of 24 (also called *24-bit color*) gives you 2^{24} colors (more than 16 million), which is good for rendering photographic images.

bitmap: A type of graphic image made up of dots (see Chapter 2).

brightness: The lightness (or darkness) of an image (see Chapter 3).

broadband: A connection to the Internet that is faster than the connection provided by the typical 56K modem that you would use with a computer and a standard telephone line. Examples of broadband connections include a digital subscriber line (DSL) connection, a cable modem, or a T1 connection.

button: An image that you click with your mouse (not the thing that holds your coat on). It often takes you to another page on the Web but can also display more information or start a Flash movie, for example (see Chapter 8).

byte: Eight bits of information. Eight bits of information is enough to represent 256 numbers, so it is enough numbers to assign, for instance, a different number to each key on your computer keyboard. *See also* bit.

CGI script: A Common Gateway Interface script; a computer program running on a Web server that can dynamically interact with a Web page (for example, to facilitate searching a database of books for a specified author).

codec: A piece of hardware or a software program that *cod*es and *dec*odes signals to and from a digital computer format.

compression, sound: A method of reducing the size of sound files (see Chapters 11 and 13).

CRT: Cathode ray tube; the giant glass tube in most television sets and in many computer monitors.

data binding: Connecting an information display to a data source that may be constantly changing, such as stock market prices or news headlines.

dithering: A method of combining existing colors in a color palette to approximate colors not in the palette.

Down state, button: The state of a button when you click it with your mouse (see Chapter 8).

download: To copy software (such as an application or a document) from one computer (usually a computer somewhere out on the World Wide Web) to your computer.

easing, animation: A way of changing the pace of tweened motion animation so that the movement either speeds up or slows down throughout the time of the motion (see Chapter 9).

editable text: Text that users can change while they view your Flash movie on a Web site (see Chapter 10).

EMBED **parameter:** The HyperText Markup Language (HTML) code required by Netscape Communicator or Navigator (and their cousin, Mozilla) to display a Flash Player movie (see Chapter 13).

fill: An object that fills in a shape. You create fills with the Brush and Paint Bucket tools. The Oval and Rectangle tools create fills and can also create strokes around the fills.

Flash Player file: The file with the extension .swf that you create when you publish your Flash movie (which has an .fla extension). You can display an SWF file on a Web site but not the FLA file.

focus: In a Flash movie, refers to the button in the movie that should receive input when the user presses Enter (Windows) or Return (Macintosh). It also refers to which text box or user interface element is selected.

frame: A representation of a small amount of time on the Timeline. By default, a frame represents $\frac{1}{12}$ of a second (see Chapter 9).

GIF: A compressed bitmap graphic file format often used on the Web. The GIF format is usually used for simple line art. (see Chapter 9).

gigabyte: 1024 megabytes; abbreviated as GB.

gradient: A fill that varies in color. Flash can create linear gradients for striped effects and radial gradients for concentric effects (see Chapter 3).

group: A set of objects that function as one object for purposes of selection and editing (see Chapter 4).

guide layer: A layer containing an object, usually a curved shape or series of line segments, that guides an animated object's motion (see Chapter 9).

hexadecimal: A number system using 16 digits (represented by the digits 0–9 and the letters A–F). The hexadecimal system is used extensively in the computer world. For instance, Web-safe colors are defined by using a hexadecimal system (see Chapter 3).

Hit state, button: The area of a movie that responds when you click the button with the mouse (see Chapter 8).

HTML: HyperText Markup Language. The code most commonly used to create Web pages.

hyperlink: A link on a Web page. Click it and suddenly you end up on another Web page — the one it hyperlinked to.

instance: A copy of a symbol that you can use on the Stage and for animation. You can change certain properties of instances without affecting the symbol (see Chapter 7).

interactivity: The ability of a Flash movie to respond to users. An example is clicking a button to turn off music (see Chapter 10).

interlacing: A way to display a GIF file while it loads so that the viewer sees the entire graphic but in increasingly clear values.

JPEG: A highly compressed, 24-bit bitmap, graphical format. The JPEG format is usually used for photographs and other graphics with many colors.

kerning: A way to control the spacing between pairs of characters, such as the capital letters A and V (see Chapter 5).

keyframe: A frame on the Timeline that contains a change in animation. For example, to create tweened animation, you need to create keyframes at the beginning and end of the tween (see Chapter 9).

kilobyte: One thousand twenty-four (1,024) bytes; abbreviated as K or KB.

layer: A level on the Stage that contains objects. Different animations should always be on different layers (see Chapter 6).

LCD: Liquid crystal display; the kind of display used for laptop computers and many flat-screen computer monitors.

Library: The storehouse for symbols, imported bitmaps, and sounds (see Chapter 2).

loop: To replay a movie over and over again. By default, movie clips loop. Also, the default setting when publishing a movie is to loop the movie (see Chapters 7 and 13).

mask: A special kind of layer that hides objects on layers below it. You can put a shape on a mask layer to reveal objects on lower layers within that shape (see Chapter 6).

megabyte: A million bytes, or 1,048,576 bytes, depending on whom you ask; abbreviated as MB. 1,048,576 bytes is 1,024 kilobytes.

method: A procedure that comes built in with an ActionScript object. (See Chapter 10 for more information on ActionScript.) Sounds in Flash, for instance, come with a built-in `setVolume` method, which makes it easy for you to control how loudly they play.

motion path: A path — created with the Pencil or other tool — that defines the motion of an object in a motion tween (see Chapter 9).

motion tween: An animation that moves objects, created by defining the beginning and end points and letting Flash automatically fill in the in-between motion (see Chapter 9).

movie clip: Animation contained in a symbol. You can then place the symbol on the main Timeline so that you are playing a movie within the main movie (see Chapter 7).

Movie Explorer: The Flash panel for discovering all the components of a movie, including objects, layers, and actions (see Chapter 12).

MP3: A highly compressed, sound-file format (see Chapter 11).

navigation: A set of buttons or hyperlinked text that enable the viewer of a Web site to move through the various Web pages.

OBJECT parameter: The HTML code required by Internet Explorer to display a Flash Player movie (see Chapter 13).

onClipEvent handler: A way to define what event, such as a frame loading, triggers the action in a movie clip (see Chapter 10).

On (mouse event) handler: A way to define what happens when the mouse interacts in different ways with a button, such as passing over it or clicking it. On (release) is an example of the beginning of an On (mouse event) handler (see Chapter 10).

Onion Skin mode: A method of viewing animation so that you see all the frames at one time (see Chapter 9).

orient to path: A setting that rotates an object in a motion tween in the direction of its motion path. A bird turning as it flies is one example (see Chapter 9).

Over state, button: The state of a button when the mouse cursor passes over it (see Chapter 8).

palette: A set of colors that are available for use in drawing or publishing a graphic file.

panels: The windows in the Flash program that allow you to view, organize, and change the elements of a Flash movie. You can collapse and expand these panels.

PICT: A Macintosh graphic file format that can be either a bitmap or a vector file.

pixel: A picture element — a single dot in a computer image. A color pixel on a CRT monitor is actually made up of three dots (one red, one green, and one blue), which blend together. *See also* CRT.

PNG: A bitmap graphic file format available on both Windows and Macs that supports transparency.

pressure-sensitive tablet: A flat surface for drawing that is connected to a computer. The tablet usually comes with a stylus that looks like a pen. A pressure-sensitive tablet responds to the pressure that you use with the stylus to create variable-width lines, for example (see Chapter 3).

publish: To create a Flash Player file (a .swf file) that can be viewed on a Web site (see Chapter 13).

RAM: Random access memory; the electronic memory in your computer. Storing information in RAM is much faster than storing it on your hard drive, but RAM is more expensive than a hard drive. Most types of RAM (except super-expensive stuff) do not continue to store any information when you turn off your computer's power.

raster: The grid of dots that make up a computer image.

relative path: A description of the location of a file, relative to another file, so that you don't have to describe the entire location. For example, if a file is in the same folder as the first file, you can just specify the filename, such as index.html.

RGB color: A method of defining a color according to the amount of red, green, and blue that it contains (see Chapter 3).

sample rate: A means of controlling the fidelity and size of a sound file. Higher sample rates sound better but result in larger files (see Chapter 11).

scene: A division of a movie; used to help organize the movie into parts (see Chapter 9).

shape hint: A means of specifying how a shape tween changes shape (see Chapter 9). *See also* shape tween.

shape tween: An animation in which one shape changes into another shape; you define the first and last shapes, and Flash automatically fills in the intermediate shapes (see Chapter 9).

shared library: A library resting on a computer server that can be accessed by a Flash Player file (a .swf file); used to make Player files smaller (see Chapter 2).

Stage: The rectangle in the middle of the Flash screen where you place objects for animation.

streaming media: Audio/video information that is heard and/or seen by the viewer at the same time that the information is being sent over the Web to the viewer. If you must download a complete audio/video file onto your computer before you can start playing it, it is not streaming media.

stroke: A line or outline. For example, a circle or rectangle can have an outline (see Chapter 3).

SWF: The filename extension for a Flash Player file. A .swf file can be displayed on a Web site. (A Flash .fla file cannot be displayed on a Web site.)

symbol: A named, saved object or set of objects, stored in the Library. You can create instances of symbols and place them on the Stage (see Chapter 7).

synchronization, animation: A means to make sure that animation in a movie clip keeps pace with the number of frames that it occupies on the main Timeline (see Chapter 9).

tablet, pressure-sensitive: *See* pressure-sensitive tablet.

tangent handle: A marker, displayed when drawing with the Pen tool, that determines the direction of a curve.

target: The object of an expression in ActionScript: specifically, a Timeline. For example, if a movie clip tells the main movie what to do, the main movie's Timeline is the target.

template: A group of settings for the HTML code used to display a Flash Player file (a .swf file). Flash offers a number of templates that you can use (see Chapter 13).

Timeline: A movie's set of frames along which the animation runs (see Chapter 9).

tween: *See* motion tween, shape tween.

type: Another word for *typography* or *text* (see Chapter 5).

upload: To copy software (such as an application or a document) from your computer to another computer (usually a computer somewhere out on the World Wide Web).

URL: Uniform Resource Locator; the standard way of specifying the location of an item on the Internet, such as the address of a Web page — for example, `http://www.infinityeverywhere.net.`

variable: In ActionScript, a named holder for a value that you can retrieve for use in a script or database.

vector: A definition of a distance and a direction. Vector graphics, such as those in Flash, are defined by equations rather than by the dots used in bitmap graphics (see Chapter 2).

WAV: A Windows sound format (see Chapter 11).

Web services: Software interfaces that are made public so that computer programs can communicate over the Web to other computer programs.

Web-safe color: A color that appears the same on all computer systems and in all browsers. All 216 Web-safe colors are defined by using a hexadecimal system (see Chapter 3).

XML: eXtensible Markup Language; an increasingly popular language for creating customized languages for designing documents, the kinds of data that the documents contain, and how the data is displayed.

Appendix D

What's on the CD-ROM

Here's some of the cool stuff that you find on the *Macromedia Flash MX 2004 For Dummies* CD:

✔ More than two dozen Flash projects from the book *50 Fast Macromedia Flash MX Techniques*

✔ Ten royalty-free Flash movies from Bigshot Media, a provider of stock Flash movies

✔ A collection of trial software from Macromedia, including Flash MX 2004 (of course), Fireworks, and Dreamweaver

✔ Swift 3D, a standalone tool for quickly creating 3-D animations that you can save as Flash Player movies

✔ A library of geometric, whimsical, and artistic vector graphics ready to be instantly opened in any Flash movie

✔ More than two-dozen additional Flash movies that you can dissect and learn from

✔ An e-book version of *Macromedia Flash MX 2004 For Dummies*

System Requirements

Make sure that your computer meets the minimum system requirements in the following list. If your computer doesn't match up to these requirements, you may experience problems in using the contents of the CD:

- ✔ A PC with a 600 MHz+ Pentium III or faster processor or a Macintosh PowerPC 500MHz G3 processor.

- ✔ Microsoft Windows 98 SE, 2000, or XP, or OS X 10.2.6.

- ✔ At least 128MB of RAM installed on your computer. For best performance, we recommend at least 256MB of RAM installed.

- ✔ A CD-ROM drive.

- ✔ A sound card for PCs. (Mac OS computers have built-in sound support.)

- ✔ A monitor capable of displaying at least 16-bit color (thousands of colors) and 1024 x 768 resolution or better.

- ✔ A modem with a speed of at least 14,400 bps.

If you need more information on the basics, check out these books published by Wiley Publishing, Inc.: *PCs For Dummies,* 9th Edition, by Dan Gookin; *Macs For Dummies,* 8th Edition, by David Pogue; *iMac For Dummies,* 3rd Edition, by David Pogue; *Mac OS X For Dummies,* 3rd Edition, by Bob LeVitus; or *Windows 98 For Dummies, Windows 2000 Professional For Dummies,* or *Windows XP For Dummies,* all by Andy Rathbone.

Using the CD

Follow these steps to access the software on the book's CD:

1. **Insert the CD into your computer's CD-ROM drive.**

2. **The interface launches.**

   Note for Windows Users: If you have AutoRun disabled, choose Start⇨Run. In the dialog box that appears, type **D:\start.exe,** and then click OK. (If your CD-ROM drive uses a different letter, replace D with the proper letter. If you don't know the letter, see how your CD-ROM drive is listed under My Computer.)

   Note for Mac Users: Click the start icon from CD to launch the interface.

3. **Read through the license agreement that appears, and then click the Accept button if you want to use the CD.**

   After you click Accept, the License Agreement window won't bother you again.

4. **The CD interface appears.**

   The interface coordinates installing the programs and running the demos. The interface essentially enables you to click a button or two to make things happen.

Software on the CD-ROM

The following sections are arranged by category and provide a summary of the software and other goodies you find on the CD. If you need help with installing the items provided on the CD, refer to the installation instructions in the preceding section.

Note that some of the software packages are trial, demo, or evaluation versions. These are usually limited by either time or functionality (such as not letting you save a project after you create it).

Dreamweaver

For Mac OS 10.2.6 or higher, Windows 98, 2000, or XP. Trial version.

Dreamweaver is one of the premier Web site authoring programs. As a result, Flash and Dreamweaver make a great match. You can use Dreamweaver to create HTML pages and add your Flash Player files to them with ease. Visit Macromedia at www.macromedia.com/software/dreamweaver/.

Fireworks

For Mac 10.2.6 or higher, Windows 98 SE, 2000 or XP. Trial version.

Fireworks is the Macromedia Web graphics creation program. Its features include both bitmap and vector graphic-editing tools. Check out the Macromedia site at www.macromedia.com/software/fireworks/.

Flash MX 2004 trial version

For Mac 10.2.6 or higher, Windows 98, 2000 or XP.

The Flash MX 2004 trial version is the 30-day trial that is fully functional. Use it to try out Flash and have fun! After 30 days, you can purchase it for exciting animation possibilities lasting a lifetime — or at least until the next version comes out.

Flash Player

For Mac 9.x or later. or OS X 10.1 or later; Windows 95, 98, Me, NT 4.0, 2000, or XP.

You use this to view all the Flash Player files on the CD, of course.

Swift 3D

For Mac 8.1 or higher, or OS X Classic; Windows 98, NT, 2000, Me, or XP. Trial version.

Swift 3D is a standalone tool for quickly creating 3-D animations that you can save in a variety of formats, including the .swf format for Flash Player. For more information, visit Swift 3D at www.swift3d.com.

Adobe Acrobat Reader

For Mac OS X 10.2; Windows 98, NT, 2000, Me, or XP.

An e-book version of *Macromedia Flash MX 2004 For Dummies* is included on the CD in Adobe's Portable Document Format (PDF), and Adobe Acrobat Reader allows you to view it on your computer.

Your Own Personal Library of Graphics

For the Mac and Windows.

We've created more than 60 vector graphics that you can use in your Flash movies. Some are geometric shapes that are hard to create in Flash. We added some fun shapes . . . some practical and others whimsical, such as our thought bubble and explosion. Finally, we included some artistic drawings of everyday objects. We hope you like them! (Please keep in mind that these files are provided for your personal use and are not to be sold or redistributed.)

All that you see when you open the Flash file is a blank screen. To see the graphics, choose Window⇨Library. To use these shapes in another Flash file, choose File⇨Import to Library and choose the file named Flash MX For Dummies Library.fla.

An even better idea is to copy the `.fla` file from the CD to the Libraries subfolder of your Flash MX 2004 folder. (In Windows, you find this at `Documents and Settings\[username]\Local Settings\Application Data\Macromedia\Flash MX 2004\en Configuration\Libraries` on your hard drive. On the Mac, you find it at `Applications/Macromedia Flash 2004/Configuration/Libraries` on your hard drive.) Then you can access this file at any time by choosing Window⇨Other Panels⇨ Common Libraries.

Flash Movies Galore

For the Mac and Windows.

Throughout this book, we refer you to the CD to look at Flash movies as examples of the features that we are explaining. These movies are organized by chapter. They help you understand some of the more complex capabilities of Flash that are hard to explain or show in a figure. Some of these movies are real-world Flash movies that come from active Web sites. Others are examples that we created for you to isolate the Flash feature. Either way, we hope that you can use them to further your understanding of Flash.

In addition to all the movies discussed in the book, the CD includes an additional 25 FLA files from our other book on Flash, *50 Fast Macromedia Flash MX Techniques.* You can analyze and modify these files to further explore quick, cool techniques for creating animations, effects and interfaces in Flash.

And we've included ten FLA files from Bigshot Media for you to study, enjoy, and use in your own Flash movies. Bigshot is a vendor of royalty-free stock Flash movies with a database of thousands of Flash movies ranging in size from 5K to 2000K. *(Thanks to Ruth Frost, at www.bigshotmedia.com, for the movie files.)*

Here are a few troubleshooting things to keep in mind when you use the Flash movie files provided on the CD:

- ✔ **Copy movie files to your hard drive.** Don't try choosing Control⇨Test Movie to test a movie directly from the CD. Copy the `.fla` file to your hard drive first and then test the movie.

- ✔ **The Flash movie doesn't play.** Sometimes when you open a Flash movie, nothing happens when you try to play the animation. Choose Control⇨Test Movie to see the animation.

- ✔ **The fonts look different.** If some of the fonts required by the Flash files aren't available on your system, you may see less-than-satisfactory substitutions when you play the Flash Player files.

E-book Version of Macromedia Flash MX 2004 For Dummies

For the Mac and Windows.

The complete text of this book is on the CD as an Adobe PDF. Now you can take it along with you wherever you may roam. You can read and search through the e-book with the Adobe Acrobat Reader, which is also included on the CD, and view it in all its glory with all the layout, fonts, links, and images just as they appear in the paper version of the book.

Troubleshooting Your CD Problems

We tried our best to compile programs that work on most computers with the minimum system requirements. Alas, your computer may differ, and some programs may not work properly, for some reason.

The two likeliest problems are that you don't have enough memory (RAM) for the programs that you want to use or that you have other programs running that are affecting the installation or running of a program. If you get an error message such as Not enough memory or Setup cannot continue, try one or more of the following suggestions and then try using the software again:

- ✔ **Turn off any antivirus software running on your computer.** Installation programs sometimes mimic virus activity and may make your computer incorrectly believe that it's being infected by a virus. You undoubtedly want to turn your antivirus software back on when you're finished installing the software.

- ✔ **Close all running programs.** (If necessary, this may even include closing the CD interface and running a product's installation program directly from Windows Explorer or the Macintosh Finder.) The more programs you have running, the less memory is available to other programs. Installation programs typically update files and programs; so if you keep other programs running, installation may not work properly.

- ✔ **Have your local computer store add more RAM to your computer.** This option is, admittedly, a drastic and somewhat expensive step. However, if you have a Windows PC or a Power Macintosh, adding more memory can really help the speed of your computer and allow more programs to run at the same time.

If you still have trouble with the CD, please call Wiley Product Technical
Support at 800-762-2974 (outside the United States, call 1-317-572-3994) or
via our Web site at www.wiley.com/techsupport. Wiley provides technical
support for installation and other general quality-control items only; for technical support on the applications themselves, consult the program's vendor
or author.

To place additional orders or to request information about other Wiley products, please call (800) 225-5945.

Index

Wiley Publishing, Inc.
End-User License Agreement

5. Limited Warranty.

(a) WPI warrants that the Software and Software Media are free from defects in materials and workmanship under normal use for a period of sixty (60) days from the date of purchase of this Book. If WPI receives notification within the warranty period of defects in materials or workmanship, WPI will replace the defective Software Media.

(b) WPI AND THE AUTHOR(S) OF THE BOOK DISCLAIM ALL OTHER WARRANTIES, EXPRESS OR IMPLIED, INCLUDING WITHOUT LIMITATION IMPLIED WARRANTIES OF MERCHANTABILITY AND FITNESS FOR A PARTICULAR PURPOSE, WITH RESPECT TO THE SOFTWARE, THE PROGRAMS, THE SOURCE CODE CONTAINED THEREIN, AND/OR THE TECHNIQUES DESCRIBED IN THIS BOOK. WPI DOES NOT WARRANT THAT THE FUNCTIONS CONTAINED IN THE SOFTWARE WILL MEET YOUR REQUIREMENTS OR THAT THE OPERATION OF THE SOFTWARE WILL BE ERROR FREE.

(c) This limited warranty gives you specific legal rights, and you may have other rights that vary from jurisdiction to jurisdiction.

6. Remedies.

(a) WPI's entire liability and your exclusive remedy for defects in materials and workmanship shall be limited to replacement of the Software Media, which may be returned to WPI with a copy of your receipt at the following address: Software Media Fulfillment Department, Attn.: Macromedia Flash MX 2004 For Dummies, Wiley Publishing, Inc., 10475 Crosspoint Blvd., Indianapolis, IN 46256, or call 1-800-762-2974. Please allow four to six weeks for delivery. This Limited Warranty is void if failure of the Software Media has resulted from accident, abuse, or misapplication. Any replacement Software Media will be warranted for the remainder of the original warranty period or thirty (30) days, whichever is longer.

(b) In no event shall WPI or the author be liable for any damages whatsoever (including without limitation damages for loss of business profits, business interruption, loss of business information, or any other pecuniary loss) arising from the use of or inability to use the Book or the Software, even if WPI has been advised of the possibility of such damages.

(c) Because some jurisdictions do not allow the exclusion or limitation of liability for consequential or incidental damages, the above limitation or exclusion may not apply to you.

7. U.S. Government Restricted Rights.
Use, duplication, or disclosure of the Software for or on behalf of the United States of America, its agencies and/or instrumentalities "U.S. Government" is subject to restrictions as stated in paragraph (c)(1)(ii) of the Rights in Technical Data and Computer Software clause of DFARS 252.227-7013, or subparagraphs (c) (1) and (2) of the Commercial Computer Software - Restricted Rights clause at FAR 52.227-19, and in similar clauses in the NASA FAR supplement, as applicable.

8. General.
This Agreement constitutes the entire understanding of the parties and revokes and supersedes all prior agreements, oral or written, between them and may not be modified or amended except in a writing signed by both parties hereto that specifically refers to this Agreement. This Agreement shall take precedence over any other documents that may be in conflict herewith. If any one or more provisions contained in this Agreement are held by any court or tribunal to be invalid, illegal, or otherwise unenforceable, each and every other provision shall remain in full force and effect.